EASING

Accepting My Gay Self

Seth Vicarson

Quarry Creek Press
St. Augustine, Florida

Thanks to Frances Keiser of Sagaponack Books & Design
and Beth Mansbridge of Mansbridge Editing & Transcription.

The material presented in this autobiography was framed by old documents, letters, and recollections, which undeniably have mutated over the years as a result of my mind's ability to edit. I have attempted to recreate as closely as possible what actually occurred, knowing that exact details of specific events and conversations are impossible to recall. In those instances where my memory has been fuzzy, I have taken a few liberties to fill in the blanks without infringing on the story's truth.

Due to the highly sensitive nature of this autobiography, I have chosen not to use actual names, even though many people mentioned are deceased. Additionally, in some instances I have changed geographic locations and the physical characteristics of some individuals. The latter is probably a moot point, given that physical descriptions are now camouflaged by the ravages of more than forty years of time and no longer within the realm of accuracy. Confirmation of this reality has been provided by my own mirror.

The Internet references and resources listed in this publication are current at the time of printing. They may be helpful but I cannot endorse or guarantee the efficacy of any particular reference or resource.

ISBN 978-1-7323501-0-6 (softcover)
ISBN 978-1-7323501-2-0 (hard cover)
ISBN 978-1-7323501-1-3 (e-book)

Library of Congress Catalog Card Number: 2018944469

BIO031000 Biography & Autobiography / LGBT
SOC012000 Social Science / LGBT Studies / Gay Studies
OCC019000 Body, Mind & Spirit / Inspiration & Personal Growth

Quarry Creek Press
St. Augustine, Florida

Printed and bound in the Unitd States of America
First Edition

This book is dedicated to those who are struggling.

"When you're different, sometimes you don't see the millions of people who accept you for what you are. All you notice is the person who doesn't."

—Jodi Picoult, *Change of Heart*

Contents

Introduction

For years, I felt desperately alone as I allowed the church and dogmatic opinions surrounding me to be my guides. This predisposed me for a destructive course that resulted in a protracted period of anguish and crippling self-loathing. My ultimate admission to being gay—and finally accepting it—freed me from the injurious effects of being immersed in an evangelical, gay-intolerant environment.

If you or someone you love is gay, let me assure you that you are not alone. You are in the company of millions who are all part of God's creation and as much loved as your straight counterparts.

The last thing I ever saw myself doing was writing a book. However, I felt compelled to do so with the intent that my experiences might bring hope to anyone who is in a lightless tunnel. I have attempted to be inoffensive, PG-rated (one section is probably closer to an R rating), frank, and humorous. The hands that wrote this are now punctuated with some wrinkles and creases—all representing the years I have been blessed to live. I am grateful for each one and view them with a smile.

While the primary focus of this writing pertains to sexuality, I have included other significant facets of my life history that are unrelated or tangential to the topic—yet they are all pieces of the puzzle. My overarching goal was to accurately chronicle who I am as a human being and to highlight the drivers that have steered my life course. This journey, led by the tip of my pen, has taken me through a "countryside" that I now view with a much wider lens than the one with which I was equipped when most of life was in front of me. Having this expanded view has given me a more objective ability to conduct a thorough self-study. This autobiography, *Easing Out: Accepting My Gay Self*, is the result.

Chapter 1

Was I Born Gay?

This question has haunted me my entire journey through life (at least the portion following puberty), and I am convinced the answer is a resounding *yes*. I think most of the unbiased scientific community agrees with my conclusion, even though the evangelical element in which I was raised does not.

Chapter 2

Background Snapshot

My life began in the summer of 1948, when my parents decided they wanted to make a baby. They already had one kid and five years had passed since my brother was born. You could say their decision to add me to the household was not rushed. Thus, I was well planned and conceived. I remained a content fetus, happily swimming around in my mother's amniotic pool until the spring of 1949 when the dam broke. And out I came—the first time, that is.

I have no memory of my entry into this world, yet my birth certificate is proof the event occurred when I was told it did. It was during a time when scads of babies were littering hospital maternity wards. They called us *baby boomers.* Back then, there was an instruction book for raising babies; Dr. Benjamin Spock wrote it. I would later discover I was born with a sexual "preference" for other boys. There was no instruction book for that, and we were labeled *queers.* It is necessary for me to explain why my use of the word *preference* is not really accurate. Here is why. If I am offered a choice of vanilla or chocolate ice cream, I strongly prefer vanilla, although I will eat and enjoy chocolate. The same principle of preference didn't apply when it came to sex. My "choice" was assigned and that assignment was purely same-sex. I figured out early on that I had minimal sexual attraction to girls; however, it took many years for me to come to grips with the reality of it.

My Town

I grew up in Jacksonville, Florida, which was characteristically southern—complete with requisite drawls, hominy grits swimming in butter, and Spanish moss dripping from the trees. The St. Johns River flows right through the heart of the city, which lies about fifteen miles west of the Atlantic Ocean in the northeastern corner of the state. Jacksonville was a "muscular" city, as many residents derived their livelihoods from shipbuilding, stevedoring, fishing, aircraft mechanics (US Navy), and other blue-collar-related jobs. The city lies a scant few miles to the south of Georgia and, from an ideological perspective, has typically identified more with Georgia than with most of Florida. Not surprisingly, "Jax," as the locals call it, was a paragon of conservatism and resistance to social change. Even so, it was a sweet place to grow up, where a small-town flavor persisted long after the city was no longer so small. Weekend attire (at least in the part of town where we lived) was primarily composed of T-shirts, shorts, and flip-flops, except when chilly weather demanded flannel shirts and jeans. It was a mellow kind of place which corresponded to my own relatively easygoing personality.

Summers in Jacksonville were hot—really hot. In fact, the "swelterness factor" was magnified when I was a kid because air conditioning was not yet commonplace in most middle-class homes—including ours. Attic fans, ceiling fans, and window fans did little to mitigate the heat; however, these devices did at least create an electrically-powered breeze that moved the heat around. At night, we slept with the windows wide open, with no concerns of an intruder coming into the house (we were too hot to care). I recollect the sultry night air permeating every pore of my body as I lay in bed, acutely aware of distinct sounds and wafting smells I will forever associate with childhood and hot nights. Most prominently emblazoned in that reminiscence were the occasional dissipating wails of ships' horns in the distance, muted roars of lions at the nearby zoo, the aroma of coffee beans roasting from the downtown Maxwell House plant, and the perfumed pungency of night-blooming jasmine. The sweet smells were reflective of growing up during a sweet time.

Our neighborhood was close-knit, "lily-white," and composed mostly of gospel-music-loving, churchgoing folks who knew and cared about each other—that was the norm back in those days. While our particular neighborhood was understated middle class, the general area of town where we lived encompassed sections where folks had less and were forced to scrape for a living. Many considered our part of town to be on the wrong side of the St. Johns River, although in my estimation, growing up where I did was a huge blessing. The attitudes and values were much like what existed in the fictional town of Mayberry from Andy Griffith fame. We even had our own version of "Aunt Bee," as well as a neighborhood "drunk" who added "interest" to our sheltered environment.

In my estimation, I was born with all the advantages. I was gifted with wonderful parents who loved each other, and that love extended to my brother and me in the form of true devotion, appropriate discipline, and emotional support.

My dad was employed in the insurance industry, and Mom chose to assume a stay-at-home role. She and my dad agreed this arrangement was the best way to ensure my brother and I didn't end up as deviants. The Vicarson household was much like the Cleavers from *Leave It to Beaver* TV fame, without the country club. The church assumed that role and it was indeed central to our lives.

We were not wealthy. Even so, I didn't understand how good we had it until after I graduated from college, and realized that only a minority of graduates in my high school class had the same opportunity. It was clear most of my classmates were not able to further their formal education due to family economics or because their parents didn't steer them in that direction. My parents provided the financial access, and instilled within me the expectation—and desire—to obtain a four-year college degree. Regardless as to whether or not college is attended, I recognize that family tone sets the stage for a child's ability to succeed in life and adapt to adversities. I am extremely grateful to my parents for all they did for me, and I frequently expressed that gratitude to them.

Spotlight on My Parents

My mother was strongly extroverted, funny, she laughed a lot, and was attractive. She had dark eyes and hair, was 5' 1" tall, and although petite, was "well put together." She grew up in Palatka, Florida, during the Great Depression and was the oldest of four kids in a family that struggled financially. After graduating from high school, she and two of her friends from Palatka enrolled in the Erlanger Hospital School of Nursing in Chattanooga, Tennessee. Three years later, she obtained her certificate as a registered nurse, and then married my dad, who had moved up there to be close to her. Subsequently, they both returned to Florida.

People were naturally drawn to my mom's sharp wit, winsome personality, and musical ability. Accordingly, she was the life of any party. She played the piano, sang, painted landscapes, and was an excellent writer. To be concise, I'll say she was into artistic endeavors. Mother had a terrific sense of humor, was fairly opinionated, and freely expressed what she thought, up to a point—she would never consciously offend anyone. She was comfortable with herself, except for being self-conscious about her height. This was mitigated by her hair architecture—a teased masterpiece that just about reached the ceiling.

In Chinese philosophy, if my mother was "yin," my dad was "yang." He was tall and thin, had blue-gray eyes, receding brown hair, a fair complexion and a good sense of humor. My dad was quieter than my mom, and was a no-nonsense type of guy. He was a deep thinker, and not one to make decisions or statements without a great deal of thought. He was nonjudgmental, a consummate gentleman, and never said anything that was unkind about anyone. I never considered him to be particularly good-looking, but in reviewing old photos, he actually was "cute as a button," with a dimpled chin and an inviting smile. To me, his most outstanding personal traits were his objectivity, unquestionable honesty, and an unerring sense of fair play. His guiding philosophy in dealing with people was that in situations where "the stick has a short end and a long end," be sure you are on the short end. In other words, give beyond what is expected or required.

My dad was highly intelligent, although his formal education terminated in the seventh grade—thus, he was largely self-educated. His school in rural southwest Georgia, where he grew up, burned down when he was entering the eighth grade, and he never went back. He grew up on the family farm and was the middle child of eleven kids. Occasionally he recounted how hard farm life was and, based on his descriptions, the entire family toiled in the fields like servants, under the blazing sun. He never disparaged his parents or the way he was raised, yet clearly disliked the captivity of farming, which back in the early 1900s was heavily dependent on manual labor. Consequently he moved to Florida as a young man, in search of a better life, and found it—plus something else, my mother.

My parents were reasonable and logical with their approach to child-rearing. They had the best interests of my brother and me in the forefront of anything they did. My dad was a disciplinarian, as was my mother, and discipline was administered out of love rather than anger—with one notable exception that I will mention later. Either parent administered the occasional spankings. Invariably, these "corrections" were prefaced by a "talk" (particularly from my dad) as to why the punishment was necessary. The talk included the "This hurts me more than it hurts you" line. Back then, I didn't believe it or understand what it actually meant. When I was an adult, I understood the meaning. My parents were on the same page when it came to discipline, and if a spanking was dispensed by one parent for a particular misdeed, the other parent didn't render a second "dose."

Both parents were kind, sweet but not syrupy, and levelheaded. They never fought in front of us, and I can never remember hearing either of my parents yell at each other. They had disagreements, although anything of real consequence was never aired in front of my brother and me. I grew up with an immeasurable amount of security.

Spotlight on My Brother

My brother Max and I had as little in common as humanly possible when we were growing up. Since he was over five years older, we spent little time together, although he derived great joy in pestering me. He loved to call me Gravel Gertie, which I didn't particularly like. I figured the name was of his own fabrication and I didn't associate it with anything other than it sounded derogatory. Years later, it was brought to my attention that Gravel Gertie was the name of a character in the *Dick Tracy* comic strip. I was not an avid reader (due to reading comprehension challenges) and never read the comics. Thus, it was plausible I didn't know Ms. Gertie on the same level as the rest of the literate world.

By the time I entered first grade, Max was already in the seventh grade; however, his entire school experience had been marked by poor grades due to basic inattention. They didn't have a name for it back then, and no treatment; I imagine he was a classic example of attention deficit disorder (ADD). He was much more of a management challenge to my parents than I was (the almost-perfect kid). My mother made the comment that even in the womb he was highly active, especially when compared to me. Our parents and Max's teachers suspected he had a learning disability, and prior to the time he was scheduled to enter the eighth grade, tests were conducted in hopes of pinpointing the problem. They revealed a most surprising discovery—his IQ punched the top of the scale and my pain-in-the-ass brother was declared borderline genius. This seemed utterly impossible: someone performing so poorly in school could be smarter than me, the kid who already was making good grades and gave no one any trouble. Nonetheless, he was judged to be bored in school. As unbelievable as his "diagnosis" seemed, it became apparent as he grew older that he indeed exhibited off-the-chart intelligence in just about anything dealing with mechanics and electronics.

Max reacted to puberty in the manner that all the child-rearing books said he was "supposed to." Unfortunately, a different template applied by the time I hit the same level of development. As expected, Max was "all boy" when it came to his appreciation for the opposite sex and had many male friends who, like him, were girl crazy. Of course, I had no idea what all the hubbub was about (and still don't). When I was thirteen years old, he flew the coop (courtesy of the U.S. Air Force), leaving me as an "only child."

So, too many years separated us in those early times and we found too little commonality that ordinarily would foster deep brotherly connections. Many years later, the hand of fate dealt a most uncomfortable set of circumstances that forced Max and me to forge an unexpected and lifelong bond.

Under the Influence

My parents were adherent Southern Baptists and, as such, we were entrenched in church doctrine. *Everything* revolved around the church, just as the Earth revolves around the sun. Back in those days, the church seemed less "in your face" than what exists today, and separation of church and state was considered sacrosanct. Accordingly, political views were never heard or even inferred from the pulpit. That seems to have changed.

Music was my favorite part of a service. Traditional hymns, southern gospel, and classically-inspired choir anthems created an inspirational mix that is now all but gone. The church where I grew up fostered a great sense of belonging among congregants, with fish fries, picnics, and ice cream socials as frequent occasions which I eagerly anticipated. Activities for youth were a hallmark of my home church and, as a result, camaraderie permeated our tightly-knit group. In short, I loved it and never imagined one day I would be compelled to leave it.

Every morning in the Vicarson household, we had a time of devotion which included a brief Scripture reading and prayer. At a minimum, we attended church on Sunday morning, Sunday night, and usually Wednesday night. Of course, additional opportunities presented themselves on other days. Any Baptist will verify this to be true. Good for us we lived a block from the church; otherwise, we may as well have pitched a tent in the church parking lot.

There was no smoking, no drinking of alcohol, and no swearing in our family. In fact, I never heard my dad speak a curse word except for one occasion. That was when someone ignored a stop sign and punched the back side of the family car. No one was hurt, but he said a loud "Dammit" upon impact, and then profusely apologized to my brother and me for the utterance. Mother was slightly less inhibited with her sometimes more colorful expressions, and occasionally selected words from the "non-approved" vocabulary list.

My parents expected me to perform chores around the house when I was old enough to accomplish them safely. Things like mowing the grass, bringing in the garbage can, and helping clean up the kitchen, and so on, were among my responsibilities. In return, my dad gave me a small weekly allowance with the requirement that I was to give 10 percent to the church and save the remainder for items I wanted to buy for others or myself. It was an early and invaluable lesson in charity and in money management.

Chapter 3
Early Indicators

Being gay and inclined toward introspection, I have studied my life's events for years, searching for answers and clues as to why I am gay, and if my "gayness" could have been avoided. I have wondered at what point in my life the directional indicator landed on the gay rather than non-gay assignment. My earliest recollections, although sketchy, begin at about the age of four. My mother, like most moms, has many pictures of me she took, beginning when I was born. (This was long before the time when fetal snapshots were possible.) In looking them over, I can remember most events represented in the photos from age five and can even recall specific emotions associated with occasions that were more noteworthy. As I perused the old photos and connected them with definite memories and feelings, I was able to identify "mile markers" that I think would have predicted my gay orientation at an early age.

A Man Crush at Age Five

I have distinct memories of a summer revival at our home church, which occurred when I was five years old. A then well-known visiting evangelist and an assisting music director, whose names I still remember, conducted it. This revival was the typical "hellfire and brimstone" series of meetings that went on nightly for a full week, and we attended them all. As was common in the mid-1950s, the church was not air-conditioned; oscillating, wall-mounted "cooling" fans were lined up like soldiers on the side walls to combat the summer heat. Of course, the fans were inept at dispersing the nonstop flow of "heat" emanating from the high-octane, fire-breathing evangelist. Fortunately, a rectangular baptistery measuring about four feet by six feet, containing a pool of three-foot-deep cool water, was positioned just a few feet behind the hoarse-throated evangelist. The promise of instant heat relief was available to anyone who went forward for salvation at the end of the service, as a complete immersion in the pool would soon follow. Night after night, I dreamed of swimming in that pool while watching many folks splash around a bit after getting dunked by the preacher. Also, I was concerned about the possibility of going to hell and, as a result, went forward at the end of a service. Subsequently, I was baptized. This is not the only distinct memory I have of the revival meeting.

Though it was next to impossible to ignore the histrionics of the sweat-drenched, red-faced evangelist, one distraction continually caught the attention of my eyes—the visiting music director. His name was James and he was around thirty years old. He sat in the pulpit area, and I couldn't stop gazing at him and wanting to be around him. James was handsome and, as a five year-old kid, I was smitten by his good looks. Since my mother played the piano for the revival, she worked with him during the week; to my thrill, I had the opportunity to meet him following a service. When the revival was over and the guest leaders left—I cried; the reason was because I had developed a crush on James, the revival music director. When my mother asked me why I was crying, I just said, "I don't know why." No doubt she dismissed my tears as being an emotional reaction to my baptism and the high-voltage revival.

I have frequently thought about this revival and have identified it as being my first recollection of being highly attracted to someone of the same gender. While at this early age there was no sexual connotation, I believe the "roll of the dice" determining sexual orientation had already occurred. Many similar crushes would follow.

My Relationship with Neighborhood Kids

Our neighborhood was overflowing with kids, courtesy of many progeny-prone folks who started making babies after the conclusion of World War II. Many kids my age lived within a stone's throw of our house, so finding playmates was no problem. I loved being with friends and playing games such as Monopoly and kids' Scrabble. In addition, I spent an inordinate amount of time alone when "safe" activities such as these changed to sports. Those solitary times were frequently fraught with boredom and even some mild depression. Of course, at that age I had no idea what depression was. When either of my parents asked if anything was wrong, I said I was bored. They were clearly frustrated and couldn't understand why I sat at home alone. After all, I could be playing ball in the park with the other neighborhood boys. What my parents didn't recognize was that I was already dealing with the early effects of being different from the other boys. It was an increasing source of discomfort. Occasionally, I enjoyed playing badminton, and that was mostly with the girls, which was decidedly comfortable.

When I was in the second grade, my first taste of mild verbal harassment was dealt on the school playground when I was called a "sissy," due to my inept performance playing softball. I also had been fitted with braces on my teeth that same year, but being called "metal mouth" didn't bother me to the degree "sissy" did. That branding followed me throughout my elementary school years, particularly during play period. This one-hour slice of hell on the playground was a dreaded daily requirement I abhorred with a passion and then some. I was much more suited for creative endeavors, like arts and crafts, than anything remotely resembling a ball and a bat. I was a painfully skinny, easy target, and my lack of aptitude for team sports—particularly softball and basketball—was not unnoticed by the guys on the playground. Being frequently called "sissy" was bad enough; the ultimate rejection—actually, a humiliation—was the all-too-familiar ritual of being the last one "selected" when sides were chosen. In other words, the last man standing—usually me—had to be taken by the unlucky team. No doubt I was correctly perceived as a liability. "Seth can't catch and he throws like a girl." Gosh, how recalling that declaration still causes me to wince.

In a futile attempt to gain some respect on the playground, I asked for and received a new softball glove for my birthday. It may as well have been an oven glove for use in the kitchen. I figured out quickly how to put it on, but beyond that it was a useless piece of equipment. My thinking was it might transfer some magic to my playing ability, and maybe the boys at school would admire it and thus admire me. Of course that logic was flawed and, as a result, my playing ability didn't improve, nor did I gain the esteem I desperately sought. Interestingly, not long ago I came across that forever-remembered item of uselessness, enshrined in the garage attic of my parents' house. More than fifty years of baking in the Florida heat had all but destroyed it. Nonetheless, I picked it up and felt the creases now petrified in the palm of my first softball glove. When I was in the fifth grade—and true to prediction—the ultimate confirmation of my seriously deficient catching ability was delivered in the form of a softball that landed squarely in my left eye socket when I was unable to catch the hurtling missile. The blow severely blurred my vision and, in an adrenaline-fueled response, I ran home (it wasn't far). My mother took me to the eye doctor, and it was determined the injury was relatively minor. My vision returned to normal by the next day.

It is astonishing how the emotional imprints of those early softball experiences have remained with me, even as I enjoy my senior years. Several years ago, I was given the opportunity to throw out the first pitch of a baseball game for our local minor league team. I feigned a shoulder condition. The truth is I declined the offer based on my supposition that "Seth throws like a girl." Not much embarrasses me, but this always will.

My entire elementary school experience is remembered more by playground embarrassment than my well-above-average academic achievements—with one exception—and his name was Rob. He was a friend throughout elementary school and, boy, did I ever have a persistent crush on him. I considered him oh-so-cute and tried to be near him. He was a perennial "class darling" with the girls, so I was not alone in my appreciation.

By nature, I was friendly and reasonably extroverted. My relationships with other kids were actually good (other than on the softball field). I "played" well with just about everybody—probably too much so—as I frequently enjoyed entertaining my friends during class. On one occasion, I had an eighth-grade teacher who didn't appreciate my efforts to assist, and, rightfully, he instructed me that "his classroom was not Seth's social hour." However, being studious and reasonably smart, I found my schoolwork came fairly easy; I made excellent grades in spite of my in-class diversions.

My parents expected a lot out of me and were hands-on with my education. If my grades were less than my capability, they were quick to schedule meetings with teachers to see what they could do to get me back on track.

Chapter 4

Defining Moments

Overall, I was an easy-to-manage kid and needed little discipline, although my parents didn't shy away from its administration when needed. As studious and obedient as I was, my parents occasionally caught me during some of my more inopportune moments. There are two disciplinary actions dealt by my dad that are particularly memorable—the first of which was a defining moment that undeniably shaped my behavior for life. The second was "dispensed" when I was about fourteen years old. It was equally memorable, but had much less of a long-term impact.

When I was about ten years old, an overweight boy who lived in the neighborhood rode by the front of our house on his bicycle. He said "Hello, Seth," and, without a thought, I responded by saying "Hello, fatty." My dad was in the front yard and overheard the exchange. He was angrier at me than I had ever seen him. Deservedly, I received a not-to-be-forgotten lecture, followed by the worst spanking I had ever received. It was a summer day, so I retrieved my red wagon, filled it with water from the yard hose, and sat in it to "cool things off." My mother observed the entire scene through the open windows of the house and took a picture of me sitting in the soothing waters of my manmade lake.

She recently showed me the picture and asked if I remembered the circumstances surrounding it. Without a doubt, I did, and we both laughed about it. I will never forget that spanking, and more important, will never forget the lesson I learned from a caring, even if angry, father. I was a tenderhearted kid, and no doubt this lesson amplified my sensitivities toward anyone different. Consequently, I can't stand to see people insulted, called names, or be put down based on their station in life or how they look. There is a disc jockey on an Orlando radio station I occasionally listen to. Every day he makes the comment, "It is nice to be important, but it is more important to be nice." I make efforts to subscribe to that philosophy, which was learned from my dad when I was a young and malleable kid.

The second act of discipline was entirely different. Most of the trouble I managed to find was usually due to petty misbehavior and being a "goofball" at inappropriate times. Sunday night church services were a ripe opportunity for a "performance"—talking, laughing, and doing whatever to amuse myself and the nearby populace. When I was in need of entertainment (which was most of the time), I chose to sit directly in front of Conrad and Ginger Biggersly, who were a sweet couple in their fifties. Ginger was blessed with an unmistakable vocal presence and rejoiced in sharing her talents during all congregational singing opportunities. She was "gifted" with a highly resonant, molto-vibrato voice, accompanied by a remarkable off-pitch singing ability. This lady actually had a gorgeous voice, but couldn't hit a note. It was a performance that several close friends and I never wanted to miss. I laughed uncontrollably, to the point where my sides ached and tears cascaded down my face. Trying not to laugh made the situation even worse. Fortunately, since most folks were occupied with their own singing, my "pause" in decorum was not as noticeable as it could have been—with one conspicuous exception.

During one such occasion when Ginger was in top form—and I was advantageously positioned for maximum exposure—my dad suddenly shot up from his pew, which was in the second row from the front of the church. In horror, I watched him purposefully march toward me along the left wall of the church, straight back to where I was sitting in row fifteen. He motioned for me to stand up, grabbed me by the arm, and ushered me back to row two, where I sat next to him for the remainder of the service. I was aghast and immersed (appropriate for a Baptist church) in embarrassment. Somehow he knew I was leading the charge in the rear of the church. It didn't take long for me to connect the dots. My mother was sitting in the choir loft and had a clear view of what was going on, even though I was fifteen rows back. The church was about half full, so visual distractions from her perch were minimal. She managed to elicit my dad's attention and, through some sort of extrasensory wavelength, communicated that I needed his immediate attention. I certainly received it and was one thoroughly mortified fourteen-year-old kid. When we arrived home, I was subjected to a sermon that included strict directives for "future event" seating at church. Sadly, from that point forward, I forever missed "The Ginger Show" on Sunday evenings. To my knowledge, Mr. and Mrs. Biggersly never knew the source of my laughter.

A Few of My Favorite Things

My tendency as a young boy to spend more time alone than most kids, continued as I approached my teens. Solitary activities were appealing because I could be the master of my own destiny and not worry about making an idiot of myself on the softball field or basketball court. I preferred being outdoors and my favorite activities were closely tied to nature. The natural construction of trees, shrubs, and flowers intrigued me. I loved planting seeds and observing in wonder as plants emerged from the ground to begin their lives, eventually bursting forth in bloom.

I was captivated by the weather, and closely followed local and national daily forecasts. Frequent thunderstorms on summer afternoons demanded my attention; I keenly watched the cumulus clouds suddenly explode into giant heads of cauliflower before releasing their payload of gusty winds, crackling lightning, and torrents of rain. Often, I got a pencil and a piece of paper to draw the clouds in their various stages of development.

Consistent with my interest in the air, another favored activity was assembling and thrusting balsa-wood glider airplanes into the "sky." In fascination, I watched them react with gyrations to the invisible air currents that guided them. (I was not Doppler radar equipped.) In the event that windy weather conditions grounded my fleet of gliders, I shifted efforts to my under-the-grape-arbor playground, where I deployed an army of toy trucks and earthmovers—something else I loved.

The grape arbor was also the site for watching something else that captivated me. When I was about ten years old, the sixteen-year-old boy who lived directly behind us consistently worked out with weights in his backyard. Of course, this was still well before I had entered the "change of life," and accordingly had no understanding of anything sexual. On many afternoons, I knew there was a good chance Benjamin would be working out, and I made sure to make myself available for the "show." I carefully chose the perfect "box seat" so my view would be unobstructed and close up. That perfect spot in my personal theater was under the grape arbor in our backyard. At last, Benjamin would appear "on stage," dressed in a white T-shirt and blue jeans, with a barbell balanced in his hands. He proceeded to do overhead presses and then bicep curls. The sight of his muscles bulging during the routine, which was probably less than twenty minutes, had my eyeballs bulging as well. Benjamin was aware I watched him and he didn't seem to mind. One day, I mustered the nerve to ask him if I could feel his biceps—and he obliged! It enthralled me and is a memory that stands out as being another milestone predictor of my sexual orientation.

One of my pastimes that was rather off the wall—and atypical for a "normal" boy—screamed, "This kid is gay." Occasionally, I enjoyed placing a small cardboard table in the backyard, dressing it with a tablecloth, and setting it for afternoon "tea" with a child-sized plastic tea set I had been given. And yes, I asked for that tea set; the winds were already blowing. I would invite a couple of girls my age in the neighborhood to join me as I served Kool-Aid along with some super-sophisticated crackers called Social Tea Biscuits. I recall once telling my mother that I liked being a "hostess." She quickly advised me that since I was a boy, I needed to refer to myself as the host—and so I did (except when joking around).

When weather conditions precluded outside ventures, I adapted to creative outlets indoors, including two of my favorite hobbies. I had several sets of American Bricks, which were a little like Legos, but more realistic in application. With these bricks, I meticulously constructed houses, churches, and office buildings from the foundation to the roof, and later demolished them for other construction projects. My crowning project was a small city, built on an expanse of open floor in my parents' bedroom. Unfortunately, zoning regulations were not compatible with the property use as a long-term development, and soon my city was the subject of eminent domain. Sadly, it succumbed to a project involving a higher use—my mother's vacuum cleaner. Prior to implosion, which I carried out according to the terms of confiscation, my mother took a photo (which I still have) of my shining city—featuring its ten-year-old architect-contractor. No doubt, the foundations I laid with the plastic bricks also served as an early platform for learning independence and self-sufficiency.

Since I loved airplanes, my parents frequently took me out to the Jacksonville airport on Sunday afternoons to watch the planes land and take off. Accordingly, putting together plastic model airplanes—particularly the commercial airliners—was my other highly favored indoor hobby, mostly in my early teen years. I had a fleet of aircraft I had assembled, and even built an airport on a 4' x 8' piece of plywood to accommodate them. The airport was equipped with painted runways, a terminal building, and an attached concourse—all constructed with my plastic bricks. This complex was housed in the garage, and so the family car could still be parked, my dad designed a way for me to suspend the airport from the garage ceiling when ground-based vehicles occupied the area.

Admittedly, my hobbies were not exactly common ones, yet they helped me to maintain sanity during times when I was frequently lonely. Unbeknownst to me, serious challenges to my emotional health awaited in the not-too-distant future. Nonetheless, my interest in airports and airplanes never waned and was an early predictor of a career choice many years later.

Chapter 5

Opportunities

In corporate America, the word *opportunity* has become a euphemism for a pain-in-the-butt work project that generally nobody wants. When I was a kid, the meaning was the complete opposite. An opportunity was something everyone clamored to capture.

Much to my annoyance, when I was thirteen I was presented with the highly prized "opportunity" to attend summer camp for a week at O'Leno State Park, just north of Gainesville. It was sponsored by a number of Baptist churches in our area, and many of the kids in the neighborhood were signing up. And why not? What kid wouldn't jump at such a fabulous opportunity? Well, me. Most of the listed camp activities were indeed inviting—like eating grilled hamburgers and hot dogs, and roasting marshmallows on an open campfire while singing camp songs like "Kumbaya." There was also the promise of daily swimming in the Santa Fe River, which incidentally was also a natural habitat for our hungry alligator friends. Fortunately, their campsite was a little downstream; consequently, they wouldn't be a deterrent to us jumping in. However, there was one terrifying word that summed up my resolve to not sign up. Softball! It received a prominent position in the billing—not a good sign. To me, softball was in the same category as hell. How about badminton? I'd be up for that. Alligators wouldn't deter me from signing up, but assuredly, softball would.

Fortunately, my parents were wise and never steered me into activities in which I had no inclination. However, the familiar song lyrics, "Hello Muddah, hello Faddah / here I am at Camp Granada," perfectly characterized my fate—my "ass" got shipped to camp. True to the camp billing, softball was the first thing on the agenda after checking in to my assigned eight-man cabin at Camp O'Leno. I was doomed. Without question, I was determined to find a way to avoid the inevitable embarrassment that surely would accompany my association with a damned softball. Fortuitously, my "hide and seek" skills were sharply honed; so my solution was to hide, which enabled me to successfully evade all softball games. Amazingly, there was no roll call on the softball field, and no one seemed to miss me. The rest of the time at camp was as promised; it was a fun week I warmly remember.

Not a Keyboard Prodigy

My parents wanted me to be "well-rounded," and to that end they presented me with the "opportunity" to take piano lessons, which I took for four years, from ages nine to thirteen. What a gift this was, even though my not-so-nimble fingers indicated a questionable propensity for the instrument. It was apparent by the time I was thirteen my middle name was not "Liberace" (at least not for musical purposes). At that glorious moment, my parents allowed me to discontinue the lessons, with one major caveat—a requirement that I join the band when I entered junior high school at the end of the summer. This turned out to be a splendid trade, because I learned to play the tenor saxophone and excelled at it. The biggest bonus, however, was being surrounded by kids with a commonality in music and, thus, a natural camaraderie. It was the first time I felt like I belonged to any group at school. Joining the band turned out to be pivotal; I gained a sense of self-worth and felt valued by schoolmates—both boys and girls.

Shortly after joining the band, I was elected to the student council. Almost overnight, my life had turned 180 degrees and it was reflected in my developing a gregarious, outgoing personality. My junior high years were a time of blossoming that I fondly remember as my happiest school years. Of course, the blossoming I experienced in junior high school also included an awareness of puberty's onset.

What a Hunk

In the summer of 1962, when I was a prepubescent thirteen-year-old, my parents began construction of a new home on the lot adjacent to our house. Another "opportunity" was in the offing. My dad required my brother and me to pitch in and accomplish whatever work we were capable of doing. There was a twofold purpose in this—to save money and to teach us the value of hard work. So, we helped dig the foundation—a task that didn't fit well within my idea of fun. Fortunately, there was one distinctly mitigating factor about the house project and his name was Elijah—a talented workman my dad had hired to lay the concrete blocks. Elijah was an African American gentleman who was built like Hercules (someone else I appreciated). My dad had a great deal of respect for Elijah and the quality of his work, which was why he was hired for the job. Unlike my dad, I was not interested in Elijah's work attributes, but was enthralled with his physical ones. Muscles on top of muscles is how I would describe this living, yet Michelangelo-like sculpture in ebony. When Elijah was laying blocks, I made every effort to be nearby so I could observe his biceps, triceps, and any other "ceps" naturally flex as he effortlessly manhandled thirty-pound concrete blocks. My infatuation with him went well beyond what I think "straight-wired" boys my age would have experienced. I wanted to feel Elijah's sweat-glistened muscles, but was now old enough to know it wouldn't be advisable—unless I wanted to get launched into the stratosphere.

It has intrigued me that even though I didn't associate anything sexual with my infatuation with Elijah, I wanted to touch him. To put things into an understandable context, the 1950s and early 1960s were an innocent time, particularly for kids. Most parents (including mine) protected their children to the hilt from anything they perceived as being unfit for discussion. Sex was not discussed to the degree it is today and sex education was nonexistent in schools. Additionally, movies and television reflected those societal attitudes and never included anything overtly sexual. At this time, at age thirteen, I had never even heard about same-sex attraction. Even if I had, it probably wouldn't have occurred to me that my attraction to Elijah was likely that. Looking back, I am convinced it was. The pattern for my destiny as a gay male was already well established since I was unavoidably and highly attracted to muscular, good-looking men.

Chapter 6

Birds and Bees, According to My Dad – Part One

When I was thirteen, after I entered junior high school, my parents knew the time had come for me to have an initial, high-level discussion about sex. My dad assumed the role of educator. The onset of puberty had not yet begun; however, the time when that phase of my development would kick in was just around the corner.

After I arrived home from school one afternoon, my dad asked me to come into his and my mother's bedroom to chat. He shut the door, smiled, and said we needed to talk about the birds and bees. So I sat in a chair next to his desk and listened. He told me that in order for a baby bird to be born, a male bird must first fertilize a female bird to make an egg that would eventually hatch. He went on to say that much like birds, men and women kind of did the same thing to make babies. This was news to me, since I had assumed—as I had previously been told—that after two people got married, a baby would come when God made it happen. My dad thoughtfully and scientifically elaborated: Babies were the result of men and women falling in love, getting married (this was the early 1960s), and then engaging in the act of sexual intercourse. He outlined that a woman was built differently than a man and he named the individual components making up a woman's sexual anatomy. He explained that a man's penis was not only for urinating—it had another function that was necessary for a woman to have a baby. My testicles were not ignored; that afternoon I learned they worked with some other sexual organs to manufacture semen—a sticky fluid analogous to seeds. Finally, he said the man would find it pleasurable to insert his penis into the woman's vagina and deposit his semen—this was called sexual intercourse. The semen would find its way to a woman's "egg," fertilize it, and in nine months a baby might be born.

I wasn't the least bit interested, but remember asking what would happen if a man's penis wouldn't fit into a woman's vagina. Dead-faced, my dad said for me not to worry because God had designed things to fit automatically. My aforementioned softball glove was a one-size-fits-all item—so I could relate to my dad's explanation. However, unlike a penis, it surely didn't provide any pleasure.

He ended the conversation by telling me that soon I would begin to have a desire to be close with girls and may even want to kiss a girl. When the time arrived, he would have another talk with me because things would make more sense then. There were additional details to our discussion, but I don't remember what they were. My dad cautioned me not to discuss anything about sex with anyone else, as it was a private matter. He further cautioned me that any information I needed should come from him and not from my friends. Thus, the lesson ended and out the door I went.

Chapter 7

Puberty Begins

When I was almost fifteen years old, puberty was knocking on my door with embarrassing voice modulations and greetings of body hair sprouting in previously "barren" places. Other things were also beginning to percolate, as the realization that I was "hard-wired" differently from the male friends with whom I had grown up began to be evident. No surprise, in keeping with established patterns, most of my close friends were girls—probably because they represented a safe haven and not because I was sexually attracted. I wasn't. I did have male friends and spent a fair amount of time with them, primarily playing board games or cards when the weather was lousy. There also was one other activity—much out of the ordinary for me—that I enjoyed with other guys.

As much as I hated softball, I discovered I had a fair degree of athletic ability for playing football—of all things. Many fall afternoons were spent playing sandlot football with the guys in the neighborhood. Mind you, I didn't have the confidence to even consider trying out for the football team at school. Yet I could easily throw and catch a football and, being physically wiry, could run like the wind with it. I was around guys more than I ever had been, and a great deal of conversation was centered on the opposite sex—yes indeed, girls.

In fact, I had a crush (sort of) on the girl who lived a couple of houses down the alley from us. Carolyn was my age, had dark hair, dark eyes, a flawless complexion, and was a majorette in the marching band.

She was undeniably a "looker" and, predictably, had plenty of suitors. She came from a large Catholic family and was the oldest of six kids. Her brother, who was three years younger than us, was also a close friend. Accordingly, I spent much of my free time at their house. I loved this family dearly, and the open door of their home was also a portal to me for opening my mind to religious thought and practices different from my own. In short, it was an early and valuable lesson in embracing diversity.

One day, I was riveted to a conversation between two guys who were comparing notes about having "hard-ons." Although I myself was beginning to experience this physical phenomenon, the initial talk with my dad concerning the birds and bees didn't include the type of gritty disclosure I was now hearing. Therefore, I couldn't relate to the context of this stimulating discussion between my two friends. I was spellbound, listening to every detail as both of these guys testified to obtaining erections when looking at a girl in a bathing suit or even just being around a girl. Unbelievably, the exchange assumed even more graphic testimony!

One of the guys said he had kissed a girl, and when he did, he "shot off" in his pants.

The other guy said, "Yeah, I even had it happen during a dream—I woke up and had stuff everywhere."

They both laughed, and I laughed with them in agreement, even though I was clueless. I knew Carolyn was considered "a hot chick" by the guys at school, and I enjoyed "palling" around with her—but paid little notice to her body as it had developed into that of a young woman. It was lost on me. I had never kissed Carolyn, nor did I have any interest in doing so. No doubt, I was at the point in my development where being around Carolyn should have elicited some sexual urges. Something was off-kilter.

Something happened shortly afterwards that exacted my attention. An athletic guy at school, who was a year older and I didn't know well, came up from behind in a crowded hallway during a class change and grabbed me.

He enveloped me with his arms, immobilizing me in an upper-body squeeze. He pulled me back so he could speak directly into my ear, and said, "I'll bet you'd love what's between my legs, wouldn't you, pretty boy?"

Then he released me and went off in another direction while snickering. The whole encounter lasted no more than five seconds, yet it left me stunned. Amazingly, no one else seemed to notice what had occurred. Although I was embarrassed, it happened too fast to scare me. I had no time to react and never told anyone about being accosted. Why my "attacker" singled me out is a mystery; no doubt he sensed something that even to me was nebulous. Nonetheless, his statement was impactful, mostly because it contained more than a grain of truth—on a visceral level, he excited me. Not long after this incident, he left school and I never saw him again.

Manifestations

One of the more perplexing manifestations of advancing puberty were "out of the blue" erections that were making themselves known at odd times and without any apparent provocation. Inexplicably, they happened suddenly, uncomfortably, and rather glaringly. The most curious of these inopportune episodes occurred in the school cafeteria just about every day when I walked through the lunch line. It felt like the *Titanic* was lurking in between my legs, and, in reality, what was floating in the pond was more akin to the *Queen Mary*. In an effort to hide the embarrassing protuberance when an "attack" was in progress, I carried my lunch tray rather low.

I never figured out the causal mechanism, and assuredly it had nothing to do with the proximity of girls in the cramped surroundings. Perhaps my most personal of members received a little stimulation from the friction created by my tighty-whities. It is still a mystery.

One unavoidable truth which puberty confirmed was that my eye automatically gravitated to the guys in school—particularly the ones who were good-looking, or muscular, or blessed with both attributes. If a "voluptuous" (what's that?) girl was standing next to a "hot" guy, I didn't even notice the girl—not that I would have, anyway. It was increasingly apparent to me I was attracted to guys, but still didn't fully understand it from a gay perspective. I considered the attraction to be a phase and didn't give it much thought. Yet.

Uh-oh

My dad had not yet presented his "continuation course in sex education," and I had reached the time when invaluable information was frequently being disseminated through the "underground." I was about to get "schooled" in masturbation, although the name given for the activity was not that. My first point of contact for an introductory course was offered by a good friend named Bart, who was in my Sunday school class (praise the Lord). Unquestionably, he was one I could trust.

One day, I spent an afternoon over at his house and we were comparing notes regarding our vast collective knowledge of sexually-related topics. Of course, I remembered the caution from my dad about discussing sex with friends, but this was an extraordinary opportunity. Bart and I were the same age, although his schedule for puberty progression was actually accelerated when compared to mine. It also was apparent his "database" was far more complete than mine. He had already augmented his initial education—received from a neighbor—with "independent study." Bart was evidently a scholar in the field; therefore, his knowledge was firsthand.

So we went into his bedroom when we thought it was "safe," shut the door, and each of us crawled into separate twin beds situated against adjoining walls. As instructed, I pulled my britches down so I could freely participate in this highly secretive exploration. Bart gave me a complete demonstration, and being a most eager student, I wanted to pass the course. I watched closely and mirrored his actions intently. Bart told me that thinking about a girl's breasts (particularly those belonging to a girl named Naomi Ferguson) would make things work faster. What? Why would I do that and kill the moment? All I had to do was touch my "member" and it would spring to attention—no need to complicate things by thinking about something I considered a buzzkill. Even though this was an at-a-distance lesson as far as Bart was concerned, I had a strong urge to get close and wanted to touch his "private zone." However, I resisted the temptation and continued as tutored. In probably less than a minute, I was catapulted into the euphoric sexual stratosphere for the first time in my life. I had no idea what had happened to my body, and felt electrified. I didn't connect the experience to anything my dad had discussed during the "birds and bees" talk. I was "dumber than dirt."

About the time we were finishing the "science project," we heard footsteps coming down the hall, and quickly pulled up the sheets. Bart's mother, who we thought had gone to the grocery store, suddenly opened the door and wanted to know what we were doing. Bart told her we were taking a nap, but the look on her face said it all; she knew. I remember feeling immeasurably embarrassed and overcome with guilt. No question, it was time for me to go home; I called my mother, and within a few minutes she picked me up. With much dread, I expected Bart's mother to fill my mother in on what had transpired in Bart's bedroom.

The day passed without any such communication—and with every ring of the phone, my heart raced. I expected it to be "the call." Much to my relief, it never came.

Not long after I successfully completed Bart's introductory course, I started to experience considerable guilt with each "practice." I fully expected God would punish me with a dreadful disease if I didn't stop. In fact, one of the guys at school said it would cause blindness if done too often—and I believed it. Did I mention my junior high student newspaper (*The Clarion*), named me as "most gullible"? When I asked my mother what it meant, she said it was another way of saying people liked me. Yes, I believed her.

Bart's family left Jacksonville just prior to his senior year in high school, and we lost contact with each other. I was delighted to locate him recently and reestablish contact after not knowing where he was for nearly fifty years. He is straight, happily married, and has a family.

Birds and Bees – Part 2

Sure enough, my parents duly noted the physical and emotional changes occurring in me. One evening, and true to his word, my dad sat me down next to his desk to conduct the second in his two-part series of my continuing Sex Ed. (There was a third, impromptu, and extremely uncomfortable installment that will be discussed later.) So, the talk began and initially was focused on my feelings and emotions, as opposed to the subject matter contained in the Part One syllabus. If you recall, that session focused on "his and hers" body parts.

My dad started the session by asking me how I felt when I was around Carolyn (the attractive girl who lived down the alley). I said I liked her.

He asked me why, and I stated, "Because she is fun to be with."

This would have been an expected answer for a prepubescent teen, but I was well beyond that stage. I believe my dad wanted to hear something different, something like, "Man, she is a fox, and I want to date her!" What I didn't say probably concerned him, and I feel my parents already perceived I might be tilting in another direction—based on how my dad ended the discussion.

My dad talked about erections, about how they were necessary to have sexual intercourse with a woman, and how wonderful the sensation was when ejaculating semen into the woman's vagina. The dive deepened as he described what semen looked like and explained it contained sperm along with other components. He exacted my full attention when he said semen was sometimes called cum. In a split second, I recalled Bart's lesson had included this descriptor. Bingo, I connected the dots and the lights came on.

Everything—well, almost everything—from *A* to *Z* was covered in my dad's dissertation, including how to prevent pregnancy and the necessity to not engage in sex until after marriage. My dad then spun the conversation in a different direction that made me squirm. He warned me about boys who wanted to "touch" other boys and even engage in disgusting acts with each other—acts that were "sinful and perverted." He didn't ask me if I had any such desires, and sternly told me "these people" were deviants and known as "queers." My stomach was churning and I could feel my face flush. Thank God, the talk was almost over, but not until an explanation of masturbation and its evils was portrayed. He did mitigate his caution by saying it was a difficult habit to break. This bullet point was covered a little too late, yet it didn't go unnoticed.

"Seth, do you have any questions?"

I said, "No, sir," and walked out of the room—but felt like running.

My dad's comments pertaining to same-sex attraction during the "birds and bees" talk have remained a curiosity. Recently, I had a discussion with my brother about his recollection of talks he had with our dad. Specifically, I wanted to know if there was ever any discussion about boys touching each other or engaging in sexual activities.

He said, "Definitely not."

His answer settled my curiosity—my dad probably suspected rather early that I might have gay inclinations.

Dreams and Themes

Specific mile markers continued to announce my sexual maturation—one in particular at a most unexpected time. Not long after the second "sex talk" with my dad, I experienced my first sexual dream. This was the one topic he had not covered. Fortunately, I had not forgotten the unbelievable account of such an occurrence that was previously corroborated by two aforementioned schoolmates. In the middle of the night when my mind was at its most unfiltered state, the dream to end all dreams happened. No girls were in the cast (what a shock), but that surely didn't stop my subconscious mind from writing a script straight from the X-rated dream catalog. There were two cast members in my private play: a guy I barely knew, and me. This acquaintance at school had beautiful hair I admired, but I was never aware of being attracted to him. There really was no apparent physical attribute (like bulging biceps) meriting his inclusion into my play; nonetheless, he auditioned for the part and got it. The dream involved a kiss and touching in highly sensitive zones. Just as our activities were getting to that "point of no return" excitement, something happened to end the dream suddenly. Much to my disappointment, I was jolted from sleep before the scene was complete—so I thought. Much to my surprise, I discovered proof the final scene was indeed physically complete, even though emotionally it was not. In disbelief, I found I had ejaculated during the final act of the play, which is probably what woke me. What a mess I had, not to mention an overwhelming sense of guilt. Once fully awake, I collected myself, cleaned up, and then prayed, asking God to never let me have such a "sinful" dream again. It was ecstasy followed by agony.

Predictably, the dreams continued with increasing frequency and began to include passionate kissing, coupled with tight embraces. Never did any of these dreams involve girls; my subconscious orientation was purely same-sex, as well as its conscious counterpart. One unerring theme was that some sort of unwanted interruption consistently ended the dream before a satisfactory conclusion occurred, even though an ejaculation sometimes occurred. Fear of being found out was, without fail, a major component of the storyline. As a result, it was usually realized in the form of someone walking in and discovering the "illicit" activity. I would wake up in a panic, and would pray—yet again—begging God to deliver me from these dreams which I felt would doom me to hell.

Talk Number Three (Oh, God!)

Nocturnal ejaculations left telltale stains on my sheets and pajamas despite my diligence in wiping them off. Mother began to notice them when doing laundry and knew what they were. She mentioned it to my dad, which resulted in "Talk Number Three." As had been the usual protocol for the previous two talks, I was summoned to my parents' bedroom by my dad and asked to sit down by his desk. I had no idea what it was about, and he looked dead serious. Never one to first "circle the corral" (unlike me), he went straight to the point and said my mother had noticed stains on my sheets and pajamas. I had never noticed them, yet quickly deduced what he was referencing. I was horribly embarrassed. My dad assumed I was "taking care of business" in the bed. In no uncertain terms, he told me if I had to do it, to please direct the "output" away from my pajamas and sheets. *Holy cannoli!* Even if I had used my bed as a platform for self-gratification, I would have had the good sense to be prepared for the eruption. So I told my dad the truth: I admitted I was indeed experiencing "releases" at night, but it was happening during my sleep and therefore was uncontrollable.

He seemed incredulous at first, and then asked a question impossible to forget: "What are you dreaming about when this occurs?"

I knew I could never tell the truth, and rationalized the sin of lying was much less serious than the resulting consequences if the truth were divulged. Therefore, I responded, "I don't know, I never remember."

My dad was not stupid, and I am sure he recognized I would remember a dream significant enough to produce an ejaculation. Thankfully, he didn't pursue it, and no further talks regarding sex ever occurred.

As previously mentioned, my nocturnal fantasyland adventures presented an unpleasant side effect—awakening to the sticky "goo" that invariably jolted me into wide-awake lucidity. It was unpleasant and disruptive. This was now exacerbated by the laundry complication my nighttime frolics created for my mother. Something had to be done, so I decided to conduct a study in hopes of finding an acceptable solution. I had not yet been exposed to corporate America, so I was ahead of my time in choosing this approach. Unlike what the studies in my corporate experiences have since yielded—usually nothing—I came up with a brilliant solution. The best way to eliminate the problem causing the unpleasantness and the stains, was to reduce the likelihood of "overflow" ever creating a mess to begin with. To that end, I employed two preventions that performed miraculously. The first of which was to ditch the pajamas and, instead, sleep in my "tighty-whities." Compared to the loose-fitting pajamas, the underwear reduced the chance for my emissions to fully escape into the surrounding atmosphere. Secondly, before going to bed, I stuffed my underwear with a copious amount of toilet paper, which did a great job of containing spillage before it became a "hazmat" site. It worked! And as hoped, no further comments were made by my dad—even though the wet dreams didn't abate.

Chapter 8

Straws and Pom-Poms

By the time I entered high school, it was apparent I had inherited my mother's wacky sense of humor and, like my dad, was analytical. I loved being around people, and the church provided a wonderful opportunity for developing social skills. For this, I remain grateful. Nonetheless, I had a yearning for more than what was provided through my church. I wanted to learn to dance, but never went to dances. Assuredly, Southern Baptist churches didn't sponsor any, as dancing was undeniably frowned on. My parents were not prudes, but would never "buck" the church. Therefore, they didn't encourage me to attend school dances (other than the benign annual school proms). I had a decent degree of musical ability and a great sense of rhythm, so dancing would have been a natural extension. I began to feel left out. Most of my close friends were Southern Baptist and in the same boat—except they seemed content.

As I neared completion of my course in puberty and began assuming the physical profile of a young man, it was concerning to my parents that I displayed no interest in dating girls. After all, it was past time; I was then a high school student in the tenth grade. To clarify, my parents were not exactly on target in their assumption I was disinterested in girls—I actually was interested, yet not in a manner that would please them. The all-girl cheerleader troop at school was a constant fascination—and not because they were attractive and had bouncing breasts. I lusted for something else—their pom-poms. So much so that I made my own set from crepe paper, cut into long, flowing strips. Boy, were they ever fabulous; however, I was smart enough to keep them well hidden. When no one was around to view the spectacle, I practiced doing cartwheels and cheers with my over-the-top pom-poms. It was just another facet of my own secret world.

My parents and, in particular, my mother, were increasingly uneasy with my sexual maturation—no doubt, something was perceived as being "a tad" askew. My mother began to make comments in my presence that I think were designed to keep me from becoming gay—as if I had a choice in the matter. I'll call it an early attempt at "prevention therapy." One such statement she made to her sister, which I distinctly remember, was that she would rather have a knife in her heart than to find out either of her two boys were "homosexualists." She frequently shared her "insights" about gays in the form of tiresome derogatory pronouncements. While these barbs were never directed at me, there was no question they were intended for my edification. Usually her editorials were precipitated by a gay-related story she'd read in the newspaper or saw on the evening newscast—but not always.

One of her funnier depictions centered on a woman living in the neighborhood who she heard had "gone lesbian." My mother railed, "I just can't understand how in the world she could decide to do such a thing; and she is a pretty girl too."

Based on her assessment, I guess being attractive should normally be an exclusion to qualify for membership. There was no question my mother was extraordinarily uncomfortable with gays and lesbians. Her "set in concrete" views were indisputably due to the way she was raised (by an over-the-top Fundamentalist Baptist father), where she was raised (in rabidly conservative North Florida), and the continuing, overwhelming influence of the church. She was one to never deeply question some of her ideas, particularly if they were rooted in church doctrine. Interestingly, my self-controlled, deep-thinking dad never made any such comments, even though I knew his stance on the subject of same-sex relationships was aligned with the church. As level-headed and rational as my mother otherwise was, she clearly couldn't handle the thought of me possibly being gay. I knew her fears were borne out of love for me, yet that didn't make my situation any easier.

In the midst of this period in my life, my mother shared two preposterous ideas that had to have come from the official "God Only Knows Where" repository. They were nonetheless consistent with her mindset when it came to the topic of gay behavior. The first had to do with drinking straws; that's right—straws. I had not given this important household item sufficient thought or study, and, gratefully, my mother informed me they were primarily for girls. I learned it was much more masculine for a guy to drink straight from a bottle or glass rather than employ a straw for conveyance. This in itself was invaluable, and the punchline that followed was worthy of framing. It was imparted, with authority, that "homosexualists" were known to use straws when drinking from glasses and bottles. *Woweeeeeee!* With the feared gay population explosion, which unquestionably was the result of successful recruiting efforts, I figured I should buy stock in a straw manufacturer. Unfortunately, financial considerations and no tie-ins with a brokerage firm precluded any such investment activity.

Another one of my mother's notions she threw from left field was her idea that a man's hair should be parted on the left. This was because parting on the right was known to be a "homosexualist" characteristic. Since it was easier for me to part my hair on the right instead of the left, I parted it on the right. As far as I knew, there was no other underlying reason dictating why I parted my hair on the right side of my head. Even if parting one's hair on the right was some sort of secret signal to others of the same persuasion, it was no longer a secret.

Much to my surprise, I later discovered my mother's ideas regarding straws and hair parting were widely-held beliefs. There was no internet back in those days, so "intelligence" along these lines typically passed through the grapevine as fact. Although on a much greater scale, the "righteous" folks in Salem had used a similar means of intelligence gathering to determine who was a witch and thus worthy of being burned at the stake. I don't think things have changed much, given the amount of vehement and erroneous political email fodder frequently forwarded to me as fact. No matter where my mother obtained her information, she believed it, like the folks in Salem did. The implication was clear: she was nervous about some of my traits and desperately wanted to change them. She mentioned on more than one occasion she was concerned some people would perceive me to be a "sissy." Had I shared my pom-pom routines, there no longer would have been a perception.

Failed Antidote

My dad was successful in just about anything he did—with one notable exception involving me. Beginning when I was in my teens, he did his dead-level best to get me involved in learning car mechanics, so I could do my own repair work when "easy-to-fix" things needed attention. And who knows, perhaps the activity could, as a possible secondary consideration, "butch" me up. My dad and my brother were enraptured by auto mechanics and spent hours under the hood, which to them smelled like a rose garden. Not for me; just about any less greasy alternative was preferable to what lurked under the dirty hood of a car. Nonetheless, my dad insisted I learn to change the oil—and I succeeded, even though I purely hated doing it. More complex endeavors like replacing belts or a malfunctioning alternator required extensive tutoring, which invariably ended in futility and frayed nerves for both of us. No doubt, my undisguised lack of enthusiasm was difficult for my dad to comprehend—particularly since my brother found grease and wrenches to be a marriage made in car heaven. My dad eventually gave up; car mechanics was clearly not in my wheelhouse and consequently a lost cause. Interesting thing: An aptitude test I took in high school showed a strong propensity for mechanical reasoning. What?

"Sweet" 16

I was a responsible kid, which included appropriate use of the family car. By the time my sixteenth birthday rolled around, I proved to my driving teacher (Dad) that I could be trusted behind the steering wheel of the car. Accordingly, he reached a sufficient comfort level to "release" me to solo driving, subject to the concurrence of the great state of Florida. Fortunately, after passing the state-mandated driving test, the Florida Department of Motor Vehicles agreed with my dad's assessment and awarded my unrestricted license.

Subsequent to that joyful occasion, the keys to the family car were frequently offered, which was a thrill, but not for the most singular of reasons that excited most guys—dating. This was a subject in which I had minimal interest, yet it was highly advisable for me to at least feign participation in this rite of passage. I frequently "took out" a couple of girls I knew from the church, and in the truest context, they were not dates. It may have looked that way to my parents; they would give me the car keys, and observe me leaving and then returning several hours later. Upon my return, they would ask, "Did you have a nice time?" My answer was usually a rather perfunctory "Yes." What they couldn't observe was my disinterested demeanor during the date.

I was a perfect gentleman with impeccable manners, which would please any parent. I was just a little too perfect. During the course of a date, there was no hand-holding, no sitting in the car at some romantic spot, and no smooching. I may as well have been with my brother. My typical date would include taking a girl to a movie, grabbing a pizza, or, more likely, attending a church function. Afterwards, I would take her straight home, walk her to the door, say good night, and quickly turn around to scamper back to the car.

There was one girl in particular I frequently "dated," although my lack of physical intent was not lost on her. I overheard her tell a mutual friend our relationship was platonic, after she had been asked if we were serious. I had no idea what the word meant and, without delay, my curiosity led me to the dictionary. It said a platonic relationship was one lacking physical or sexual desire. Damn! The dictionary knew me well—and so did my date.

My mother had taken note that I had never been particularly interested in any girl, unlike every other testosterone-charged guy in the neighborhood. No doubt, my testosterone tanks were fully charged—and laced with a lot of "sugar." Nonetheless, my mother insisted I just had not found the right girl. She said convincingly that one day soon, some girl would "knock me off my feet." She added that some guys mature a little later than others in this regard and for me not to be discouraged. I rationalized she may be right, and my "gay tendencies" would end at that "knocked off" point—which hopefully wouldn't result in a "knocked-up" situation. Years later, I discovered my mother was at least partially right when I was indeed "knocked off my feet."

The question, "Seth, do you have a girlfriend?" or even worse, "How is your love life?" was frequently asked by various people, particularly at church. Gosh, how I detested that distressing question. An exaggerated smile and a couple of eye winks frequently added drama to the facial expression of the individual asking the question. Instantly, I would feel the familiar yet uncontrollable flushing in my face. I wanted to yell, "I have no girlfriend, desire no love life with a girl, and please mind your own business." Of course, I merely smiled and said something like, "It's fine, thank you." Invariably, my mother's response, when describing my dating life to her inquiring friends, was, "Seth is still a little shy with the girls, but we are sure that will be changing soon."

At about the same time, an older cousin got married in The Cathedral of St. Augustine. (That part of the family was Roman Catholic and without a doubt less uptight.) A woman my mother knew sauntered over to a group of us during the reception, with her glass of champagne strategically balanced in her hand. I was turned off by her affected demeanor and perusing eyes. I had no recollection of ever having met this "Mrs. Robinson" (from *The Graduate* movie) type of woman.

Nonetheless, she said to my parents, "This must be Seth."

I smiled and admitted to her supposition, at which point she made the remark, "I bet you have the girls lined up to date you."

My mother beamed and said, "Yes, he has plenty of opportunity."

I interjected, "Not really."

Of course, the "champagne lady's" comment was complimentary, but it was not something I welcomed, particularly in the presence of my parents. It served to add more fuel to my parents' fire.

By the time I entered my junior year in high school and neared my seventeenth birthday, I was aware of my overwhelming sexual attraction to guys, and more noteworthy—still none for girls. My lack of desire to look at a *Playboy* magazine centerfold was clearly an indicator my compass was pointing in a different direction. Not surprisingly, I had never seen photos of a nude female (other than in *National Geographic*) and am certain most of the guys my age had already ravenously consumed any *Playboy* that could be surreptitiously obtained. While the guys in high school were riveted by the likes of Jill St. John and Raquel Welch, I was equally enthralled with Sean Connery and John Gavin—and imagined being kissed by either of these two "gods." The female anatomy was of little interest to me—nothing about it was appealing.

Even so, I continued to believe my lack of interest was a phase, and hoped for that much-heralded "knocked off my feet" moment. I prayed daily and waited patiently, believing the phase would soon end. My anxiety was compounded by a great deal of guilt when I found myself frequently daydreaming about certain guys in a sexual context. I became sexually excited, and like most other guys on the planet, took matters "into my own hands" to relieve the "tension." My actions resulted in increasing guilt; so much so that I kept a small calendar where I would mark an *x* on the days where I couldn't resist the natural urge. My goal was to go as many days as I possibly could without "doing it." On the days when I succumbed to the temptation, the *x* signified failure and thus the need for more prayer. It was a vicious, self-destructive circle. I was deeply troubled, felt alone, and my course was vectored for an unavoidable, soon-coming crash. Surely, I was no more sexually charged than my straight counterparts, but my charging station was clearly from a different outlet and even that was short-circuiting.

Two rather improbable sources of sexual interest were, of all things, the J.C. Penney and Sears catalogs. Back in those days, the catalogs were huge and typically delivered by U.S. Mail to the door. I couldn't wait for the latest edition to arrive, so I could pore over the pages most interesting to me—the glossy ones containing good-looking men modeling physique-revealing sportswear, swimsuits, and yes, even underwear! Needless to say, the magnificence of the male architecture printed on those pages was of supreme interest and demanded close scrutiny. The catalog was obliged to give equal space to the ladies modeling their panties and bras, and as far as I was concerned, those pages were pointless (they were not printed in 3-D). The catalogs represented my first foray into printed material eliciting a sexual response. They in fact served as my *"Playboy,"* even though there was no nudity or "redeeming" literary contribution. It is doubtful the intent of these iconic retail establishments was to provide such a voyeuristic opportunity, yet it was not something escaping my inquiring, wide-open eyes.

A Guy Named Hector

The terms "queer," "sissy," and "69er" were commonly heard in school, usually in nonsexual contexts. Other than being called "sissy" in elementary school, seldom were any of these words aimed at me other than in joking around. I had a well-developed sense of humor and a knack for getting along with just about anybody; thus, any jokes at my expense were easily deflected. Even so, I abhorred these three aforementioned terms, even when dispensed in a joking, nonsexual context. In particular, "69er" became highly detestable because of an inexcusable situation at school I am confident would be categorized today as gay harassment.

There was an unassuming, relatively quiet guy in my class, Hector, who was continually picked on by a small group of jerks because they perceived him as being "queer," whatever that meant. He was verbally bullied, which went largely ignored because it was probably not considered serious, and awareness was not heightened as it is today. Whether or not he was gay, I will never know. For whatever reason, this group of guys had it in for him. Hector was a lot like me—studious, not a jock, not confrontational, and a little soft around the edges. He was quiet (unlike me), a sweet kid, and an enemy to no one. Afraid to say anything for fear I would be the next target, I watched in silence as two or three jeering guys frequently chased Hector down the halls while yelling "Sixty-niner" at him. I never understood the choice of terms; nonetheless, the inference was that he was gay. Occasionally they cornered him, yelling that he better "haul butt," or he would be "racked in the nuts." His assailants laughed uncontrollably and scooted off to their next class. Hector just took it and would hang his head, never saying much of anything, which was his best defense. I don't know if any teachers ever witnessed these episodes, which were usually between classes. If they did, nothing ever changed. In one of my school yearbooks, someone wrote "69er" across Hector's picture, which infuriated me then and still does today when I look at it. For all I know, someone may have done the same thing to my picture in someone else's yearbook. It has haunted me that I didn't stick up for him when no one else did. Sadly, Hector was killed in an automobile accident a few months after high school graduation.

Chapter 9

Disaster Hits—I Enter My Senior Year in High School

At the beginning of my senior year in high school, I entered a period of personal struggles that marked what would be the most unhappy and challenging period of my life. I was never bullied in high school and was more or less ignored by the guys in my class. It was the same feeling of being left out I had experienced in elementary school (and beyond), when I was the last person chosen to participate in a ball game. Even so, it was preferable to the hell Hector endured.

There was one unforgettable exception to being ignored that resulted in my being injured as a result of a practical joke. One of the guys in the band, whom I had considered a friend, pulled the chair from behind me as I was about to sit down with my tenor sax in hand. The floors in the band room were concrete, and I landed extremely hard, squarely on my tailbone. While a few of my classmates viewed the deed as comical, I didn't. My usual reaction of laughing things off with everyone else was replaced with an angered response I can't remember exactly. The immediate effect, other than the insult, was intense pain emanating from a bruised coccyx. It took me over a year to recover from it, and the event signaled the beginning of intermittent back problems that plagued me from that point forward.

The chair incident was coupled with my general dissatisfaction with the band director's lackadaisical attitude. In fact, I had become disenchanted with the band in my junior year, and overall was in a better frame of mind then, to handle it. Our band was commonly referred to as the "marching snakes," due to our inability to stay in straight lines when marching. Honestly, I found the "marching snakes" moniker humorous, yet still rationalized it to be a valid reason to quit. So, as a perceived panacea to my deteriorating mental stability, I quit the band during the second week of my senior year. My parents didn't overly object, which in itself still remains a question mark. In reality, leaving the band was probably the worst action I could have taken, as far as my mental health was concerned.

The general unhappiness that raised its ugly head toward the latter part of my junior year had rapidly spiraled down into a full-blown depression—in fact, a severe one. My interest in life had degraded to the point where I loathed the dawning of each day. My primary escape was sleep, which came easily and was a daily event I greatly anticipated. When awake, my world was consumed with introspection, fear, and being miserable. If my junior high school years were Mt. Everest, my high school years had descended into Death Valley. I was seventeen years old, had developed an inferiority complex, and was in an out-of-control downward spiral.

My grades had been excellent, and as a result I was inducted into the National Honor Society during my junior year. Unfortunately, my senior-year depression handicapped me with a vengeance and initiated a cascade of events, not the least of which was difficulty concentrating on my studies. Even worse, my efforts in studying were continually thwarted by dark, scary thoughts enveloping me like a fog. As a result of lousy grades in trigonometry, I was put on probation by the National Honor Society, and when that occurred, my parents consulted with the school to locate a tutor. As luck would have it, a good-looking guy in my class volunteered to tutor me, and, not surprisingly, my interest level in the subject perked up—so did my trigonometry grades. As I had hoped, the National Honor Society restored my good standing. Nonetheless, the depression tenaciously remained, and my parents didn't recognize its gravity. They knew I was troubled, at least on some level, but clearly didn't understand what I was experiencing. Accordingly, they were at a loss in handling it. I didn't understand it either and, when asked by my parents why I was unhappy, I said, in all honesty, "I don't know." I didn't possess the mental maturity to connect the dots.

My Parents' Response

My dad was ahead of his time in his belief that physical exercise was an excellent antidote to anxiety. Every morning before I went to school, he required me to ride my bicycle through the neighborhood for about a half hour to relieve my "stress." I thought it was a ludicrous idea, but psychologists today have validated his belief to be true. I can't say the bicycle riding had a significant impact because it didn't address the cause of my depression. Psychological intervention would have been in order, but during those times, such remedies were largely frowned on by many—including my parents. Additionally, my dad's brother had gone through electroconvulsive therapy some years prior for a depressive disorder, which all but destroyed his life. As a result, my parents were hesitant to consult a psychologist or psychiatrist. When I was in high school, the type of counseling—and understanding—I needed was not available. Even if it had been, any uncovering of my sexual desires would likely have resulted in my being referred to our pastor or someone else connected to the church. No telling what "remedies" would have been employed, and I shudder to think what could have happened. I had no place to turn to other than myself.

Along with my daily bicycle excursions, I also received "encouraging talks" from my parents, designed to elevate my somber mood. They urged me to look on the bright side and reminded me my senior year in high school should be one of the happiest times of my life. They said how fortunate I was to be college bound, which I fully recognized, but being reminded of something wonderful coming in the near future fell on "deaf ears."

The ultimate attempt to elevate my mood came in one oft-repeated statement that drove me near the brink of the cliff. "Seth, you would feel much better if you dated girls. I am sure any girl would love for you to ask them out. What about Trish? Her mother said she would love to go out with you."

I wanted to scream, since this statement, with a few variations, was made with such predictable regularity that it became a mantra—creating even more anxiety. Astonishingly, I didn't fully recognize my lack of interest in girls was a significant clue to the source of my depression.

Another contributing factor to my depression was my church and its "our way or you go to hell" philosophy. Being gay, even if it was a "temporary" condition, caused me to begin questioning—although with much guilt—everything I heard coming from the pulpit. I began to consider if I really was gay, then God surely made me that way because I had no say in the matter. Why would God send me to hell for something with which I had nothing to do? This was one thought that comforted me, though slightly.

Light in a Lightless Tunnel

During this time in my life, my parents frequently took me to our family physician, Dr. Hiram Edwards. I was plagued with acid reflux, nausea, sometimes vomiting, sometimes diarrhea, light-headedness—you name it, I had it. I was a raging hypochondriac, a consummate worrier, and imagined every ache, every pain to be a harbinger of a life-threatening illness. Gosh, did my parents ever have their hands full. The most curious part of this was, as afraid as I was of being deathly ill—I was considering suicide. This would have been the ultimate escape from myself.

My trips to Dr. Edwards were much more than being told by him there was nothing seriously wrong physically. This much-beloved man was counseling me by addressing my real and imagined physical maladies. He was in his late thirties, a little shorter than average, bordering rotund, with thinning hair, and as laid back as a beach blanket. Nothing ever seemed to faze him. Oh, and one other detail—according to my mother, he was rumored to be gay. Dr. Edwards gave me ample time to talk and served as a ray of light in the endless dark tunnel where I resided most of the time. He repeatedly assured me my physical symptoms were a result of my mental state, which my parents had also told me; more important, he gave me substantive hope. He challenged me to not dwell on things I couldn't change. We didn't talk about sex—at least not then—but I am convinced he knew I was gay and that most of my struggles were hinged to that fence post. He extended a lifeline—his personal phone number—and told me to call him if I needed to talk; I did on many occasions. Obviously, I didn't kill myself, much in part to Dr. Edwards' unheralded care. Over time, he became a close, life-changing friend.

Thank God—I Graduate

My grueling senior year finally ended and I graduated in June 1967. No doubt, depression—regardless of the reason—feeds on itself like misery breeds more misery. It was a vicious circle. When I recall my last year in high school, my primary recollection is it was anything but "the happiest time in my life"—I have almost no pleasant memories.

Nonetheless, I lived through it and left with survivor skills greatly contributing to my ability to withstand life's storms. My depression was a wide-open avenue whereby I had no choice but to start questioning the church, myself, and life in general. That component was positive.

Following my high school graduation, my parents wisely required me to find a job for the summer. The income would be welcome and, more important, the diversion would occupy a good bit of my time and provide a fresh, positive focus. Actually, I had cut neighborhood lawns to earn money since I was old enough to push a lawnmower; however, the structure of a steady job would offer more stability and responsibility. As luck would have it, Carolyn (the appealing girl who lived down the alley) had a lead for my possible employment. Her parents had a close friend who was a manager at the J.C. Penney store near our house; through them, I landed a job working in the shoe department. This was an early lesson in the value of networking. In addition to working at Penney's, I frequently went surfing with my two "buddies," Carolyn and Rosemary. Rosemary, who was a close friend from the high school band, had a beat-up van perfect for hauling our surfboards. My long-established pattern of usually hanging out with the girls rather than the guys had not changed. I didn't have any male friends who ever asked me to surf with them (except for Carolyn's younger brother). Through the kindheartedness of Carolyn and Rosemary, I was "adopted" and they taught me how to surf.

While the summer of 1967 marked a slowly improving mental state, I was not particularly happy. Something was missing. Unfortunately, it would take me several more years to come to terms with myself.

Chapter 10

College Bound (Sort Of)

After much soul-searching, my parents and I made the collective decision that I would remain living at home and enroll in the local community college (then called Florida Junior College) to begin my college years. Clearly, I didn't possess the maturity or mindset to go off to a four-year university, and since I had not yet chosen my major, it was a relatively easy decision. Most of my closest friends elected to leave Jacksonville to attend college, and admittedly, I was a little embarrassed to be staying home.

Although I didn't view it positively, FJC (jokingly called Fruit Juice College) was a huge blessing to me and also to my parents. It was affordable, the quality of teachers was good, and the student-teacher ratio was low. The "campus" I attended was a former military housing complex which spread across fifty or so acres. Abandoned 1940s-era duplex housing units had been retrofitted into spartan classrooms. The drabness of the buildings didn't bother me, but the major downside to attending FJC was that it was a commuter school. There was little camaraderie among students, and I was pining for connectivity.

While at FJC, I made a surprising academic discovery about myself—an affinity for subjects relating to the arts. I aced courses in humanities, art appreciation, psychology, human relations, and philosophy. This was a surprise, as my aptitude tests in high school suggested I should pursue a science degree. Interestingly, I encountered some difficulty with science courses, whereas the non-science, arts-related courses were a joy. These courses proved valuable; they greatly contributed to my overall "rounding." In addition, they imparted a respect and appreciation for things in life that are less statistically measured—and I was a statistics hound.

As I began my second year at the community college, the choice of a major had been narrowed down to two possibilities. Meteorology was my first consideration, and ornamental horticulture was a close second. Both complemented my interest in nature, although the curriculum required for a degree in meteorology was heavy in courses where I struggled—physics and calculus. I chose ornamental horticulture, with the goal of working in the nursery industry after obtaining my degree.

While at FJC, I made a few friends, but none resulted in any long-term connections. My outside-the-classroom experience was nonexistent; even so, FJC was the right fit for me. I graduated with an associate of arts degree in June 1969. During those first two years in college, my depression became more transient, yet still simmered in the background. I was active in my church (even though I didn't agree with the dogma), studious in school, mowed lawns, and worked at J.C. Penney on the weekends. My various involvements helped to keep my depression from assuming the full-blown proportions that hamstrung me in high school. There was one other significant positive—my dating life was an absolute zero (thankfully!) because my "girlfriends" from church were away at school.

Even though my first two years of college were not a mountaintop experience, the world view to which I was exposed greatly expanded my perspectives. Today, I realize those years at FJC were significant contributors to positive growth.

College Bound (Really!)

The University of Florida (UF) in Gainesville was the most logical place for me to obtain the degree I was seeking. The school boasted the large, highly-regarded Institute of Food and Agricultural Sciences (IFAS), and was affordable. It was seventy miles from Jacksonville, which was far enough to be out of town, yet close enough to get home promptly if necessary. The application process was straightforward, particularly for a transfer student with good grades from an in-state community college. Accordingly, I received a letter of acceptance on January 11, 1969, which was about nine months prior to commencement of classes in the fall. As the September report date approached, I experienced a degree (actually, several degrees) of apprehension. Fortunately, I was much better equipped to enter a major four-year university than two years prior.

UF required incoming first-year students to check in to their dormitory—mine was North Hall—several days prior to the beginning of classes. This would allow me to become familiar with the campus, register for classes, and meet the guys with whom I would be sharing space. The day arrived—Sunday, September 14, 1969—and off to Gainesville we went (after church) in my parents' 1962 Chevrolet Impala. The trip took a little over an hour. During that brief time of captivity, I received last-minute encouragement and advice, including the suggestion that I join the Baptist Student Union (BSU) as soon as possible. (The BSU had already sent me a welcome letter, which I still have.)

My mother added, "It is a wonderful place to meet nice girls."

This "warning" was all the reason I needed not to affiliate.

By the time we arrived at my dormitory, which was within a stone's throw of the football stadium, I had become anxious. The three of us entered an almost-empty building with a few hang-up items, a bag containing my shoes, two overstuffed suitcases filled with underwear, jeans, shorts, and knit shirts, and a dopp kit fully stocked with daily hygiene necessities. We walked into my lifeless, Dumpster-view, first-floor room, which contained two desks, two single beds, two tiny closets, and two chests of drawers. All were positioned on a tan, worn-out vinyl floor. My new surroundings were devoid of any decoration other than venetian blinds hanging in front of a bank of large casement windows. The room was a wide-open blank canvas. My parents helped me transfer my worldly goods into one of the chests and a closet. They made sure I had my registration papers and prepaid "meal ticket." They didn't tarry after I was settled in the room, and my dad issued last-minute instructions for me to eat all my meals.

The three of us walked to the car as I fought to choke back tears. Before leaving, my mom and dad expressed their love and assured me my experience at UF would be the most wonderful time in my life.

In my wildest dreams, I had no idea how prophetic their prediction would be.

The Phoenix Takes Flight

I didn't know who my roommate would be, and a day later a lanky guy named Allen entered the room, ending my suspense. He and most of the other residents, like me, were transfers from various in-state community colleges. Allen was an engineering student from West Palm Beach and within a few minutes of meeting him, I sized him up as being affable—and much quieter than me. I perceived the personality difference could be a problem, given my propensity to socialize.

The hubbub of the first week on campus allowed my trepidation to be supplanted with growing confidence as I met new friends, registered for classes, and looked forward to pursuing my course of study. My meticulously constructed outer shell was cracking; in fact, I was bursting out of it. One of the most wonderful aspects of my new environment was that nobody knew me. Best of all, nobody knew I threw a softball like a girl; plus, there were no required physical education classes whereby this embarrassing secret could be exposed! The blank slate of my room was representational of the blank slate with which I entered UF. Likewise, I knew nothing about anyone else in the dorm, and therefore the stage was set for an equal playing field. I entered UF with more than my share of emotional baggage, yet now had the golden opportunity to ditch my encumbrances for a new, unfolding world of discovery.

It was a quick assimilation to dorm life, and at last I was experiencing the type of camaraderie and sense of belonging I had felt in junior high band. For the first time since entering high school, I was experiencing joy and not dealing with some degree of depression. The guys in the dorm were focused on their respective fields of study while still being sociable. I made friends easily. A welcome and unexpected personal renaissance was in its fledgling phase.

The dorm was filled with guys from different parts of the state, the nation, and even foreign countries. The diversity to which I was exposed initiated a much-needed pivot from my previously restricted "understandings" of different religions, beliefs, and customs. I discovered with a degree of shock that not everybody ate grits, fried chicken, and collard greens. To my edification, most of my friends in the dorm (except for one) were not Southern Baptist. By golly, there were Catholics, Lutherans, "no prefs," and just about everything else thrown in this melting pot called a dormitory. In fact, one close friend was Jewish and, as it turned out, I had more in common with him than with most of the other guys in the dorm. What an enriching experience his friendship proved to be as our closeness soon extended to his family—and still does.

Shower Concerns

One of my worrisome yet necessary daily activities centered on the dormitory's community shower. It was one big room with multiple shower heads lined against the wall—in other words, zero privacy. A concern about taking a shower with other men may sound a little odd coming from me, as the adventure should have been highly entertaining—but in those close quarters loomed a potential problem. A number of good-looking, well-built guys in the dorm were impossible not to notice—particularly a Cuban guy for whom I had great "admiration." Nonetheless, the source of my apprehension was the possibility I might obtain an erection while in the "eye-candy store." I was usually able to prevent such an embarrassing situation by timing my showers to avoid being in such a compromising situation. Occasionally, I was not successful. In those instances I remained circumspect, but even so, couldn't resist the opportunity to occasionally steal a peek at the various Adonis-like creations showering nearby. Thankfully, I was able to sufficiently thwart my attention (by quoting Bible verses under my breath); I never embarrassed myself.

Affiliations

My world was changing fast, and, as my parents suggested, I visited the Baptist Student Union—one time. It was evident that involving myself would likely cause painful internal conflicts to resurface. I felt—rather strongly—the BSU was not in my best interest at this juncture, when I was finally in a state of emotional equilibrium. I was hungry for new opportunities to broaden my thinking and add to my limited world exposure; my gut feeling was the BSU would be a deterrent. Of course, I had not forgotten my mother's "warning" about it being a great place to meet girls. Regardless, I didn't want my college experience to revolve around a church-related group, particularly one I viewed, right or wrong, as narrow focused. Without question, the BSU provided a wonderful service to college students and was a home away from home for many. However, joining the BSU would have been counterproductive; I needed to loosen the church noose.

My parents had encouraged me to join a fraternity if I desired to do so. I all but dismissed the idea, until being asked by a classmate at UF to visit the fraternity house where he was a member; I accepted the invitation, which included an evening dinner. The guys at the frat house were overwhelmingly welcoming and, without question, I had a great time. Like the BSU, I didn't feel it to be the right fit for similar and dissimilar reasons. The atmosphere was indeed collegial, much like what I was experiencing in the dormitory. However, one of the fraternity "selling points" was access to dating "super-groovy babes" at the sororities. Spreading my wings in this regard had not been included in my envisioning process. Besides, I had heard stories about bizarre hazing incidents involving fraternities at UF and didn't want to be subjected to such humiliation. Call me chicken. One last consideration in deciding whether or not to join was the cost. My parents had not budgeted for fraternity membership, and I was sensitive to the financial implications for them. For all the right reasons, I didn't join.

Irreconcilable Differences

The initial compatibility concerns I had with my roommate were soon confirmed. We were like oil and water, particularly when analyzing study habits. Allen was studious, more mature than me, rather serious-minded, and actually a heck of a nice guy. On the other hand, I was undoubtedly a challenge to him; my radio was sometimes turned on while I studied, my attention span was much shorter than his, and I tended to talk. Admittedly, the majority of problems we had emanated from me, not Allen. As it turned out, a good friend down the hall, Terry, and his roommate were having similar issues, so we did a roommate swap. My new roommate was Baptist and was enrolled in the College of Agriculture; we shared a good bit of commonality. Additionally, our personalities and study habits were similar. The arrangement was successful, and Terry allowed me to put some personal decorating touches in our room. When the ornamentation was complete, the room had travel posters suspended from the ceiling, fishnets on the walls, and a turquoise rug on the floor. Such a triumph demanded that our room be appropriately named. Thus, it was worthily christened (by me) as "The Atmospherium."

Terry and his girlfriend (who lived in Orlando and later became his wife, then ex-wife, then wife again, and finally, ex-wife again for good) determined I needed to be set up with a date. It was concerning to them that I was not dating, so they took it upon themselves to address the situation. Accordingly, they paired me with a UF co-ed from Orlando they both knew. We went out one time, and I don't remember the name of the girl or even what she looked like. Nonetheless, the date was considered a failure and, fortunately, no further attempts were made for an "arrangement." It was comforting that many guys in the dorm didn't have girlfriends, so it was easy for me to not date—and not worry about what anyone else might think. The guys in the dorm were compatible, and we all hung out together. My contentment had never been greater.

Life in the Too-Fast Lane

The conservative sensibilities instilled by my parents were not for naught, as I had little interest in experimenting with drugs and alcohol, which were commonly available. I watched in horror one night as a guy in my dorm, named Andy, went to a party and came back so drunk that he had to be carried into his room. Then he passed out and nearly asphyxiated when, during his state of unconsciousness, he started throwing up. He turned a bluish-green color while another dorm buddy worked with him to keep him from aspirating his retch. I believe Andy came close to dying and probably would have, had it not been for attentive friends. He survived it (and ultimately graduated), and had no memory of his wild night when he was greeted later in the morning with a wicked hangover and transient lucidity. One reminder of his "excursion" was the stench of stale "leftovers" remaining in the room—which he had to clean up.

That night was a frightening experience, and it remains as one of my most memorable at UF. Gladly, I never again witnessed such an overdose of alcohol.

The sexual revolution was in full swing on campus, as members of the opposite sex were occasional overnight guests at just about any all-male dormitory on campus—including ours. Security was lax; it was not difficult to scoot anyone in or out at just about any time of the day or night. Additionally, such open access was no secret; in fact, one of the members of the Florida Board of Regents (the now-defunct governing body exerting control over state universities) disgustingly labeled state university dormitories as "taxpayers' whorehouses." Truthfully, the situation was far from what was suggested by the colorful label; and to almost everyone on campus, including me, it was a hysterically funny characterization of dorm life.

Hell No, We Won't Go

When compared to other universities in the South, the University of Florida was said to be more liberal and informal. Dress codes were becoming relaxed: shorts and flip-flops were commonly seen and a few students even went barefoot to class. It was a time of great social unrest and protest. Strong anti–Vietnam War sentiments resulted in demonstrations, which were not out of the ordinary in Gainesville. Typifying this, a banner hung outside a nearby dormitory window declared: "FIGHTING FOR PEACE IS LIKE SCREWING FOR VIRGINITY." It made complete sense to me and contained more than a modicum of truth. Much of the way I think and view world events today was shaped by those years of lost innocence. Views I held prior to going off to college were shed as I learned to objectively analyze and weigh facts. I realized many of my former opinions were really not my opinions; they were a compilation of what other people thought. I became less afraid to question and was no longer satisfied to blindly accept others' philosophies when formulating my own. I was developing intellectual maturity and learning to think on my own.

My dad was not one to appreciate the "Hell, no, we won't go" antiwar sentiments and demonstrations in Gainesville, which were frequently shown on the local newscasts in nearby Jacksonville. He once told me if he ever found out I had participated in any such event or had gone barefoot to class, he would yank me out of school so fast it would make my head spin. I adhered to his admonition (mostly), but still was opposed to the war. I had friends who didn't attend college and ended up being drafted into the army; several were killed in Vietnam shortly after high school graduation. I fully expected to be drafted soon after my projected graduation from UF in late 1971, and this black cloud hung over my head like a guillotine. I didn't want to be another soon-to-be-forgotten statistic in what I considered a senseless war. Nonetheless, I was resigned to the possibility I might end up over there.

December 1, 1969

There are many mile markers in life, and this date denotes one that is among my most memorable and life-determining. Toward the end of my first quarter at UF, a draft lottery based on birth dates was executed on December 1, 1969. My understanding is it was the first such lottery since World War II. Birth dates representing each day of the year were inserted into small capsules, which were placed in a container and drawn at random, one at a time by a designated individual. It was a nail-biting experience ... every guy in the dorm was huddled in small groups in front of nearby radios or a community TV, intently listening to each birth date methodically and slowly called. My brow was not the only one beaded with sweat; we all nervously listened to each birth date announced, hoping not to hear our own until somewhere after the 190th birth date was called—the point at which we were told the chances of being drafted following graduation started to diminish. Early in the process, all up and down the dormitory corridors, I frequently heard someone yell or groan "Oh no!" or "I'm a dead man!" following the calling of a particular birth date. These guys would likely end up being drafted after graduation, which undeniably was viewed as a potential death sentence—and for some, this terrible prospect became reality. After the 190th birth date was finally drawn, tensions began to slowly subside, one birth date at a time. The entire drawing, from the first birth date drawn to the last, took about an hour or so, and it seemed an eternity of high anxiety. When my number was finally drawn, it was well beyond number 190. I sat in quiet relief, grateful it would be unlikely for me to be drafted (and possibly killed). At the same time, it was excruciating to witness the anguish on the faces of my dorm buddies who were less lucky. I was "saved by the bell."

Gays Make the News

Most students read the widely-available *Florida Alligator*, a tabloid-style school newspaper. While walking to class one morning, I picked up the latest edition and focused on an article that stopped me in my tracks. It covered an informal event that had been held on one of the campus lawns—an event designed to bring gay awareness to students. I was captivated. Even so, such an event on campus was shocking to me, and I would never have been near it for fear of being seen. This was in the infancy of what was then frequently dubbed the "gay liberation" movement, and few gay men were "out." Two other liberations were also gaining flight at the same time—women's liberation and black liberation. It seemed everybody was getting liberated from something—and I was afraid to raise my hand.

What actually caught my eye, though, was the picture in the middle of the article. It showed one of the attendees in the foreground, who happened to be a well-built, attractive guy. Later in the day, Terry saw my copy of the newspaper in our dorm room and made an unforgettable comment.

He emphatically stated, "There is no way the guy in that picture is gay; muscular guys are not that way."

I considered the possibility that if I started working out, my attraction to guys would fade away. Maybe my hormones would be jolted into some sort of untapped sphere, thus creating an attraction to girls. I began to believe the solution to my "problem" may be a relatively easy fix after all. Based on these erroneous suppositions resulting from Terry's expressed opinion on muscularity being a gay exclusion, I resolved to start working out. I had to! I desperately wanted to be straight and "muscling up" might be the key. I needed to gain weight, anyway—I was 5' 10" tall and weighed a slight 135 pounds.

So the infant project began as I read materials regarding gaining muscle weight. Additionally, I consulted with some guys in the dorm who had already accomplished what I desired in myself. Easy access to weightlifting equipment was not an option, so the next-best alternative was calisthenics and isometrics. Thus, my "makeover" began with push-ups, chin-ups, and sit-ups, along with static-tension isometrics. Coupled with my exercise program, I started eating more regularly (as my dad had commanded) and over a period of several months, my weight reached 148 pounds. Gaining thirteen pounds may not seem like a lot, yet to me it was huge. One weekend I went home, and my mother asked if I had been lifting weights. I hadn't, at least not yet, but her observations confirmed my efforts had been effective—except in one regard. My attraction to men was still present. Being the consummate rationalizer and not yet equipped to accept what should have been indisputable, I came up with a brilliant extrapolation: if I started working out with weights, those desires would end—particularly if I met the "right" girl.

My confidence was bursting. I had started playing tennis on campus with dorm buddies and actually won more matches than I lost. One dorm buddy in particular, a guy named Georgi, was my most frequent partner and in fact became a close friend. He eventually was forced to drop out of school for family reasons, but would play an unexpected role in my life some years later. More about him and his influence on me will be explored in later chapters.

My First Year Ends

The early part of June 1970 marked the end of my first year at UF, which without question had been the happiest year in my life. My growth had been exponential: I loved my course of study, had done well academically, and flourished personally. UF had rescued me. Consequently, the imminent summer hiatus back in Jacksonville was not particularly welcome. Nevertheless, I returned home to take advantage of summer work at J.C. Penney and to mow lawns. Mistakenly, I figured it would be the last time I would be living at home, so I made the most of it. That summer marked a return to regular church attendance—which I had largely abandoned while at school—and the same tired "You need to be dating" expectation. Fortunately, I was busy and the summer passed quickly. I returned to UF relatively intact for the fall 1970 quarter.

Much to my disappointment, prior to the end of my first year at UF, most of the guys in the dorm had already chosen different living arrangements for the coming year. Some would be living in fraternity houses, some in apartments or private homes, and a few were leaving school. Terry was engaged to be married and chose different arrangements. Andy (the guy who had vomited over himself while passed out) knew two other guys who were interested in getting an off-campus apartment. The four of us signed a lease beginning with the fall 1970 term at the fairly new La Bonne Vie apartment complex on SW Sixteenth Avenue. It was about two miles from campus and nestled in an area known as "Sin City." It was no more or less sinful than any other area of town, but, for whatever reason, that's what it was called.

Chapter 11

My Second Year at UF

I returned to Gainesville as a drastically different individual than I was a year prior. I was self-confident, had a high degree of expectation, and was looking forward to the adventure of living in an apartment with three other guys. I had met my roommates before signing the lease and at least had an idea of the personalities mixing in this cohabitation experiment. We all arrived at the apartment within a day of each other and embarked on our year together. The year proved to be invaluable as we learned the importance of respecting privacy and the necessity to compromise.

Fall also meant the return of football and, with it, the excitement of watching the Florida Gators play. The air in Gainesville was electric on those weekends when games were played at Florida Field. As much as I anticipated the games, some associated activities were just as wondrous—the cheerleaders, of course! However, the source of my infatuation no longer had anything to do with luxurious pom-poms. It was the guys on the squad that now drew my admiring eyes, with their athletic builds and good looks. When the Gators were not doing too well on the field, the cheerleaders stepped in to provide their brand of entertainment. Surely, any void otherwise existing was filled by them.

One of the highlights of my second year was, oddly enough, an outcome of making a low C on an organic chemistry test given by Professor Benjamin Portman. Surprisingly, when he returned the graded test, he asked me to speak with him after class. Without hesitation, I obliged. Admittedly, I was a bit nervous, but mostly curious. Dr. Portman gave me a pep talk, almost in a paternal fashion, and then went over some suggestions for study. The conversation impelled me to study harder—much in part because I didn't want to disappoint him; subsequently, my grades improved. Additionally, I loved his class lectures; his highly animated and sometimes humorous teaching style was unique, particularly considering the deeply scientific subject matter. As good as he was in the classroom, his intellect was most evident in his research lab. My knowledge of his prowess there was firsthand since he later hired me to be a part-time lab assistant. Among other responsibilities, I occasionally assisted him in conducting all-night experiments that required the use of radioactive materials, managed according to strict protocols. I followed his directives to the letter and never glowed in the dark. He later entertainingly quipped that he hired me because of my attitude, not necessarily because I was the brightest star in the classroom—which I obviously was not.

Weights and Measures

One of my roommates in the apartment obtained a set of free weights (which I later found out had been stolen), and I began to work out with them in addition to continuing my calisthenics regimen. Within a few short months, I "ballooned" from 148 to 165 pounds, which was by far the most I had ever weighed—still not a "heavyweight," yet for me, a noticeable change. Weight lifting alone didn't account for the gain; I had upped my caloric intake by drinking milk shakes containing raw eggs. There were no precautions stamped on eggs back then, regarding raw consumption, and I didn't convulse—or die—from eating them. Maybe the birds in those days practiced cleaner hygiene. Even so, what excited me most about my weight gain was that it was concentrated in "all the right places"—my waist measurement barely increased. I surely preferred my new and improved self and believed anyone who may have suspected I could be gay, no longer viewed me as such. Sadly, I had duped myself into believing I might not be gay. Sublimation and suggestion do work—for a while.

All Good Things Must Come to an End

I didn't graduate in June 1971, which was the expectation when I had entered UF in the fall of 1969. As it turned out, an additional course was required, and part of my degree requirement—completion of a research project—was still under way. Consequently, I stayed in Gainesville during the summer to work on my project, which was a study of how rapidly weed-killing herbicides move through various soil types. Believe it or not, I was not sniffing anything when I chose this topic.

Fortunately, my roommates were also staying in Gainesville for the summer, so we continued to share the apartment through August. During this time, I continued to work for Dr. Portman in his lab. The "mad professor" was becoming a trusted friend, and we enjoyed frequent jocular conversations about growing up in the evangelical South (he was from Tennessee). Gladly, my friendship with Dr. Portman continued well beyond my UF days, which resulted in our discovering an unanticipated shared commonality many years later.

The 1971 summer was one I remember with much fondness. Weekends were frequently spent around the apartment pool and sometimes included a day-trip to Crescent Beach (the unofficial beach for UF). It has been said that all good things must come to an end, which was never truer for me than during this time. I was beginning to look toward my graduation in December with a great deal of sadness, mixed with the excitement of beginning my career in nursery management.

The fall quarter of 1971 arrived, and my graduation in December loomed ever so soon. Too soon. Since I was not able to sign a long-term lease at an apartment, I rented a room with kitchen privileges in a spacious private home for my final three months in Gainesville. While there, I scrounged a set of weights for $5 at a garage sale, and was able to continue my workouts on an outside porch. Admittedly, graduating a little late provided for one more highly savored, last gasp of life as a UF student—the fall football games.

My final quarter coursework was light, and in what seemed like the blink of an eye, I completed my research project and classes. At 10:00 a.m., Saturday morning, December 11, 1971, commencement ceremonies proceeded in the UF gymnasium. Alongside several hundred other soon-to-be-paraded graduates, I was draped in my black cap and gown—a neophyte about to be released into the real world. The protective cocoon UF signified was being removed in a few short minutes. My emotions were visibly raw and are forever enshrined in a picture my mother took of me as I stood in front of the gym prior to the commencement program. The picture displays an unsmiling, rather unhappy-looking sort. While most of my classmates seemed elated (at least, outwardly) to be graduating, I was less ebullient. It was largely an unsuccessful effort to hide my true feelings; reddened eyes and telltale tracks of occasional tears were not well concealed. Nonetheless, my understanding parents were proud beyond words when it was my turn to walk across the platform and receive my degree. That moment, for them, was the culmination of a lifelong dream they had for me, not to mention the financial relief my graduation promised. What they did for me I could never repay. What UF and the college experience in Gainesville did for me is incalculable, since, in many respects, I feel UF saved my life.

Chapter 12

The Reality of Graduation Hits—I Get a Job

Prior to graduation, I interviewed with two firms in southwest Florida: one was a land development company involved in a massive project in Port Charlotte; the other was a large, rapidly expanding wholesale nursery and landscape operation in Naples. Both cities were small, but fast-growing with an influx of retirees primarily from the Midwest. Of the two, I preferred Naples, which was undeniably beautiful and adjacent to wide-open, nearly vacant beaches. I was offered positions at both firms. A few weeks prior to graduation, I accepted the job in Naples—based on verbal assurances given to me—and moved there to begin work on Monday, December 14. It turned out to be an ill-advised move and ended in eventual disappointment for many reasons.

On my first day at work, I was steered to a draftsman's table and asked to begin designing a landscape plan for a home under construction. What? My degree had focused on plant production and nursery management—I was not a landscape architect, nor could I pretend I was. Without delay, I was ushered into the office of the company's owner and informed of their understanding: that my degree included considerable coursework in landscape architecture. My gaping mouth underscored the shock painted all over my perplexed, flushing face. The mystery was solved within a few minutes and it exposed an enormous mistake. I had a classmate, soon graduating with the same degree, who had taken elective courses in landscape design. I hadn't. We both interviewed within days of each other—plus we had similar first names. Incredulously, the owner confused the two of us. The position awarded to me was actually intended for the other guy. I was caught in the crossfire and my world suddenly flipped upside down.

The owner's solution was to make me a salaried sales rep with the primary responsibility of marketing plants to retail nursery outlets and landscape companies in the Miami-Ft. Lauderdale-West Palm Beach region. The job would require I spend the majority of the week on the road, staying in motels, and eating a lot of fast food. Furthermore, I considered it a derailment of my desired career path. To add insult to injury, I was advised the beginning salary initially promised couldn't be honored and accordingly was offered 12 percent less. It was clearly a take-it-or-leave-it scenario. By then I had already declined the other offer in Port Charlotte, had signed an apartment lease in Naples, and felt I had no choice but to accept the job. My parents had reservations, yet agreed with me, particularly since I wanted to live in southwest Florida and had no other prospects. My hope was the job would be short term and lead to a position at the nursery, which would be compatible with my education.

My hope became reality—the job lasted six months. I was laid off due to financial losses the company was experiencing. The owner was apologetic and even offered to assist me in obtaining a job at a local bank. I declined his initiative, and did something I had sworn would never happen—I moved back to Jacksonville. As fate would have it, an opportunity presented itself in a wholesale nursery there. After speaking to my advisor at UF, I decided to interview for the position. I secured the job, but had mixed feelings about returning to Jacksonville. I couldn't help but associate my hometown with painfully difficult times in my not-too-distant past.

Who Is That Guy?

Right after I moved back to Jacksonville, my five-year high school class reunion was held in a fairly new downtown hotel. The affair required dressy attire—coats and ties for the men and cocktail dresses for the women. I made sure to "gussy up" and, as expected, everyone else did the same thing. No one wanted to be outdone—it was almost like a revisit of the high school prom, except we were now "grownups." While my recollection of some event details is faded, certain aspects are wonderfully and distinctly remembered.

The self-transformation project I began while a student at UF had continued in Naples; my appearance was drastically different from how I looked in high school. I had gained a considerable amount of muscle weight, and changed my hairstyle from a rather severe, slicked-back look to a longer, more casual "expression." The painfully skinny, geeky kid everyone remembered was gone, and I couldn't wait to see the reactions of my classmates. I was not disappointed—it surprised even me as to how many classmates didn't recognize me. The comments I received ranged from, "I can't believe how you have changed," to "Where were you in high school?" It was an evening of validation that had me grinning from ear to ear. My former UF dorm mate's comment that "muscular guys are not that way" ricocheted in my head. Certainly, none of my classmates would now wonder if I was gay. Because I wasn't.

Back in the Harness Again

I returned to Jacksonville and moved in with my parents, with the intent of staying long enough to get settled in my new job and find an apartment. I agreed to pay them $15 per week to cover my grocery costs—a good deal.

While in Naples, I became active in First Baptist Church; it was the best way to meet people and make friends since I was not into the bar scene. Unfortunately, I found relatively few people my age in the church (or in Naples); most had left the area to capture employment opportunities. Subsequently, there were few prospects and thus no pressure for me to date. That was about to change.

I knew the expectation of my parents and friends was for me to transfer my church membership back to my home church. This is a nonnegotiable commandment for those of us who are "dyed in the wool" Southern Baptists. In fact, this obligation to unite with a Southern Baptist church when moving to another area is stated in the *Church Covenant*, which, in those days, was plastered conspicuously on a prominent wall in all Southern Baptist churches. The covenant consists of several paragraphs and exhorts practitioners of the faith to live by the "agreements" as set forth in the document. Truthfully, most of the tenets are a model for daily living, and I know few individuals who follow them to the degree outlined. So, being obedient and observant of the customs of my faith, I rejoined my home church on Sunday, June 11, 1972. I was twenty-three years old. I also joined the church choir, which was a group composed of about fifty people, many of whom were my age. It was a great place for anyone who loved religious music and enjoyed camaraderie. Back in those days, the music in my home church was uplifting, sometimes classical and reverential, sometimes on the spirited side, yet still conducive to reflection and contemplation. It was not electronic; it was vastly dissimilar to the "rock concerts" featured in many churches today.

My trepidation aside, it was good to be home with the folks I had known my entire life. The pastor of the church was a young, charismatic gentleman named Josh Jacobs, who practiced what he preached, and demonstrated in his life how loving Christ translated into loving people of all walks. Josh was a rarity and not the fire-and-brimstone kind of pastor so frequently associated with the Southern Baptist Church. I had great respect for this man and have no recollection of his ever speaking ill of other denominations—or against folks who didn't fall within the Baptist definition of acceptability. Of all my pastors, he probably was the most impactful—because of the way he lived his life and for what he didn't say from the pulpit. Following a rich ministry, he passed away in his home state of South Carolina in 2016 at the age of eighty-three.

Chapter 13

Conveniently Blind

My home church was relatively large and, as is typical, had an active youth and singles program. On Sunday morning, June 25, Gail Triplett, a good friend with whom I had grown up, asked if I was planning on attending the singles social that night after the evening service. I told her I was, and, without any further thought, dismissed the question. It was never in my nature to miss any occasion where food and fun were offered, particularly in such a protected, amicable environment.

Gail was attractive, with light brown hair, brown eyes, and an infectious smile. She was intelligent, fun, personable, and single. What a catch for some lucky guy! My mother had asked numerous times why I didn't ask Gail out, and I would regularly whip up some bogus reason that seemed to placate Mom's inquiring mind. Fortunately, time was on my side. Anthony Petrini, a new friend and fellow choir member in the church, reeled in Gail.

He and I had both recently celebrated our twenty-third birthdays, which were a few weeks apart. To say Anthony was good-looking is an understatement. He had thick, wavy, blonde hair, icy blue eyes, an olive complexion, was a little taller than average, and reasonably well built, although not particularly muscular. He was charming, had recently graduated from a major university in the Midwest, and every single girl and probably some married ones in the church were after him. He was a sales representative for a major national clothes brand, which required him to take frequent trips to New York City. He also did modeling of expensive-label suits as part of his job duties and frequently appeared in the center of large newspaper ads for a leading department store. Admittedly, I was attracted to him, but kept those feelings well hidden and sublimated—well, for the most part.

The previous Saturday evening, Anthony, Gail, Millicent Baker (a close friend of Gail's), and I went on a double date—if you want to characterize it as such. My friendship with Millicent was long-standing and platonic, as were all my relationships with girls, and neither of us expected anything beyond that. At least, I didn't. Millicent was a little on the plump side, had sparkling blue eyes, deep dimples in her cheeks, perfect teeth, and was the life of any party. Everybody loved this girl. That evening, we all ended up in the pool of the apartment complex where Millicent lived. This was preplanned, since the June air was sultry and the water an inviting respite. However, I had no idea how hot (at least for me) this benign outing would become.

We all enjoyed sharing a bottle of fine-vintage Blue Nun wine, which in those days was a revered brand. Sure enough, we soon succumbed to its effects and our Baptist inhibitions were replaced with us feeling mighty fine. We did the typical pool things: engaged in fun conversation, splashed around, and conducted ourselves appropriately. Before the pool adventure was over, Anthony and I ended up with the girls on our shoulders in about chest-deep water and engaged in the requisite tussle of water wrestling to see who would fall into the water first. My recollection is we all fell into the water at about the same time, at which point Anthony and I continued to wrestle. After about thirty seconds of grabbing, pushing, and holding with slippery hands and arms, I became horrified to discover during this engagement with Anthony that I had obtained a raging erection. *Holy mackerel, what do I do now?* I orchestrated the story that I had thrown my back out and had to stop. Water wrestling is over, folks. Fortunately, it was nightfall and the water in the pool was reflective rather than transparent, so I was able to regain my "composure" in a few minutes without anyone else noticing. I had a subsequent miraculous healing of my back spasm.

My sexual reaction to Anthony troubled me; nothing like this had ever occurred when in physical contact with a girl. It was more than ample food for thought, which caused me to remain awake much of the night in a deeply conflicted place. The thirty-second adventure with Anthony was ecstatic and torturous. Still, I refused to come to terms with my true self, which dictated my living in a continual lie. Church teachings and social mores in a highly conservative city had paved the way for me and many others to conveniently and blindly adopt such a defensive, misguided posture.

Not long after the double date in Millicent's pool, Anthony and Gail announced their engagement, much to my disappointment. I had hoped (at least, on some level) the day would arrive when I would overcome my "feelings of perversion," fall in love with Gail, and live happily ever after with her in Camelot. On a deeper level, I knew my disappointment was more related to Anthony getting married—I had developed feelings for him. I rationalized, however, that through prayer and properly directed "mind control," God would lead me to the mate He had chosen for me, and I would automatically be cured. I continued to diligently pursue the prayer route, read my Bible, and remained convinced my attraction to men was a phase and would pass when I met the right girl. Genesis 2:24 (KJV) says: "Therefore shall a man leave his father and his mother, and shall cleave unto his wife and they shall be one flesh." Matthew 7:7 (KJV) says: "Ask, and it shall be given you; seek, and ye shall find; knock, and it shall be opened unto you." It was spelled out, and I believed it.

I was getting more desperate as time passed. My friends were getting married, and I was continually being asked why I was not dating. My parents were clearly perplexed, and my living at home made my situation—actually a self-imposed entrapment—exponentially worse. To placate my parents, church leaders, and friends, I occasionally asked a girl out and "dated" the same girl a few times. As soon as the girl gave any indication of desiring the slightest physicality, such as a kiss, I became terrified and never asked the girl out again, without any explanation. Truthfully, I knew this kind of behavior was cruel, but on the other hand I didn't know how else to make an exit. Frequently, my parents asked what happened, and I would tender a manufactured explanation. Interestingly, I can't ever remember being asked by a girl I had dated why I lost interest. I could never divulge to anyone there was never any interest to begin with.

My prayers every day included the same request to God. The request was actually a plea to God to take away my physical attraction for men and to replace it with a desire for women. I really believed my prayer would be answered, and also believed God expected me to take action. In other words, I had to act in a manner that reflected my prayer had been answered. One particular verse rang in my head incessantly: "I can do all things through Christ who strengthens me" (Philippians 4:13 KJV).

Blindsided

Following the Sunday evening church service, I walked over to the social hall with a group of my friends and, much to my surprise, ran into Millicent. She attended a nearby Baptist church, and it was not unusual for a handful of youth from the smaller area churches to occasionally attend our functions. The social hall, which was sparsely decorated yet commodious, occupied the space of the former church building. It was built in the 1940s and had black-and-white checkerboard vinyl floors sloping down to the original pulpit area. It was in the same pulpit area where I, as a five-year-old kid in the mid-1950s, remembered being captivated in a revival by a handsome visiting music director. Fortunately, there were two major differences in the room: the atmosphere was now wonderfully cooled by air conditioning, and the source of "pulpit heat" had been eliminated.

I was drawn to the white sheet–covered tables at the front of the room where there was an offering of self-serve Baptist punch (lime sherbet floating in ginger ale), an assortment of pimento cheese, tuna fish, and deviled ham sandwiches, plus crowd-drawing homemade chocolate chip cookies. The sandwiches were made of white bread (that's about all there was back then), cut in half on the angle, and prettily arranged on large platters. To add a touch of flair to these beloved, high-glycemic-indexed delicacies, the crusted edges had been trimmed off. Incidentally, "catering" was provided by various church volunteers (usually our mothers). Without hesitation I excused myself momentarily from Millicent (who subsequently went to the ladies' room) and made a beeline to the food altar, where I poured myself some punch and filled a paper plate with sandwiches.

I didn't notice Millicent had brought one of her sorority sisters from Jacksonville University, or that there were two girls to each guy in the room. After all, it was a good-sized room, right? My attentions were tuned to another channel, and the channel didn't include girl watching. A moment later, Gail walked up to the food table and asked if I had met Charlene Harrelson. I had no idea who she was and surely hadn't met her. I was embarrassed to realize Charlene had been standing alone, near my side, waiting for Millicent to return from the ladies' room.

Gail introduced us, and I apologized to Charlene for not being more observant.

Charlene smiled widely, displaying beautiful teeth, and said, with a little giggle, "I knew who you were, based on Gail's description, but was more comfortable waiting for an introduction."

She was soft-spoken, had shoulder-length light-brown hair with blonde highlights, blue eyes, and was slender. Her flawless "peaches and cream" complexion was complemented by her lovely light-blue dress. In other words, she was easy on the eyes and not at all aggressive—a quality that would have me running for the exit. She mentioned she lived with her parents, was twenty years old (three years younger than me), was an elementary education major at Jacksonville University, and they were originally from Dallas, Texas, which they sorely missed.

We engaged in light conversation for a few more minutes, at which point I excused myself to go to the men's room. I had been in the men's room for no more than a few seconds when Anthony came in, which in itself caused my heart to beat faster.

He knew I had just met Charlene and asked if I thought she was attractive.

I answered, "Yes," and said nothing more.

He disclosed that Gail thought Charlene and I would be a good match. I recalled Gail's question earlier in the morning, asking if I was going to attend the social. In retrospect, my surprise in learning the whole thing was a setup was classic Seth—naïve and oblivious to the obvious. My mind began to bounce all over the place as I dismissed the tuna fish and, instead, deliberated on how to handle the developing situation. I became uncomfortable, if not nervous, and wondered if Charlene could be "the one" God had picked out for me. After all, we were at a church function, and Charlene had shared with me when we briefly spoke that she was Baptist. The echo kept playing in my mind: *She could be "the one."* I was not one to believe in omens, but all of a sudden this thought invaded my internal processer and I couldn't escape it. More than likely, Anthony and Gail's engagement factored into my mindset.

Anthony and I left the men's room together and walked back to Gail, Charlene, and Millicent, who were standing at the opposite end of the room. My mouth quickly became uncomfortably dry and my hands noticeably chilly. These physical manifestations of nervousness were a source of embarrassment to me, and I frequently kept my hands in my pockets in a fruitless attempt to warm them up. By now my heart was pounding, as a feeling of entrapment enveloped me and my adrenal glands screamed *Run for your life!* There was no easy way out.

We all engaged in the usual insignificant chitchat until the social ended—and I felt the clear expectation from my circle of friends that I should ask Charlene out for a date. Any "normal" guy would have pounced on the opportunity, and why not? Charlene was sweet, well presented, and attractive. I couldn't bring myself to do it, and at about 10:00 p.m. we went our separate ways when the social ended. Since I had not driven to church, I sauntered along the sidewalk for the nearly two blocks separating the social hall from our house. My mind was in overdrive and I felt frantic—I strongly felt this chapter was just beginning.

I opened our front door, which entered directly into the living room where my parents were sitting, watching TV. They typically didn't go to bed until after watching the late-night news, so it was not surprising to find them up. Given the floor plan of the house, there was no way to access my bedroom other than walking through the living room. I hardly had the front door of the house closed behind me when my mother inquired about the social and asked if I had met any nice girls. I had anticipated the question while walking home. Accordingly, I adhered to my predetermined answer and said something to the effect that there was a good crowd of people and I stuck with the usual gang.

It then occurred to me my parents may have known about the setup. If so, they didn't pursue the topic any further. I didn't welcome an opportunity for further discussion and scurried to my bedroom.

Repercussions

On the Tuesday evening following the "ambush" at the Sunday evening social, I was standing in the kitchen helping my mother wash and dry dishes when the phone rang. As was usually the case, she answered it. My dad was not one to talk on the phone and deferred such opportunities to my mother, who was prone to carry on phone conversations. Mother passed the "telephone gene" to me, although I didn't receive the high-test version granted to her.

Nonetheless, the first thing I heard was my mother saying, "Oh, hello, Anthony. Seth is right here."

The phone was affixed to the kitchen wall and had about 10 feet of stretched-out coiled cord attached to the receiver. My mother passed me the receiver while continuing with her kitchen employment. Since the other phone in the house was in my parents' bedroom, where my dad was working at his desk, there was little opportunity for privacy. Anthony called infrequently, and the timing of his call was curious. Admittedly, I had an idea what the call was about—Charlene. So, with a healthy dose of trepidation, I walked the receiver around the kitchen counter separating the open end of the kitchen from the dining room.

To maximize privacy, I purposefully sat in a dining room chair with my back to the kitchen wall. The reason Anthony called was to find out if I had Charlene's phone number (he knew I didn't). I gave the transparent excuse that since I had nothing to write with, I didn't ask for it. What an idiotic response.

Anthony responded with a laugh, and said, "Sure."

I knew what was coming next; he gave me Charlene's phone number, with the assurance it was permissible for me to have it. My interpretation: "Hey, stupid, Charlene wants you to ask her out."

Gulp. I grabbed a pencil and pad lying on the counter by the phone and wrote down the phone number.

Anthony was not going to let me off so easy and finished the conversation by saying, "Gail and I are going out for pizza on Saturday night, and we thought you and Charlene could double with us, so give Charlene a call. I doubt you have any plans."

We both knew he was right. I had no plans, and there was no way for me to wiggle out. It was a fait accompli—I was toast.

After I hung up the receiver, my mother's interest was piqued and she inquired about the phone call. Here is my recollection, surely not exact, of the ensuing exchange.

"Anthony wanted to know if I would be interested in going out with him and Gail on Saturday night."

My mother responded, "What a wonderful idea. Is anyone else going?"

In an effort to say as little as possible, I replied, "There may be someone else. They have a friend named Charlene who might go."

As expected, my mother's inquisitive nature honed in on this nectar like a bee, and, not surprisingly, she probed deeper. "Do you know this girl?"

Instantly, I remembered not giving full disclosure when my mother had asked on Sunday night if I had met any nice girls at the church social. I grudgingly answered, "Yes, she is a friend of Gail's who was at the social this past Sunday night."

With a long pause, my mother asked, "Oh, so you have already met her? I thought you said the other night you had not met any new girls at the social. Did you talk with her?"

God, help me! My mother should have been a private investigator. At this point, I was about to "lose it" while on the witness stand, but remained fairly composed throughout the interrogation.

Admittedly, I was irritated, and my voice no doubt reflected it as I tersely said, "Yes, we met briefly, but didn't have much of a conversation. She is a student at Jacksonville University and goes to First Baptist downtown."

Her church affiliation would be of utmost importance to my mother, so I thought throwing out this morsel would thwart any further inquisition. It almost did; my mother sandwiched one more question and comment in, which was the one I was desperately trying to avoid.

"So my guess is Charlene might go out with you if you ask her. Do you have Charlene's phone number?"

To which I reluctantly answered, "Yes, I do."

My mother then gave me a few words of encouragement. "Seth, I imagine Charlene would be thrilled to hear from you. I know you're a little nervous, but she'll probably jump at the chance to go out."

I said nothing else; the court session was over. I still wondered if my mother had known more than she let on.

I later found out she actually didn't. Her intuition was dead-on, as usual.

There was no way under the shining sun, or in this case, the "kitchen lights," I was going to call Charlene at this point. Truthfully, my mother was not an intentional eavesdropper and she couldn't avoid hearing my end of any conversation without inserting earplugs.

Fortunately, I was rescued by *Hawaii Five-0*, which was about to come on TV. This show was never to be missed, much because we were captivated by the magnificence of the Hawaiian landscape. However, the real attraction for me was James MacArthur (he played the part of "Danno"). Interestingly, my infatuation with him was a holdover crush from 1960, when I was eleven years old, and James played a rather "fetching" character in the classic Walt Disney movie, *Swiss Family Robinson*. Without delay, I walked over to the TV set in the living room, turned it on, and flipped the dial to channel 4. Back in those days there was no remote control in the house, and there were only three TV channels available. Even so, there was no lack of great things to watch on TV, and all programming was wonderfully free.

I called for my parents to come watch the program, and soon the three of us were comfortable in our "assigned seating," which consisted of my mother on the sofa, me in an easy chair, and my dad in a dining room chair. My dad suffered with back problems, and the dining room chair afforded him more comfort than anything else in the house. By the time our TV viewing was complete, it was too late to call Charlene—thank God.

I retired to my bedroom and remained awake for what seemed an interminable amount of time, while considering when I was going to call Charlene and what I would say once I made the call.

The Call

Anthony didn't give me a time frame in which to call Charlene. I realized, in fairness to everyone, I needed to make the call soon. I was naturally prompt, and even though the prospect of calling Charlene was disconcerting, I knew I had to "bite the bullet" and get it done.

When I woke up Wednesday morning, I had a gnawing feeling in the pit of my stomach; it was the same familiar discomfort that had greeted me before I had to take a test in school. Even so, I was still prepared to eat and went to the kitchen for my breakfast consisting of eggs, grits, and toast, which my dad usually made. My mother was brewing the coffee she and my dad drank—I didn't like coffee and instead opted for 4 percent cholesterol-building milk. We sat at the kitchen counter, had a brief morning devotion, and then ate breakfast. Our conversation during breakfast was inconsequential, and there was no mention of calling Charlene. Afterwards, I was out the door and off to work. Since it was Wednesday, I knew my parents would be attending church services that evening. It would be the perfect time for me to make the call.

I had all day at work to think about what I would say when calling Charlene, and the more I thought about it, the more anxious I became. For someone who was fairly glib, I was rendered discombobulated by this simple task. Nonetheless, I was resigned to do it. Fortunately, the physicality of my work ameliorated my anxiety and offered some relief. One of the most important lessons I ever learned from my dad and later, from experience, is how physical work and/or exercise is an excellent antianxiety prescription. (Even now as an older adult, I still employ this simple principle and maintain a fairly rigorous exercise program on a daily basis. It works, and pays many benefits.)

The drive home from work took about fifteen minutes, and I pulled into the driveway about five thirty. My first order of business upon entering the house was to check the status of our evening meal, as usual.

"Hey, I'm home. How long will it be before supper is ready?" were my first words after closing the front door.

I was advised it would be about thirty minutes. Accordingly, I took my shower, and dressed in my usual evening attire—a white V-neck T-shirt, a pair of shorts, and sandals. I set the table and helped my mother fill the three plates to hasten the process. I saw to it my plate had about double the amount of food than what was contained in the other two plates. Fortunately, Mother was prepared for my King Kong appetite and, at last, supper was ready. I called for my dad, who was completing paperwork at his desk in their bedroom, to come join us. By the time we finished supper and the kitchen was cleaned up (by me), it was time for my parents to go to Wednesday night services. Nothing was said about my calling Charlene; my parents knew nothing needed to be said. They left for church, and I knew it was "do or die" time.

In a state of nervousness, I sat down by the wall-mounted rotary-dial phone (a what?) next to the kitchen counter to make the call. I fumbled through my wallet, which contained more folded papers than currency, and soon found the paper on which I had scribbled Charlene's phone number. Being thoroughly undone by the prospect of calling her, I wrote down on a napkin what I wanted to say. My heart was about to jump out of my chest … so, having my "script" lent a degree of comfort. I took a deep breath and methodically dialed each digit of her phone number.

Her phone rang once … twice … and before the third ring, it was answered by someone other than Charlene. The deep-voiced "Hello" on the other end undoubtedly emanated from her dad.

My intimidation magnified, but nonetheless I summoned my courage and said, "Hello, this is Seth Vicarson. May I please speak to Charlene?"

He was cordial, and said he would be happy to pass the phone to her. I heard him whisper to Charlene, "It's Seth Vicarson."

There was a little pause before I heard her voice. "Hello, Seth, this is Charlene. It's nice to hear from you."

Her voice tone confirmed what I already knew—my call was welcome.

"Hi, Charlene. I hope you don't mind me calling you. Anthony gave me your phone number." I started to read my next line and my voice cracked, which embarrassed me. Even though rattled, I continued: "Anthony, Gail, and I are going out for pizza on Saturday night, and I was hoping you could join us. Would you like to go?" Clearly I was asking her out for a date.

Charlene promptly responded that she would "love to go."

Whew! I was glad this part was behind me. I offered to pick her up around 7:00 p.m., which was agreeable. She seemed excited and gave me directions to her house before the call concluded.

Mercifully, the deed was done. To calm my nerves, I went to the refrigerator's freezer compartment to retrieve a hefty portion of vanilla ice cream and turned on the TV—two of my favorite stress antidotes.

I can't remember what was on TV; my focus was unavoidably distracted—"What the heck have I done?" continually played in my mind.

My zone of preoccupation snapped to a state of consciousness when my parents came in from church. I was ready for the "elephant in the room" question, and to my surprise it was not asked. My first thought was to say nothing, but I decided to go ahead and hang it out.

"Hey, I won't be having supper here on Saturday night because I'll be going to the pizza place with Anthony, Gail, and Charlene."

It didn't take long, though, for my mother to respond by saying, "Oh, how wonderful. Did you call Charlene tonight?"

I answered, "Yes, I did."

My dad, too, was pleased at my "swift" action. That was it. Nothing more was said, but I knew their excitement exceeded mine. It surprised me the exchange was so brief, given my mother's penchant for details. My dad was not one to ask a lot of questions unless it was required. It wasn't that he was disinterested, as the opposite was the case. He was an involved father and aware of my comings and goings.

Saturday Arrives

On Saturday afternoon, I played tennis with Georgi—my former dorm buddy at UF. During his junior year at UF he was needed at home, to work on the family farm near Jacksonville, and never returned to school. Even so, we remained in contact. When I moved back to Jacksonville from Naples, our tennis games gave him—and me—a much needed outlet. We were evenly matched and played tennis regularly on the neighborhood courts near where I lived. During our numerous matches, we had conversations that inevitably revolved around dating—

and girls. No doubt, Georgi was 100 percent straight and, unlike me, was looking for girls to date. He welcomed any opportunity for a setup and, in fact, asked me to help him find girls to date. Of course I was of little help; still, we enjoyed each other's company. Georgi was not tall; he was swarthy, intelligent, extraordinarily strong physically, and personable. Unfortunately, he had few opportunities to meet girls. My parents were fond of him and felt sorry for his circumstances, which kept him pinned most of the time to the farm.

Georgi was, without argument, the product of extraordinary circumstances. He was born in a Communist country, and when he was a child, the family escaped, ending up on a farm in the Jacksonville area. I greatly admired Georgi and found him to be a selfless individual, giving up personal opportunities for the good of his family.

Nonetheless, on this particular Saturday we played tennis for about an hour or so, until the time arrived for me to go home and clean up for the "big" date.

Georgi was a supportive friend, and as unlikely as it seemed then, our friendship would come to an unfortunate and sudden end four years later.

The tennis game, played in the summer heat, had transformed me into a sweat-soaked mess and also served to keep my nervousness under control for the time being. Soon, my anxiousness was returning and I flooded my surging adrenaline (and unclean body) with a long shower. While in the shower, I practiced what I was going to say to Charlene and her parents when I met them. No doubt, they would be home to greet the guy who was taking their daughter out on a date—this expectation compounded the nervousness now invading my body. The hour to leave had arrived, and there was nothing to thwart the inevitable. I made sure I had enough money in my wallet to cover the evening's expenses and that my clothes matched—I sometimes had challenges in coordinating apparel. My parents gave me the usual assurances the date would be a lot of fun and encouraged me to relax and just be myself. Heck, I *was* being myself—and relaxing was not part of the program. Lastly, my mother advised me to drive carefully over the high and narrow Mathews Bridge spanning the chocolate-colored water of the St. Johns River. This bridge was an unforgettable reminder of where a good friend of theirs had been tragically killed in an automobile accident several years back.

I calculated the drive over to Charlene's house would take about twenty minutes since Saturday traffic would be light. Another plus:

there were no thunderstorms around to cause wrecks and associated road calamities. As I crossed the "bridge of death" and gave fifteen cents to the lady collecting the toll (and a "Thank you, Jesus" for safe passage), it was apparent my heart was beginning to beat harder. I hated the all-too-familiar feeling. It was only ten minutes farther to Charlene's house, which wouldn't be hard to find since Jacksonville was easy to navigate.

I arrived a few minutes early to the entrance of the subdivision where the Harrelsons lived. The area was heavily forested and had winding streets and beautifully manicured lawns. It was on the "right side" of the river; most homes were large, new, and embellished with double front doors—a sure indicator of "high-end" real estate. To be candid, I felt threatened, but tried to not let it distract me.

Chapter 14

The Beginning of an Odyssey

I easily found the house and parked my 1968 Ford Galaxie 500 next to the curb in front of the Harrelsons' house, rather than in the driveway. Stepping out of the car, I was about knocked over by the unmistakable rotten-eggs smell emanating from the pulp mill on "my side" of the river. The wind direction was westerly, which allowed for "them" to share in the delights of Jacksonville's then most notorious source of air pollution. I walked up to the door, took a deep breath of stinky air, and rang the doorbell once. No one came to the door, so I stood there debating whether or not to ring the bell again. I noticed a lady across the street watching me and smiling, so I naturally smiled back. As it turned out, she and her husband were destined to become close friends of mine for life. I heard the click of the door being unlocked, and waited for the door to be opened … which it was, by Charlene.

She looked beautiful and was immaculately presented—no doubt from exposure to upscale shopping opportunities and coiffuring. Charlene warmly greeted me with her dimpled smile and invited me in. I couldn't help but wonder why she would be going out with me; my self-confidence left a lot to be desired.

Charlene ushered me into the family room and, no surprise, her parents were there. I introduced myself to Mr. and Mrs. Harrelson (Ted and Liz) and shook hands with her father. Charlene's parents were affable and made me feel at ease. Her mother and dad were younger than I had expected (probably mid-forties), both taller than average and good-looking. They asked me where I worked, what kind of work my dad did, and where I was taking Charlene. It was the type of conversation normally occurring when meeting a girl's parents for the first time. We chatted for maybe ten minutes before Charlene and I left for the pizza place, which was a five-minute drive from their house.

We pulled into the parking lot of Angelo's Pizza, and I recognized Anthony's vehicle—predictably sporty and nicely appointed. I popped out of the car, went around to Charlene's side, and opened her door. Inside the restaurant we found Anthony and Gail settled in a booth next to one of the windows.

We joined them and engaged in the usual exchanges and discussions of the day's events. Charlene was conversational and shared that she planned on teaching in an elementary school after she graduated in about two years. We ordered pizzas: one for Gail and Anthony, and the other for Charlene and me. There was no lack of conversation, as reticence didn't seem to apply to any of us. Gail and Anthony talked about their workweek and, naturally, we all talked about church since it was a group commonality. Gail had recently graduated from the University of Georgia and had landed a position at an insurance company. My work at the wholesale nursery paled in comparison to Anthony's career, so I minimized any conversation pertaining to soil chemistry and plant reproduction.

The pizzas were brought to the table, and the aroma of pepperoni and cheese permeated our cozy space. I served Charlene the first slice of pizza; if nothing else, I was polite and well-mannered, thanks to my parents' tutelage. My recollection is Charlene wanted two slices. So without hesitation, I ate the other four. The time passed quickly; we were having an enjoyable evening.

We had been in the restaurant for about an hour and a half, nursing what was left of our Cokes, when Gail and Anthony left us to our own devices. I had assumed our double date would be for the entire evening, so their exit took me by surprise. It was about 9:00 p.m. and clearly too early to take Charlene back home. I had told her parents to expect us back around 10:00 p.m., so I needed to think of something to fill the void.

There were not many options, and going to a bar or club was out of the question—we were Baptists, after all. It occurred to me Friendship Fountain would be a good choice. This circular fountain was huge and spectacular for the time. It was about a fifteen-minute drive from Angelo's and located in a city park on the river, opposite the downtown skyline. The center of the fountain featured geyser-like jets of water shooting up in the air about 100 feet, while other arcs of water shot from the periphery about 75 feet toward the middle, falling short of the center water jets. Illumination was provided by bright lights with alternating colors changing every thirty seconds or so. The water jets were on a programmed schedule causing frequent changes in height and intensity of flow. The fountain was locally famous and attracted many onlookers. I suggested to Charlene that we go to the park to watch the fountain, and she agreed it would be fun.

So off we went to watch the water gyrations and ever changing colors. It was a beautiful evening with a delightful breeze off the river, which created a romantic setting. Admittedly, I enjoyed being with such a darling girl—whom other guys clearly noticed. This was new territory for me. My insecurities were subsiding a little; still, I felt awkward about any physical contact and didn't hold her hand. We stayed at the park for about a half hour and then drove back toward her house, to arrive just before ten.

My heart was racing as the car approached her house. Surely, I would walk Charlene from the car to the front door of her house, but the culmination of the evening should probably end in some form of a kiss. This was unnerving; I felt inept when it came to the slightest expression of intimacy.

We pulled into the driveway and chatted for a couple of minutes before getting out of the car and walking to the front door. Charlene turned around after putting her key in the door lock—plainly, this was my cue.

I took both her hands and expressed how much I had enjoyed the date. I also asked if we could go out again.

She said, "Absolutely."

I summoned the nerve to kiss her—on the cheek. I declined Charlene's offer to come inside and we wished each other a good night.

A feeling of accomplishment—and immense relief—enveloped me. My confidence level took a leap, and the thought that Charlene may be part of God's plan for my life resurfaced.

My evening prayers before crawling into the safety of my bed centered on the all-too-familiar plea for God's will in my life to be realized and for my "perversion" (gay desires) to be replaced by a desire for Charlene. It was the beginning of a three-year odyssey destined to end in shattered hearts.

Now What?

Sunday morning dawned in its usual hot and humid late June fashion, but nonetheless I put on a coat and tie, which in those days was expected for church attendance. The College and Career Sunday School Building was a block from the house, so I easily walked the distance without getting soaked with perspiration. I was anxious to find out if Gail had talked to Charlene after our date. Much to my disappointment, she and Anthony weren't there, so I would have to wait to obtain any feedback. Of course, probably any other guy would have picked up the phone and called Charlene—this was not in my playbook. After church was over, I went home with the intention of calling Gail, but my parents arrived right after I did. Therefore, I didn't make the call due to awkward privacy concerns overriding my sense of reason.

As soon as my mother changed out of her church attire, she began the Sunday ritual of broiling steaks in the oven, frying frozen crinkle-cut French fries, and heating up some canned peas. Sunday dinner was a feast, in my eyes, and I could hardly wait for church to be over in anticipation. Plus, the Tarzan movie reruns were a staple on one of the local TV channels at 1:00 p.m. I *never* missed the Tarzan movie, particularly if the over-the-top-handsome Gordon Scott—a source of infatuation—was the Tarzan "du jour." He represented one of many hurricane warning flags—the wind was howling, and I stubbornly ignored it.

As expected, one conversation during lunch pertained to my date with Charlene. I had already mentioned during breakfast that Charlene and I had a good time, and said as little as possible. After all, what's to be said about eating pizza? It tasted Italian. However, the one thing mattering most to my parents was if I intended on asking Charlene out again. They knew me well, and during lunch they pressed me to make a move—knowing I was inclined to let the grape wither on the vine. I assured them I would call Charlene. My plan was to ask Gail if she had heard from Charlene and, if so, what she had said about the date. Then I'd decide whether or not to make the call. Of course, this was nothing but a delaying tactic and, predictably, I went to bed Sunday night without doing a thing.

I went to work Monday morning, and my entire day was preoccupied with the thought of calling Charlene. True to form, I got as nervous as a squirrel crossing the street. Why was I so tentative? Our first date went exceptionally well, and at the close of the date, Charlene said she would welcome going out again. What additional affirmation was necessary? My newfound confidence was already waning, so I decided to delay calling Charlene until Wednesday. I had choir practice Tuesday night, so of course, Tuesday was out. And today, being Monday, was just too hasty. My logic made perfect sense—to a fourteen-year-old.

Tuesday morning arrived and the parental lobby for me to call Charlene was in full-court press during breakfast. I vowed to call Charlene "soon." When I arrived home from work that afternoon, my mother advised me to call Gail, who had called earlier. My dad was not yet home from work, so I used the phone on his desk to make the call. Not surprisingly, Gail told me she had spoken to Charlene on Sunday, and Charlene "would be thrilled" to go out with me again. I assured Gail I would call Charlene on Wednesday, and she insisted I not procrastinate—in other words, do it now! Gail confided that Charlene had been asked to go out with a guy she had previously dated, but preferred to go out with me. There was no hiding place, and I agreed to make the call posthaste.

As soon as the call with Gail ended, I went to my file cabinet—my wallet—and retrieved the crumpled piece of paper with Charlene's phone number scribbled on it. This go-around, I didn't have a script in front of me and had less time to work myself into the usual nervous tizzy.

I picked up the phone receiver and started dialing. With each swirl of the phone dial, my heart beat a little heavier, a little faster. When I finished dialing, my underlying anxiety manifested itself as I started to pace (my dad's phone was also equipped with miles of accordion phone cord). Being true to myself, I about wore a path into my mother's new—and disgusting—multitoned pink shag carpet. The thought crossed my mind that I simply was not cut out for this type of activity (duh); it was dispelled when the phone was answered—this time by Charlene, thankfully.

I continued to pace, even though she seemed pleased to hear from me. We engaged in predictable chitchat for what seemed like an eternity (probably two minutes) before I mustered the courage to ask the "date question."

"Charlene, would you like to go with me to a movie Saturday evening?"

She paused, sighed, and said she was sorry but couldn't go; she had plans for Saturday.

I dropped into my dad's desk chair and sat, stunned. This was not at all what I had expected to hear. I don't know why being turned down was so startling, given my general lack of self-assurance. My mind went into overdrive and rendered me temporarily speechless. There was no exit strategy, no Plan B, and I had no idea what to say. I needed a script!

Finally, I collected my thoughts, expressed to Charlene I was probably a little late in asking her out, and apologized. She was gracious, and said she would love to go out another time. I took a chance and asked her out for the following Saturday. Without hesitating, she said yes. We chatted another few minutes, and I told Charlene to expect a call from me in a few days.

My parents were elated to hear she and I had another date scheduled. I can't say I experienced the same exuberance, yet felt I was doing what I was supposed to do (according to everyone else's expectations).

Since choir practice was that evening, I was looking forward to sharing my news with Anthony. As it turned out, I was too late—he already knew I had a second date planned with Charlene. He added she was "ecstatic" to be going out with me again. Surely, hearing this was ego-boosting, and at the same time disconcerting since I was dealing with a seemingly never-ending internal conflict.

My misgivings chewed on me like termites—and being continually slapped in the face by my inescapable attraction to Anthony was at the least a distraction. I was desperately attempting to sublimate those (and other) feelings. I believed practicing sublimation would lead to elimination of same-sex attraction and thus effectuate the "cure." Once this happened, God would surely replace my same-sex attraction with opposite-sex attraction. I believed the puzzle pieces were somehow going to magically fall in place. Accordingly, I couldn't dismiss the thought that Charlene was part of God's plan for my life.

The Second Date Renders a Surprise

As promised, I called Charlene several days later to confirm our upcoming date. When the day arrived for our date, I felt a general uneasiness creeping in; I couldn't avoid dwelling on those date-related "protocols" giving me heartburn. Should I hold Charlene's hand when walking by her side? Should I hold her hand in the car? Should I kiss her on the lips? I was a classic example of arrested development and desperately needed some help. These were not the types of things I felt free to discuss with my parents. Without a doubt, I couldn't admit this awkwardness to any male friend—I didn't have many to begin with, anyway. It was embarrassing: at the age of twenty-three, I felt like a fourteen-year-old. It never occurred to me that simple things like holding hands should happen naturally, without anxiety or forethought.

I found time for some much needed, stress-preventing exercise by mowing the grass with the push mower. This was followed by seventy-five pushups and some weight lifting. I was in a better place emotionally than I was before the first date, wasn't overly anxious (at least not yet), and tried not to overthink the date. *The Godfather* started around 8:00 p.m., and I had arranged to pick up Charlene at 7:30 p.m.

Again, I arrived a few minutes early and easily spotted Charlene in the front yard across the street from her house. She was talking with the same woman who had smiled at me a couple of weeks prior, while I was waiting at the Harrelsons' front door. I parked in front of the Harrelsons' house and walked across the street to meet Charlene and her neighbor. I greeted Charlene and introduced myself to her neighbor, whose name was Leona Langley. Leona was about fifty, plump, and had color-enhanced teased hair that was blondish. She was beautifully dressed and had the appearance of someone going out for an elegant evening. What an interesting, engaging lady she was, and I loved her. It was evident she and Charlene were fond of each other, and we continued to talk for a few more minutes.

We went back into Charlene's house to let her parents know we were leaving and to expect us back around 11:00 p.m.

The theater was no more than ten minutes away, so we arrived early enough to locate good seats. We nestled into our spaces with popcorn and Cokes in hand, ready to meet the Corleone family. As the movie plot began to unfold and some of the scenes got a little hair-raising, Charlene edged closer to me. At one point she grabbed my arm, holding it tightly for a minute before relaxing her grip. It was a signal even I recognized. I suspected Charlene would welcome me holding her hand. I found my courage … and did so for most of the movie. It likely was a nonevent for Charlene, yet a milestone for me.

We also held hands as we walked from the theater to the car. It felt right—like a cleared hurdle. Since the evening had already whizzed a little past eleven, I took Charlene straight home, before her parents could initiate a search party. During the short drive back to her house, we talked about the movie and had no uncomfortable pauses in the conversation.

As I wheeled into the driveway, it occurred to me the evening had been so enjoyable that I had not obsessed about the biggest of my perceived hurdles—the good-night kiss. We walked up to the front door of the house, holding hands. Charlene turned toward me, displaying a big smile; the cue she gave was unmistakable, so I asked permission to kiss her. She said yes. So I leaned toward her and kissed her—on the lips. I could instantly tell Charlene was kissing me as well. This kiss was more than a peck, and not of the French variety. Nothing else needed to be said, other than "Good night," and she went inside the house.

On the drive back home, I thought about what a gem of a girl Charlene was. She was sweet, attractive, a good conversationalist—but not a magpie—affectionate but not aggressive, intelligent, and fun. I thoroughly enjoyed her company and wanted to go out with her again. No doubt, Charlene was probably on every guy's "A-list" at Jacksonville University. For the first time in my life, I was interested in dating a girl. I was interested in *this* girl—what an unexpected surprise!

I arrived home from the date about 11:45 p.m., which was a late night for me. Not too late for my parents, though, whose bedroom light was dimly visible under the bottom crack of their door. This was no surprise; I knew they wouldn't go to sleep until I was back home. Before going to bed, I said my evening prayers and thanked God for "leading" me to Charlene.

I Surprise Myself

My early to bed, early to rise sleep pattern had long been set. Even though I had been out late, sleeping in was not part of my internal body clock. Predictably, I woke at my usual time and smelled the familiar aroma of coffee, eggs, toast, and grits wafting through the house. No encouragement was needed for me to bound out of bed for breakfast; my morning appetite was in no way diminished by the less than usual amount of sleep.

The conversation at breakfast was not, surprisingly, centered on the date. Nothing personal (like kissing) was discussed, nor would it ever be. My parents were taken off guard when I volunteered I would be asking Charlene out again soon. Assuredly, this was not what they were expecting to hear, and it surprised me the breakfast conversation was actually comfortable. I wondered what was happening to me—I had never had any desire to date anyone more than twice.

After breakfast I spruced up, donned my Sunday coat and tie "uniform," and walked the short distance in the humidity-laced, thick-as-syrup air to Sunday school. Gail and Anthony were already there.

They greeted me with bigger smiles than usual, curious to hear how the date had gone.

I responded, "*The Godfather* was a terrific movie and we really enjoyed it."

Anthony wisecracked, "That's it? The movie was great?"

I enjoyed playing a little naïve, and soon enough communicated the main attraction was not the projection on the movie screen. It was apparent to them (and me) my interest in Charlene was more than passing.

Later in the afternoon, following Sunday lunch, my parents went out to run a quick errand, which presented the perfect opportunity for me to call Charlene. There were no prerequisite script rehearsals and no floor pacing to accompany this phone call. A different Seth was emerging, and my newborn confidence energized me.

I dialed the now-memorized phone number without hesitation. This time, Charlene's mother answered, and we briefly engaged in cordial conversation until Charlene picked up, using another phone.

Charlene seemed pleasantly surprised I called so soon following our date. She wasn't the only one—so was I. I expressed to Charlene how much I enjoyed our time together and then asked if she would consider going to church with me that night. I also invited her to come over to our house following church. As luck would have it, she had no pressing plans and agreed to both requests. This would be the perfect Baptist-approved date.

My parents walked in a few minutes after the phone call ended and were astonished to hear Charlene and I had a church date. Excitedly, I looked forward to the evening for two reasons. First, I wanted Charlene and my parents to meet. Secondly, I had an inkling our relationship was going to be more than a "fling" and wanted to spend a few minutes getting to know her parents a little better. With this I mind, I proposed to Charlene that I come to her house a few minutes early. She liked the idea. All that was left to be done was for me to show up.

With heightened anticipation, I rang the doorbell of the Harrelsons' house around 6:30 p.m. Charlene's father answered the door and invited me into their spacious, wood-paneled family room where Mrs. Harrelson was sitting. For the time being, it was just the three of us; Charlene was not ready. Mr. and Mrs. Harrelson were engaging, and it was hard for me to ignore how good-looking Charlene's dad was. Not that her mother wasn't, but my natural inclination was to notice him first. They told me how pleased they were Charlene and I had met. I complimented them on raising such a special daughter and stated we were enjoying each other's company. They asked me a few questions about my job and were curious as to whether or not I saw a future in my work. My answer was truthful; I admitted my job was an eventual dead end, yet it provided invaluable experience. (This answer would prove to haunt me in a few months.) Charlene came into the room, and we left for our G-rated church date.

We arrived at the church a few minutes early, and my parents were already there. They were eager to meet Charlene and curious to see who this girl was who had me so captivated. As Charlene and I entered the vestibule of the church, I could see my parents standing in the left aisle, conversing with two of their closest friends, Jean and Lee Davidson.

I proudly walked Charlene to the group and wasted no time introducing her to my parents and then to the Davidsons. It was impossible not to see how delighted my parents were. I could read their minds: *Our Seth, brought a girl to church. Thank you, Jesus, our prayers have been answered—finally!*

The Davidsons were complimentary of Charlene and asked where I had found such a gem. I agreed she indeed was a catch and thanked them for their observation. We talked for a few minutes, until just before the service started. My mother vamoosed to the choir room (I played hooky), and Charlene and I sat next to my dad in the second row from the front (where my behavior could be monitored).

Following church, we traveled the one-block distance to our house, which was an ideal locale for my parents and Charlene to get better acquainted. It was apparent we didn't live in an expensive neighborhood, yet all houses were neat and well maintained. I was concerned the apparent difference in our social strata could be a future consideration for Charlene and her parents; time would answer that.

Knowing an evening "feeding" was in order, my mother had previously made tuna fish sandwiches. True to form, they were cut in half diagonally, with the crusted edges cut off—extra-fancy fare. My parents were genuine to the core, easy to be around, well-spoken, polished, and gracious. I have little recollection of the conversation, but remember Charlene stating how much she liked my parents.

In a Whirlwind

In the coming weeks our dating continued, and it was becoming apparent our relationship was more than the "puppy love" variety.

Charlene and I saw each other without fail every Saturday and Sunday and sometimes in between. We were in the phase of courtship that in those days was called "going steady," except we were no longer in the applicable age group for this term to be appropriate. Yet for me, the term applied; I was playing catch-up. Thankfully, having reached this level of comfort with each other meant the awkward stage of asking Charlene for dates was over. It was assumed we would be doing things together. We usually went to church together and attended either my church or hers. We had become inseparable, and this head trip had me riding the crest of a wave. It was apparent Charlene and I were "involved," and her parents seemed to approve of our relationship—at least initially.

Chapter 15

Dinner at the Harrelsons'

It is interesting how details of certain life experiences can become ensconced in one's memory banks, whereas others fade into oblivion. My first dinner at the Harrelsons', two disagreements with Charlene, and a harrowing reptile encounter are three memories still firmly entrenched in my cerebral files. Funny thing, the two disagreements Charlene and I had were kitchen related, and they were actually symptomatic of disparate backgrounds.

On one Saturday in early August, the Harrelsons decided to grill steaks in their backyard and they invited me to join them. At this point, Charlene and I had been dating about six weeks. I lost no time in accepting the invitation and looked forward to the cookout, particularly since the neighbors across the street (the Langleys) would also be there. The prospect of eating steak was a source of excitement, although smoke signals from hamburgers would have lured me there as well. I arrived a little earlier than the planned eating time so I could help out. No real help was needed. Even so, I received points for the gesture.

The Langleys arrived a few minutes after I did. As I had surmised, Leona was entertaining and the perfect accompaniment to her reserved yet affable husband, Burt. It isn't that Burt wasn't interesting, but Leona possessed the type of sass and personality making her the star of any show. She was unfiltered, laughed a lot, and I was fascinated. Additionally, she had an impressive command of spicy, carefully placed vocabulary words, making an impact on my eager ears. The Langleys were Methodists. By the time the evening was over, I decided I should visit their church. They could even drink wine—in moderation, of course—and remain in their church's good graces.

In between Leona's curtain calls, Burt and I talked a lot about his yard, which was impeccably landscaped and groomed by him. The cookout was my first real opportunity to meet him. He relished working with his many specimen plants, which belied his profession as the area manager for a major linen supplier. His yard was full of azaleas, camellias, orange trees, and bird-of-paradise, with a backdrop of towering oaks providing picture-perfect framing. We enjoyed instant commonality since my profession as a wholesale nurseryman dovetailed beautifully with his yard hobby. The Langleys and I developed an affinity, even though they were about twenty-five years older than me. They were not able to have children, though they were particularly close to an adored teenage niece who lived in South Carolina.

The afternoon was hot and sticky, and tending to a grill in the glare of the western sun was nothing anyone would envy. Even so, I spent a good bit of time talking with Mr. Harrelson while he was parked by the pyre. He had marinated the steaks earlier in the day to ensure they had ample time to absorb all the secret adulterants by grill time. In many families in the South, the ingredients in barbeque sauces and marinades are closely-held secrets—thus considered holy. However, Mr. Harrelson gladly shared his recipe with me while we chatted. He threw the steaks on the grates, and they were briefly engulfed in a fiery spectacle, followed by clouds of grease-fueled smoke that swirled around us. The grill cover was flipped down, and we ran for breathable air. A few moments later, the smoke cleared, allowing us to return to the grill. I watched intently as Mr. Harrelson turned the steaks several times, moved them around, and frequently reapplied the not-so-secret secret marinade. The steaks were soon done. He carefully inspected each one to insure the peak of perfection had been reached before methodically placing them on an oversized platter I firmly held. Finally, they were covered with tinfoil for the brief trip to the kitchen. There was an art to this entire process which was unfamiliar to me. The outcome was displayed in the sheer impeccability of the steaks—without a doubt the best I had ever eaten. Some people are skilled at grilling steaks and Ted Harrelson was an artisan.

Dinnertime came as promised, and we gathered at the beautifully set, chandelier-lit dining room table. The steaks were adorned with stuffed baked potatoes and a salad (what else?). Charlene and I sat next to each other and occasionally held hands when they were not otherwise engaged in balancing cutlery. What a fun time. It felt so easy, and so socially appropriate. There was never a loss for conversation, and it was clear the Harrelsons and the Langleys were the closest of friends. We talked about everything under the sun, and before I knew it the evening was over. Charlene's parents and the Langleys were a joy to be around, and they went out of their way to make me feel comfortable. Before the Langleys left, Burt asked me to come over to their house the next time I was in the neighborhood; they wanted to ask me some questions about their orange trees. I assured them I would love to do it and fulfilled the commitment in a few days.

After dinner, I offered to help with the kitchen cleanup. Mrs. Harrelson thanked me for the overture and insisted I not lift a finger. Charlene placed the plates in the dishwasher while her mother washed the steak platter. The piece of tinfoil that had covered the steak platter was lying on the kitchen counter, and I made the comment that it could easily be used again after a rinse. It had not occurred to me this type of thrift was not observed in all families. When it came to reusing tinfoil, I found out the Harrelsons were aligned with the non-observers.

Charlene laughed, crumpled up the tinfoil for disposal, and quipped, "Are you serious?" She was clearly surprised I would suggest something so seemingly absurd.

I laughed and said, "I am used to saving reusable items, but surely am agreeable with a proper burial in the garbage can."

Her mother didn't say anything, yet my comment regarding tinfoil reuse didn't go unnoticed, as I would later find out.

It had been a wonderful evening, and I heartily thanked Mr. and Mrs. Harrelson for including me. Charlene walked me to the front door, where we kissed each other good night, and I drove home.

During the twenty-minute drive home, I reflected on the evening and considered the possibility Charlene was going to be my wife. No doubt it was early in our relationship, yet the "road signs" sure seemed to be pointing in that direction. It was an exhilarating time—and unsettling.

While I didn't consider Charlene and me to have a class difference, I was aware we came from different perspectives on money and spending, in general. I started earning money in junior high school through various "enterprises" including selling Christmas cards and mowing lawns. Accordingly, I developed an appreciation for money management and understood the importance of exercising prudence when spending. My dad had a little to do with this as well; he was an exceptional mentor. On the other hand, Charlene had dissimilar experiences and, not surprisingly, held different viewpoints concerning money. This in itself could create some marital rockiness, but, looming larger, my concerns about us being sexually mismatched were downright frightening. I kept reassuring myself that God would work out this detail, and I managed to keep my doubts sublimated.

A Day to Remember

One of our most unforgettable dates was slated to be an ordinary Saturday outing at the beach. I suggested we go to Talbot Island State Park, which was renowned for its beautiful, uncrowded beaches. However, Charlene preferred we go to the Ponte Vedra Beach Club where the Harrelsons had a family membership. This club was a haven for some of Jacksonville's most influential families, and it was clearly outside my comfort level.

I had never been there and had no desire to go. Nonetheless, I didn't admit to a deep-seated apprehension and acquiesced without any argument. I had no idea what to expect and offered to pick up some hamburgers on the way. Charlene advised me it wouldn't be necessary because "the best hamburgers in town" were available at the club.

She assured me, "It will be a blast."

I had $10 in my wallet, which should have been more than enough to cover a couple of hamburgers (with cheese), fries, soft drinks, tax, and a tip. Right? Wrong! No doubt, my eyes were bulging from sticker shock, and Charlene wondered why I had suddenly become so quiet.

All I could say was, "Gosh, this place is expensive."

She told me not to worry about it; her dad would be billed for anything we ate or drank.

While I was relieved, this arrangement disturbed me—I never wanted to give the impression I was "on the take." Even so, I followed Charlene's suggestion and ordered the hamburger (without the cheese extravagance). Later, I offered to reimburse the Harrelsons; they emphatically refused. Of course, I thanked them for their graciousness.

After eating lunch, we ambled to the beach to catch a little sun and go swimming in the surf. One of the most bizarre and frightening things that has ever happened to me occurred while we were frolicking in the ocean. We were swimming in about chest-deep water when I felt something bump me in the back. I thought it was the foot of another swimmer since there were a few other people in the water, and it's not uncommon for waves and currents to occasionally push people into each other. It happened a second time, so I turned around, expecting to see a kid having difficulty with "rudder" control.

Much to my shock, I was face-to-face with a large rattlesnake right on top of the water! I knew rattlesnakes were strong swimmers and was aware they were common in the palmetto-studded sand dunes dotting the area. Nonetheless, I had never heard of one being seen in the surf—until now. I screamed for Charlene to get out of the water and then realized the snake's movement was dependent on the whims of the waves—it was dead. Better it than me. Nonetheless, we frantically "got the heck" out of the snake pit and decompressed in the club's unthreatening pool water. (I had nightmares about rattlesnakes for years after this never-to-be-forgotten incident.)

Upon arriving back to Charlene's house, she and I went across the street to visit the Langleys. They were working in their flawless front yard, so we all walked around to the back for me to look at their ailing orange trees. I easily observed the trees looked as if they had been sprayed with a thin coat of black paint. Easy diagnosis. They had sooty mold, which renders the trees unattractive, and is a commonly occurring malady with an easy fix. The Langleys were relieved to hear the favorable prognosis. Following treatment, the trees continued to produce large volumes of oranges for more than thirty years.

Blame It on Breyers

One of my food "vices" has unceasingly been vanilla ice cream, which I am convinced can be traced to some vagrant genes spinning around during my fetal development. There were some other things spinning around, or I wouldn't be writing this thesis. Nonetheless, I pride myself in the amount of will power I have exercised when sweets cross my path. It isn't that I don't want them; I do. But being a health enthusiast superseded my desire to eat many sweets, particularly since I would never accept anything other than a 32-inch waistline (and still won't).

Charlene was well aware that, to me, a vanilla malted milk shake was the equivalent of the apple Eve gave to Adam—an irresistible temptation. One afternoon at the Harrelsons' house, Charlene offered to make one, which had me salivating. She retrieved the requisites: malt, milk, vanilla extract, and a carton of vanilla ice cream. My eyes about popped out of my head when I beheld the ice cream was Breyers.

To put this into perspective, Breyers was probably the first of the "all natural," close to homemade-tasting ice creams to hit the market in Jacksonville. I adored it. It was a paragon then, deserving of "shrine status" in the freezer. Relative to the other brands available, it was also expensive. You probably already guessed it—here comes another story akin to the tinfoil incident.

As Charlene scooped the ice cream from the carton, I made the statement, "Wow, I know this ice cream is expensive. Are you sure it is okay to use so much of it for a milk shake?" My real concern was I would be perceived by her parents to be taking advantage of a good situation by decimating this prized ice cream.

Charlene was sharp in her rebuttal and advised me it wouldn't have been offered if there was any chance of there being a problem. She was clearly ruffled.

I apologized for the misunderstanding and thanked her for making the milk shake, which was of course delectable.

It was a brief skirmish, and the topic never came up again. The ice cream and tinfoil memories will likely never leave me.

Chapter 16

Could It Be I'm Falling in Love?

Charlene entered her junior year at Jacksonville University in early September. She was looking forward to her graduation and beginning a career as an elementary schoolteacher in two years. She had been active in her sorority at JU; however, our dating put those activities on the back burner. In fact, I never attended any events with her that were related to the university or the sorority. We had become inseparable. As September morphed into October, we recognized our relationship had blossomed into a serious phase, and our feelings for each other were deep. I had evolved to the point where I felt I was in love with Charlene.

After church one Sunday night, I drove Charlene home and parked the car in front of her house. Instead of going inside, I suggested we stay in the car. We were snuggled up in the front seat, listening to the radio when my emotions overtook what little reason I had going on at the moment.

I turned the radio down, leaned toward Charlene, and told her I was falling in love with her. This was the first time the word had been uttered. She said nothing; briefly there was unsettling silence.

Without anything being said, Charlene leaned toward me, and we tightly embraced. We then exchanged long, passionate kisses.

When our kissing ended, Charlene said, "I have been waiting to hear this. Seth, I love you too."

I asked her if she was surprised our relationship had developed so quickly in the four months we had been dating.

She said, "No." She added that fairly soon after we started dating, she knew I was different from most other guys she had known.

Naturally, I was curious to know what made me different. She told me they had been less respectful than me; they were in a hurry to pursue a physical relationship. I hadn't done that.

Based on previous conversations, I knew she was a virgin, and she knew I was. True, I was a respectful twenty-three-year-old guy, but no doubt, the maintenance of my virginity had not been difficult.

Premarital sex was frequently condemned from the church pulpit, so not having sexual relations was understandable (although probably not the norm) back in those days. It was the perfect reason for me to not make any sexual advances toward Charlene.

However, the thoughts of having sex post-marriage greatly troubled me. A popular song, "Please Go All the Way," sung by The Raspberries, frequently played on the radio. Wow, did this song ever hit a nerve every time I heard it. While it was clear what "go all the way" in this song meant, the only "all the way" interesting me was the accompaniments on my hamburger.

Oh, God! What Have I Done?

The month of October proved to be pivotal for Charlene and me as our relationship continued to mature at a dizzying—and frightening—pace. My parents recognized Charlene and I were getting serious. I know they were surprised, given my history of nothing long term with any girl. They were supportive and liked Charlene, yet had some concerns about the durability of our relationship. They didn't discuss those concerns with me until later.

Not long after Charlene and I had expressed our love for each other, I began to seriously consider the possibility that the next step, if things continued to progress, would be our engagement. My self-acknowledged concerns regarding sex and, to a lesser degree, potential money management issues, continued to be distressing. I also deliberated whether or not I was good enough for Charlene.

In spite of these misgivings, I perceived the planets were aligning, and believed love would conquer all. There was nothing foreseeable to dissuade me from asking Charlene to marry me at some point fairly soon. I rationalized if our marriage was not God's will, then Charlene would perceive accordingly and decline the proposal. Thus, the "trap" was carefully and thoughtfully set by me, and I was ready to jump in, eyes wide open. I talked myself into the idea that marrying Charlene was God's will, and believed the handwriting was on the wall. I continued to pray for discernment and pleaded for an honest-to-goodness sexual desire for Charlene.

On a mid-November Saturday, I felt the time was right to ask Charlene *the* question. We had been dating about five months—probably on the short side of the usual time spectrum for a marriage proposal. There was no doubt we got along wonderfully, savored each other's company, were both considerate of each other, and had all the outward hallmarks of a couple in love. I had no idea how to approach the subject, and undeniably, the direct route of just throwing it out there was not within my comfort zone. "Tap dancing" around the topic seemed to be the appropriate method of delivery.

That night, Charlene's parents went out for the evening, leaving us alone in the house. We sat close together on the couch in the family room, holding hands and kissing. I was experiencing an erection—nothing like what I'd experienced in the pool with Anthony—but nonetheless, it was sort of there. Surely, this was a sign from God.

I stammered around trying to find the right words. I told Charlene I loved her, and continued my discourse by saying our relationship had reached the point where we needed to talk about our future together. I acknowledged I had never experienced such strong feelings about a girl. Ever.

Charlene probably discerned I was nervous and looked at me with a pensive expression. I asked if her feelings for me were as deep as mine were for her, and she said yes. At this point, she had to suspect what was coming.

Finally, I took a couple of deep breaths and asked her if we should consider getting married. I didn't come out and say, "Will you marry me?" This would have been waaaaaaay too direct, too risky for my bones.

With a huge smile, she said, "Are you asking me to marry you?"

My answer was yes. That was it. The deed was done. By the way, she said yes. We were engaged.

When the Harrelsons got home later, neither of us said anything to them regarding our engagement. I knew Charlene wanted to prep her parents for the news.

The following morning, after a sleepless night, I called Charlene. Not surprisingly, she had not slept much either. My sleeplessness was a "good-grief-what-have-I-done" reaction, whereas hers was from exhilaration. She had not yet said anything to her parents, and planned to tell them later in the day, probably after church. We didn't expect them to be taken by surprise since they were aware we loved each other.

Charlene and I had already planned to be together Sunday evening, so it would be a logical time for us to deliver our news to my parents after church—assuming no prior fireworks came from Charlene's side of the river. If Charlene's parents voiced no objections to our intent to marry, it would be appropriate for me to soon have "the chat" with Charlene's dad. Too soon. My intestines were already in a twist.

Extra, Extra, Read All about It

I was eager to report to the world that Charlene and I were engaged, but needed to keep my mouth shut until our parents had been apprised of the development. I was not altogether successful. In fact, the first folks to be "sort of" notified were Anthony and Gail, since I had the unavoidable opportunity during church on Sunday morning.

In passing conversation, I "mentioned" to them Charlene and I would soon be imparting some significant news.

With a coy grin on her face, Gail asked, "And just what might this be?"

Of course, they both knew what was being insinuated and promised to keep this breaking news confidential until Charlene and I had spoken to our parents.

On Sunday afternoon, Charlene imparted the big—really big—news to her parents. Shortly afterwards, she called me and excitedly reported their reaction was positive. She said her parents were fond of me and they were not too surprised.

I guess the most surprised person, in fact, was me. I was engaged and believed God would handle my personal issues.

Charlene attended evening church services with me, and afterwards we went over to my parents' house in anticipation of making "the announcement." Nestled close to each other in the middle of the living room couch, we were about to burst. My parents were in the kitchen and, for once, I was less concerned with the sandwiches my mother was preparing than with the other business at hand.

I called for them to come into the living room for a minute. Asking them to come out of the kitchen was out of character for me, so this was curious. As soon as they sat, I said, "We have something to tell you."

My mother's eyes were transfixed on me, and my dad had a slight smile. Neither said a word.

Charlene had a schoolgirl beam on her face, as I made the declaration: "Charlene and I have decided we want to get married."

My parents knew our relationship was continuing to evolve; nonetheless, they were astonished. They wanted to know if Mr. and Mrs. Harrelson had been told. When Charlene answered she had broken the news to her parents earlier in the day and they were pleased, my dad advised me to talk with Mr. Harrelson as soon as possible. I promised him I would tend to the detail, probably the next evening.

My parents congratulated us and warmly welcomed Charlene into our family; we celebrated with a tuna fish sandwich feast.

I drove Charlene back to her house and as we were about to exchange good-night kisses at the front door, it opened. As it turned out, the Langleys had been visiting and were just leaving as we walked up. Judging by their over-the-top smiles, the Harrelsons had probably implied Charlene and I were engaged.

We cordially greeted each other and exchanged brief, inconsequential conversation. The Harrelsons were also at the door and invited me to come in.

The last thing I wanted was to go inside—surely, it was a trap! I thanked them for the invitation, and gave myself a way out by saying I realized it was late (about 10:00 p.m.). It didn't work.

Mrs. Harrelson countered by saying, "It isn't *that* late, Seth. Come on in and chat with us."

Holy heart attack! I was in no way ready to have *the* conversation, which unavoidably was about to happen. I needed to rehearse "my lines," which at this point were not even written. This was not listed in my daily activity planner for Sunday night. Maybe Monday night.

Nonetheless, I reluctantly went inside and felt a hot, flushed feeling in my face and a lump in my throat. I felt like a kid who had just been caught doing something bad, like chewing gum in class. (Yes, this was considered bad back then.)

Mr. Harrelson smiled at me and asked if there was anything I wanted to discuss with him. Mrs. Harrelson was of course in the vicinity and also had a smile on her face.

My quick summation was that the signs were actually good. I sort of laughed and said, "Well, I guess now is as good a time as any."

We sat in the family room while Charlene and her mother scampered into the adjacent kitchen. Mr. Harrelson surely sensed I was befuddled and broke the ice by asking what was on my mind.

I took a deep breath and started talking. "Mr. Harrelson, I am sure you and Mrs. Harrelson are aware Charlene and I have fallen in love with each other. I realize we have been dating a relatively short time—five months—yet we both believe God brought us together for a reason." (Blaming God would undoubtedly lend credence to my speech.) "We strongly feel we are being led into marriage, and I would like to ask you and Mrs. Harrelson for permission to marry Charlene." There it was, short and sweet.

He responded by saying they knew Charlene and I were in love, and they had even discussed the possibility we may be headed for marriage. He gave me their blessing, at which point we stood up, shook hands, and went into the kitchen where Charlene and her mother were on standby.

Of course, they had heard the conversation. Mrs. Harrelson hugged me and told me how excited they were for us. I was almost in tears and Charlene was smiling from ear to ear.

I was home before 11:00 p.m., the usual worry-point time for my parents if I was not within their eyesight. They had not yet gone to bed, so I updated them on the evening's events. They were surprised, and pleased, I had already spoken with Charlene's parents.

Next-Day Repercussions

When I got home from work on Monday, my mother shocked me with the news that she had spoken with Liz Harrelson earlier in the day. The rapidity at which this conversation took place was not expected. Undoubtedly, I knew our mothers would talk, but for whatever reason, didn't anticipate their communication to occur so fast. It probably was because my own nature was to be less hasty when it came to such matters. Nonetheless, Mrs. Harrelson had called my mother to express Mr. Harrelson's and her approval of our engagement. She gushed that they couldn't have handpicked anyone more perfect for their daughter than me.

Wow! Her approving remarks put me on cloud nine.

My mother echoed similar sentiments to Mrs. Harrelson regarding Charlene and expressed a desire for the two families to get together soon.

Since all major "stakeholders" had by now been appropriately advised of our engagement, there were several friends I was waiting to tell, and my close friend Georgi was on top of the list. We had not played tennis in a while, so I called him to schedule a match for the coming Saturday afternoon.

I divulged nothing until we met at the courts around 2:00 p.m. As we were playing, I told him Charlene and I were engaged. He was astonished at how quickly this had occurred, and, as expected, was wonderfully supportive and congratulatory. At the same time, he lamented his single condition and stated how desperately he wanted to get married. Without question, Georgi was on a concerted mission to accomplish his goal, and I wished his dream would soon become reality. (Happily, he succeeded in finding a tailor-made wife—but not for another five years.)

Together, Charlene and I excitedly told Leona and Burt Langley we were getting married. They feigned a modicum of surprise. We all laughed, knowing the news had already been inferred by Mrs. Harrelson. The Langleys expressed a desire to give us an engagement dinner, which was a rite I had assumed would never be experienced by me. I was in love with being in love.

The news of my engagement to Charlene spread speedily among my friends and, predictably, the church communication channels were buzzing. A lot of folks were stunned, which was not surprising given my well-known history of avoiding female relationships. Even so, the rain of well-wishes falling on my shoulders was intoxicating, and, for a moment in time, I feasted in the delusion that I was being transformed into a "normal" guy—a socially acceptable heterosexual.

Next Steps

Within two weeks after we became engaged, Charlene and I went downtown to one of the city's most respected jewelers to look at engagement rings. Charlene was reasonable and definite in what she wanted, which resonated well with me. She selected a beautiful ring with a diamond slightly less than a carat. Since there was no need to look further, I purchased the ring she wanted. The ring had to be sized, which necessitated waiting a week or two before it could be picked up.

At about the same time, Mrs. Harrelson and Charlene obtained a book containing samples of wedding invitations. Charlene and I perused them one evening, and, as far as I was concerned, the invitation could have been on a paper table napkin and it would have been acceptable. We considered a summer event. After getting married she would still have another year of schoolwork before graduation. Her parents didn't seem to object, although it was clear they would need to continue paying for Charlene's education at Jacksonville University, which was not an inexpensive school. We didn't rule out waiting until she graduated, which would give me more time to save money. I had a goal of accumulating $5,000 in savings before our marriage, and, without question, this was a sticking point for Charlene. She felt I was placing too much emphasis on the financial aspects of getting married, and we shouldn't delay a wedding in order to reach a financial goal. She was probably right, at least partially.

Wedding Bells Ring for Gail and Anthony

Anthony and Gail didn't wait too long to get married, once announcing their engagement. They had already obtained their degrees from respected universities and had embarked upon promising careers. The entire church loved this "golden couple" who were held in high esteem and looked like they belonged on a bridal magazine cover. They seemed to have it all, including a coffeepot I gave them as a wedding gift.

The wedding was held at the church on a Saturday evening in November. Charlene and I paid closer than usual attention to the details of the affair, given our recent engagement. Gail made a beautiful bride and Anthony made a ridiculously handsome groom. When they were exchanging vows, I gazed at him and reflected on the time when he and I had wrestled in the pool. It was a harsh reminder my attraction to him had not waned. Fortunately, my relationship with Charlene was sufficiently distracting to allow my true feelings to be mostly sublimated.

At the conclusion of the service, the pastor introduced Mr. and Mrs. Anthony Petrini to the congregation. As they marched up the aisle and passed me, I was overcome by a rush of emotion. The beaming couple embodied everything I yearned for Charlene and me. For some reason, at that moment I experienced honest, albeit fleeting, lucidity. Could I really have a successful marriage with Charlene? With any woman? This thought petrified me, yet my "forward ho" mindset was driven by the belief I was following God's (and everyone else's) expectations.

During the reception, a number of people congratulated Charlene and me on our engagement. One of my parents' friends made the remark to Charlene that she had to be a special lady because no one else could corral me.

Without hesitation I said, "She is."

It was exhilarating. The congratulatory messages and supportive comments fed right into the continuing delusion that my innate sexual orientation was in the process of being changed. I still expected to wake up one morning—and poof—my transformation would be completed.

Gail and Anthony's wedding event was a euphoric evening for both Charlene and me.

Afterwards, Charlene made the remark, "I am so happy, I can't stand it."

This statement has never left me.

Of all places to live, Anthony and Gail initially rented a small house about 100 feet from the nursery where I worked. I could have thrown a baseball into their yard, except I didn't throw baseballs under any circumstances. Occasionally, I went over to visit them, particularly after their first child was born. This event occurred about nine months after they were pronounced husband and wife.

Chapter 17

A Bombshell Drops

Shortly after Gail and Anthony's wedding, Charlene called me one evening in a highly emotional and distraught state. Something had happened, and she needed me to come over; it was something she couldn't discuss over the phone. Of course, most guys receiving this type of call would go into a panic, but there was surely no concern Charlene was pregnant. This would have been an impossibility in the post–Virgin Mary epoch in which we lived. We hadn't "done it," as waiting until marriage to "do it" had been easy—too easy for me. Admittedly, I was curious about Charlene's sexual apparatus; unlike Lewis and Clark, I had no real desire to explore new territory.

Without delay, I went over to the Harrelsons' house. Upon arriving, I found Charlene alone in the house and visibly shaken. She shared with me that her parents (primarily her mother) had been miserable in Jacksonville ever since they arrived several years earlier.

I was already well aware of this. Mrs. Harrelson had made no efforts to hide her disdain for the area. She found it devoid of good restaurants and acceptable shopping. Compounding her displeasure was the annoyance created by the too-frequent stench coming from paper mills. These were valid points. Still, her misery was largely self-imposed since there were many positives she chose to ignore.

Charlene disclosed it was likely *they* were going to be moving back to Dallas. This was no real surprise either; I knew her parents eventually would return to their home state. Prior to the Harrelsons moving to Jacksonville, promotional opportunities moved them from Texas to New Jersey to Arkansas. They were unhappy in New Jersey, yet satisfied with Arkansas since it was close to Dallas. For some time, Charlene said, her mother had been pressing for a return to Dallas, and the situation had now suddenly escalated. As fate would have it, a position in Dallas had opened up. Mrs. Harrelson gave her husband an ultimatum to go after it—or else—even though it would initially be a lateral career move.

The full meaning of Charlene's revelation went right over the top of my head; I didn't initially grasp the meaning of the word *they*—until she clarified it included her. If Mr. Harrelson was awarded the position, Charlene would be moving to Texas with her parents. This possibility had been brewing for a brief time and the coffee was ready to be poured. I sat dumbfounded—in disbelief—in one day, things had so drastically changed for us. It made no sense to me that her parents would force Charlene to leave JU, particularly in her junior year. Besides, we had just become engaged. The apple cart looked like it may not only be overturned but the wheels knocked off as well. When asked what her dad's chances were of landing the position, Charlene said it was all but a done deal. In fact, the deal was done and preparations for their move were well under way prior to Christmas.

Charlene and I discussed possible options that would allow her to remain in Jacksonville. The first was an appeal to her parents to allow her to remain at JU and live in a dormitory on campus or perhaps in a nearby apartment. This would allow her to complete her degree without disruption. The second consideration was to throw caution to the wind and proceed to marry. In the coming days, we would hash and rehash these two options, but as it turned out, her parents turned a deaf ear to our pleadings.

I never understood the Harrelsons' stance because their attitude was a complete 180 from the apparent elation they had displayed when we announced our engagement several weeks prior. The tenseness of our situation heightened considerably when Charlene was instructed that all financial support for her education would come to a halt if she remained in Jacksonville. In other words, if we proceeded to marry, we were on our own. This was a proviso neither of us was prepared to counter. We were forced to capitulate, although we briefly toyed with the idea of elopement. This would have required Charlene to drop out of school, secure employment, and, at some point, go back to school when we could afford it. We didn't elope.

Christmas was fast approaching, but the joys of the season were overshadowed by the pall associated with the Harrelsons' imminent exit from Jacksonville. Charlene's somber mood was countered by her mother's irritating elation. Her dad didn't display any real emotion, and I imagine he was relieved the contention between him and Mrs. Harrelson was over. (Some years later, Leona Langley shared with me that the situation in the Harrelson household leading up to their move back to Dallas was probably worse than what even Charlene knew.) Through it all, I felt sorry for the Harrelsons. I held no ill will against them, but felt their actions toward Charlene during this time were harsh.

It became apparent our engagement was in serious jeopardy. The dynamics had drastically changed and the Harrelsons' blessing of our engagement had turned into a let's-back-off-and-see-what-happens attitude. Charlene and I remained engaged; however, her parents prevailed upon her to not accept the engagement ring—which was to have been her Christmas present. I called the jewelry store to advise them I wouldn't be picking up the ring, and they gave me a complete refund. Charlene was plainly in a state of devastation to see her entire world crumble. Even though the whole situation was highly upsetting to me, I can't say I was devastated.

Other than me, Charlene's primary outside sources of support were Burt and Leona Langley. They were objective, wonderful listeners, compassionate and wise. Without question, they loved Charlene and were saddened to see their close friends and neighbors move away. Unlike Burt, Leona was plainspoken and said what she thought—most of the time. I loved that in her. She was also smart and knew when to hide her cards. As far as I know, they were never displayed throughout this entire episode. I don't know what their true feelings were and am confident she and Burt advised Charlene to do what her parents asked. The advice was borne out of their love for Charlene and me; I will never forget that.

Christmas 1972 is largely a blur. I don't remember what I gave Charlene, other than a framed picture of me. She gave me an engraved bracelet with her name inscribed. During this period of turmoil, my parents were perplexed at how fast the Harrelsons' attitude toward Charlene and me had changed. Nonetheless, they didn't disparage them and remained fond of Charlene. As it turned out, my parents never met Ted and Liz Harrelson.

When I hear "Summer Breeze," sung by Seals and Crofts, it takes me back to that poignant season in my life in 1972, which was a profound period of searching, growth, and discovery.

Our Last Day Together in Jacksonville

Charlene's parents remained warm toward me during the days leading up to their departure. They were upbeat about Charlene and me getting married once she finished her education, which would be at a yet-to-be-determined university in Texas. There had not been time for a school to be selected, and the stress this created for Charlene was apparent; it was already late December.

The night before the Harrelsons left to go back to Texas was an emotional roller coaster. I took Charlene over to my house so she could tell my parents goodbye. Predictably, they were outwardly optimistic and reassured us everything would work out. We all bravely hid our misgivings behind the façades of false smiles.

The memory most tenaciously remaining of our last night together is of Charlene and me sitting in my car, parked in the Harrelsons' driveway. We just sat there, encapsulated in a fog while we talked and cried (mostly, she cried). We bemoaned the apparent unfairness of her parents forcing her to leave JU in the middle of the year, and discussed the difficulties she would likely encounter when transferring to a new school. We clung to the hope that time would pass quickly, and we could be married (as her parents promised) as soon as Charlene finished college in Texas. We stayed in my car, our "for the moment" safe place for as long as we could, commiserating about our disbelief in what was transpiring. We kissed one more time in the car and pledged our love for each other.

At about midnight we went into the house, where I bade Mr. and Mrs. Harrelson farewell one last time. They seemed sympathetic; however, I suspected their true feelings were not as they appeared. I wished them a safe trip and gave a final hug to Charlene's parents.

Charlene walked me back to the front door, where we exchanged our last kiss. She cried again, and my eyes were welling with tears. Whew, what a tough moment! Even so, I managed to remain fairly composed.

I walked to my car, fell into the seat, and backed out of the driveway. I looked toward the house, only to see Charlene with her head buried in her hands. She looked up briefly as I drove away and displayed an anguished face dimly lit by the porch light. It ripped me apart to see her so distraught and helpless. It was a terrible time for Charlene, having to bear the brunt of this transition back to Texas. Her life was unmercifully upended.

As I crossed the Mathews Bridge, Led Zeppelin's "Stairway to Heaven" was playing on my car radio, and the tears started coursing down my face; in fact, they came down in floods, almost obscuring my vision. I wondered if I would ever see Charlene again and recognized I was no match for her parents, who were in total control of the situation. My emotions were raw, and one of the thoughts running rampant in my muddled brain was to turn the car around, rescue Charlene, and elope. The logical side of my brain instantly countered this knee-jerk idea as ill-timed and destined to be a tragic mistake.

There was no question that I loved Charlene. There was also no question that I had never developed a normal sexual desire for her, and for this reason I sensed a degree of relief that Charlene would be at a distance. However, my lack of emotional maturity and stubborn refusal to accept who I was continued to obscure the "unthinkable" truth that I was gay.

Tenaciously, for some time to come I allowed myself to be guided by destructive religious beliefs and societal expectations.

When I got home, there was the least possible conversation with my parents, who were still up. They could tell I was upset and didn't pursue any particulars. They knew it was the last time I would see Charlene in probably a long time, if ever.

Even though forty-five years have since passed, when I hear "Stairway to Heaven," the details of that night flash to the forefront of my thoughts.

Troublesome Dream

As if the trauma of the night was not enough, a postscript awaited me. Predictably, I had a difficult time going to sleep and squirmed in bed, reflecting on the evolution of the previous six months with Charlene. Eventually, I managed to drift off and, at some point during the night, experienced a dream that without a doubt was my inner voice attempting to give me a message. My subconscious state took control and, like a whirlwind, gave me an unbridled spin. I worked with a good-looking guy at the nursery, and made concerted efforts to keep my attentions directed otherwise. This didn't matter at all; my dream world scripted a scene where he and I became passionately engaged at work in the tool shed. Just as the torrid fling was winding down, we were discovered by a stunned coworker. I awoke in a state of panic. The timing of the dream was particularly disturbing; it created yet another seed of doubt taking residence with many other seeds I was doing my best to keep from sprouting. My same-sex yearnings had to remain quashed, but my dreams served to fuel them.

The Long-Distance Courtship Begins

Following the Harrelsons' move, Charlene and I began to write each other and occasionally talked on the phone. Long-distance telephone calls were relatively expensive when compared to costs today, so our primary communication was via U.S. Mail. The cost of a first-class stamp was a mere eight cents; we splurged and spent the eleven cents required for airmail, which typically ensured receipt within two days of mailing. Initially, Charlene wrote several times a week, and I dutifully responded, sometimes not as frequently. She bared her soul in correspondence and the overall theme was one of being forlorn and heartsick. It was evident our separation was tearing her apart. In comparison, the tone of my letters was not commensurate. I wrote more about what was going on at work, at church, with Gail and Anthony, with my parents, and the weather. Of course I wrote that I missed and loved her—which I did—but this message was not the focus of my letters.

It concerned me that I didn't have the same level of intensity in our relationship as she did. Our separation was having less of an effect on me than her, which made me feel ashamed. Maybe it was just a guy thing? One other complication continued to burden Charlene—she still had not completed the transfer process into a university. Consequently, she was likely to lose some time in the process, which could possibly delay her graduation. Her transition to Texas had to be overwhelming, and I could do nothing to ameliorate the situation.

One afternoon, I received a phone call from Charlene that is seared into my memory. When I came home from work and entered the kitchen from the door in the garage, I heard my mother say, "Oh, he just walked in." She handed me the phone and left the kitchen.

Charlene began the conversation by saying, "Seth, I just can't stand being away from you, and I really needed to hear your voice. I love you so much, I could die."

She was not being literal, yet the comment was disconcerting. She started to cry and said she was miserable. I suggested she could come back to Jacksonville, and it would give us a chance to figure things out.

I can't believe such a suggestion came from my lips, but the talk was highly charged with emotion rather than reason.

In one of her letters, written shortly after I made the suggestion, Charlene wrote that her mother had recently commented, "Why don't you and Seth go ahead and get married? However, if you did, he couldn't afford it, so you are better off to stay here and finish college." The remark upset Charlene and was the catalyst prompting her to ask me to consider coming out to Texas on a temporary basis to look it over.

I was unhappy with my job, which Charlene and her parents knew, and they felt it would be a golden opportunity for me. She was right; a lot of opportunity existed in Dallas, which was well known. Even so, the possibility of moving gave me stomach cramps. I replied that I would give it a lot of thought and prayer. In retrospect, had I not been gay, I would have said yes with little deliberation and likely moved to Dallas.

I contemplated Charlene's request and decided what she asked was reasonable. If our relationship had any chance of survival, I needed to make the trip; she deserved no less. I called to tell her I would come out there for a visit and do so with an open mind, as she had requested—she was ecstatic. We determined the best time for me to fly there would be in late May or early June. I would be eligible for a few days of vacation, and she would be between school terms. Additionally, my willingness to go should prove to her parents I loved their daughter.

Charlene conveyed that her parents (and she) would expect me to stay with them, although I was uneasy about the proposed arrangement. My planned visit, even though four months out, gave Charlene hope and made her days more bearable. I assured Charlene things were going to work out, while ignoring my own doubts when making the statement.

A Brief Respite

I knew the Harrelsons would be returning to Jacksonville sometime in the spring for a brief visit. I think their trip was relating to the sale of their house or to tie up other loose ends associated with their move. On a Friday afternoon in early March 1973, I came home from work to find a big surprise—Charlene was sitting at the kitchen counter, talking to my mother. I knew she and her parents were coming down for the weekend, and didn't expect to see her until later that evening.

The Harrelsons didn't have to bring Charlene with them. Yet they did. It was a positive sign and signaled to me they were perhaps not as hard-nosed as I had perceived. When I saw Mr. and Mrs. Harrelson that weekend, they warmly extended the invitation for me to stay with them when I visited Dallas. I felt they were sincere, which made me more at ease about making the trip. The puzzle pieces were beginning to fit into place. I came to the conclusion the Harrelsons would be happy with me being their son-in-law, as long as I played in their ballpark. My upcoming visit would be telling.

We had a short-lived weekend and it was over before we knew it. When Charlene left, her frame of mind was noticeably better than it was the night before they moved away. The sky had not fallen. She was enrolled at East Texas State University, located in Commerce. And undoubtedly, my upcoming visit was giving her a boost.

Our letter writing and phone calls to each other continued unabated over the course of the next several weeks. Even so, it was apparent the tone of Charlene's letters was changing, particularly with the approach of my visit to Texas. Understandably, she was busy in school and had college-related activities to distract her attentions. Her letters were less focused on being heartsick and contained clear signals her parents were making inroads. She wrote they were encouraging her to date other guys, and said if her love for me was real, dating other guys would serve to validate it. Charlene clearly didn't want to hear what they were suggesting, and I was angered at her parents.

In addition, it was becoming a recurring theme in her letters that my desire for us to live in Florida was selfish on my part—she would be giving up everything. She went on to write: If I would move to Dallas, it would prove my devotion to her and my commitment to her happiness. Moreover, it would likely result in obtaining her parents' approval (once again) of our marriage, which she desperately wanted. As far as Charlene was concerned, this was the perfect solution. She would be married to me and be living within the shadow of her parents, which would greatly please them.

It was difficult for me to contemplate moving to Texas, even though I was most unhappy with my job and had agreed to go out there with an open mind. My rationale was that Charlene and I met in Florida, my work was already established there, and when we became engaged she didn't voice any objections about where we would likely live. My degree in ornamental horticulture obtained at UF was specific to requirements and practices for growing plants in Florida. In addition, I already had a working relationship with the UF Agricultural Extension Service, which is vital to anyone in an agricultural business. It would have been arduous to transfer my knowledge in subtropical agriculture to the sometimes extremely hot, extremely cold, extremely dry, and capricious north Texas climate. Also, Charlene and her parents knew my plans were to go into business for myself in the not-too-distant future. None of this seemed to matter. It was even proposed her dad could assist me in landing a job where he worked. (Ted Harrelson was a regional sales director for a major food manufacturer.) Nonetheless, as uncomfortable as I was with Charlene's suggestions, I deeply considered her appeal and earnestly prayed about it.

Chapter 18

Enough Is Enough

My position at the wholesale nursery required I work from 8:00 a.m. to twelve noon most Saturdays. We were not open to the public, so it was inessential for someone to be there during those hours. Additionally, anytime a freeze was predicted, I had to go to the nursery late at night to make sure the greenhouse heaters were operating. Nonetheless, these were job requirements I agreed to without any negotiation when I was hired nearly two years prior. I had now reached the point where these work conditions were becoming intolerable, and I was earnestly searching for a new position, even if elsewhere in Florida. Charlene was cognizant of this and, consequently, she knew I had no objection to leaving Jacksonville.

There had been no conversation with the owner, Rich Halverson, regarding my job dissatisfaction. I clearly felt, for whatever reason, I was considered a lower-class citizen when compared to the other guys working in the office. They were not required to work on Saturday mornings, and the owner occasionally took them out for lunch or even to play racquetball. I was never asked, and it bothered me.

All nurseries in Florida were subject to periodic inspections by a representative from the State of Florida Division of Plant Industry. During a routine inspection, I shared with our assigned examiner that I would be interested in a position, should one become available in the area. A few weeks later, he called to tell me a position had opened up—in

Fort Myers. This was tempting; I had lived in nearby Naples and loved Southwest Florida. The job required a bachelor's degree in a plant-related discipline, which I had. Having a degree awarded by the University of Florida was a huge plus. I applied, interviewed with a Mr. Gonzalez, and was awarded the position on May 2. It didn't involve Saturday work, had better insurance benefits, a pension program, more days off, and an equivalent salary. I accepted the offer and looked forward to returning to the lower Gulf coast.

Soon after, I received a confirmation letter which specified my start date would be in two weeks, on Friday, May 18—just prior to my scheduled trip to Dallas. This presented an inescapable conflict; I would have to delay the trip for several months, when I would be eligible for a few days off. This placed me in a real pickle with Charlene, who reacted with less than positive emotions. Luckily, I had not yet purchased the plane ticket.

The next morning after arriving at the nursery, I anxiously asked the secretary for a meeting with Mr. Halverson as soon as possible, which was out of character for me. With a puzzled look, she asked why I needed to see him, and I replied it was personal. I had a good working relationship with this no-nonsense lady, and she didn't pry; I did see her glance at the envelope in my hand. She checked Mr. Halverson's calendar, and he was available.

He requested that I sit down in the chair on the opposite side of the desk from him and asked what was on my mind. With no hesitation, I advised him I would be leaving the company in two weeks to accept a position with the Division of Plant Industry. I thanked him for the employment he had provided and handed him the envelope containing my resignation. My resignation clearly caught him by surprise. As anticipated, he asked why I was leaving. I enumerated the reasons, minus my irritation in not being asked for lunch. He responded by predicting the Division of Plant Industry would be a dead end, and I thought, *This place isn't?* I didn't grace his unappreciated remark with a response, and with his kids already coming into the business, I knew there was no long-term future for me at the nursery, either. He asked if I had already accepted the position and seemed startled when I told him I had. He had to leave for an appointment and asked me to meet with him in the afternoon. As far as I was concerned, there was nothing left to discuss.

I briefly stopped by his secretary's desk on the way out and told her I would be leaving in two weeks. She was not at all surprised and said she surmised the envelope contained my letter of resignation. Interestingly, she shared that she had recently advised Mr. Halverson to not expect me to stick around, given the stringent work conditions.

That afternoon, Mr. Halverson walked into the area of the nursery where I was working and asked me to join him in the conference room in a half hour, which I did. When I entered the room, he was already sitting at one end of the long conference table, with a legal pad in front of him. He asked me to sit next to him in one of the side chairs. It was apparent the meeting was assuming a different dynamic than what I was expecting. Mr. Halverson had drawn up a counteroffer (which I still have), and placed it in front of me. It included a salary increase, a guarantee of future raises, two weeks of vacation (instead of one), and the opportunity to participate in a profit-sharing program. Additionally, the Saturday work requirement would be dropped. He met my primary reasons for leaving with a palatable, generous package.

I now faced a quandary. Even though I had a basic distrust for the long-term viability of the offer, I had to consider it. I discussed it with my parents and, after a lot of soul-searching, decided to take it—knowing my plans were to start my own business eventually.

The following morning I advised Mr. Halverson I would accept his offer, and then called Mr. Gonzalez at the Division of Plant Industry to rescind my acceptance of their offer. I was apologetic and embarrassed, and he was gracious. In a subsequent letter, he encouraged me to contact him if my situation didn't work out since other positions in the state were expected to become available.

Chapter 19

The Visit

After rescinding the job offer with the State of Florida, I bought a round-trip ticket on Delta Air Lines for the trip to Dallas, which was about three weeks out. Charlene was thrilled. It would be the second time I had ever flown, and my fear of flying was overwhelming.

A few days before Christmas in 1955, when I was six years old, an Eastern Air Lines Constellation crashed in the woods just short of the Jacksonville airport. The four-engine, propeller-driven aircraft was large for the time and was considered the "queen" of many airline fleets. The pilot was attempting to land the plane in the blackness of the wee hours in foggy conditions when it crashed. The consensus was either the pilot had become disoriented by the fog, or there was an altimeter malfunction. As a result, the plane was flying too low and clipped the pine tree tops about a half mile from the runway. It plummeted to the ground and exploded. There were no survivors. We lived about five minutes from the airport, and the next day, after hearing the news of the crash, my dad took my brother and me to see the wreckage. It was a horrific scene and largely unsecured, although a few policemen were present to keep onlookers at a safe distance. The site was smoldering, with a stench I will never forget. Pieces of the aircraft and strewn luggage were easily visible a short distance from where we were standing. Two wheels were sticking up several feet off the ground, still supported by the inverted landing gear imbedded in the sand. Viewing this site of mass carnage and destruction at such a young age left an indelible imprint. My fear of flying was born, and so crippled me that it almost prevented me from getting a great job with Delta Air Lines in 1977.

My parents said little about my trip to Texas, even though they had serious reservations about the ultimate outcome—even if I moved out there. The day finally arrived for my morning flight to Dallas, which required a plane change in Atlanta. The weather was clear and promised to be the same all the way out there—no fog, no storms. My parents took me to the airport, waited while I checked my baggage, and accompanied me—a twenty-four-year-old man—to the gate. (There was no airport security to worry about and anyone could walk to the gates, even if to just watch airplane activity.) No doubt they knew I was in a state of high anxiety about flying, and did their absolute best to calm me down.

It didn't work, yet I bravely boarded the plane as I took long, slow, deep breaths, as instructed by my registered nurse mother. Not long after I was buckled into my window seat, a flight attendant made the instructional announcements. The dissertation on safety precautions was inescapable and had me ready to abandon the ship before it even left the ground. It was prudent for me to not act on this consideration, so I remained chained into the seat and waited for the plane to take off. The Boeing 727 jet taxied to the end of the runway, and accelerated to flight speed, resulting in a quieter than expected, smooth takeoff, clearing the pine tree tops by probably 500 feet.

The flight was flawless, plus breakfast was served. This was the perfect distraction, even though I had eaten breakfast at home before leaving for the airport. The forty-five-minute flight to Atlanta passed quickly, and predictably, I became panicked as we prepared to land. The plane dropped lower and lower, finally to the point where the treetops seemed perilously close. I shut my eyes and clutched the armrests while my heart pounded like a pile driver. A few moments later, the tires briefly kissed the runway and bounced the jet a couple of times before settling securely on the pavement. I had survived, albeit in a cold sweat. There was still one more flight to go, but I managed to talk myself off the wingtips while the pilot navigated the plane to the gate. The connecting flight to Dallas was uneventful and took about an hour and a half on a DC-8 jet. Fortunately, this leg didn't include any visible treetops upon landing. Soon I found out why—there were few trees around.

Charlene was waiting for me at the gate, and it was wonderful to see her. It had been three months since we last saw each other. We hugged, kissed, held hands, and walked to baggage claim. Our conversation was upbeat, and Charlene reassured me her parents were excited I had come out there.

After we retrieved my baggage, we walked outside and were greeted with a blast of desert-like heat. It was starkly different from the humidity-laden, tropical air that permeated Jacksonville. We drove to the Harrelsons' new home in Dallas, which was about a twenty-minute drive. The north Texas landscape didn't escape my attention. It was a stark contrast from the lushness I had left in Florida. The trees looked stunted and many lawns were burned from an in-progress drought. The neighborhood where the Harrelsons lived was much like the one they had left in Jacksonville. Lawns were well manicured and green where irrigated and, as expected, houses were upscale.

When we arrived at the house, I was apprehensive, not knowing what to expect. Our relationship was shrouded in uncertainty, and I recognized the cards were stacked against us. However, the most significant card was in my hand, not the Harrelsons'.

Mrs. Harrelson greeted me warmly and asked about the flight—my fear of flying was no secret.

"It was great, no problems," was about all I said. There was no admission on my part the landing in Atlanta nearly scared me to death when I perceived the plane was too close to the pine trees.

She took Charlene and me to lunch at a new place called TGI Fridays and mentioned there were many other fun places in Dallas. Walking through the front door of Fridays was analogous to being time-warped into the year 1890. I was enthralled by the décor (well, of course), which included Tiffany-style lamps, oodles of antiques, stained-glass windows, gorgeous wood floors, and polished brass rails. This place was a totally "happening" establishment, with a decidedly young, good-looking crowd of folks. It would be an unforgivable oversight to not mention the oversized, drippy, medium-rare hamburgers that arguably were the best in the history of the universe. There was no TGI Fridays in Jacksonville, and my stomach was already persuading me to reconsider my "can't leave Florida" stance.

It was evident Mrs. Harrelson was going out of her way to make me feel at home. She mentioned Charlene was going to show me the area and predicted I would surely love it. Understandably, a good degree of salesmanship on Texas was on the agenda.

My visit with the Harrelsons spanned four days, including travel time. I stayed in the guest bedroom, which was tucked away in a corner of the house away from the other bedrooms. The brick house had an alley running behind it, which offered easy access to the rear of the structure and garage. Rooms in the house were spacious and beautifully decorated; in a word, it was impressive, even though the backyard was small. In the short time I had been there, it was impossible to miss that Mrs. Harrelson seemed much happier in her new surroundings in Dallas than she had been in Jacksonville. North Texas was her home and she loved it. Her love for Dallas, as well as her disdain for Jacksonville, was being transferred to Charlene in what I felt was a concerted effort.

My first of three full days with Charlene in Dallas was lighthearted and free from any worries. Charlene planned a day replete with varied activities, and it was apparent the five-month separation following the move had not diminished Charlene's affection for me. The first day was spent riding around some knock-me-out, dazzling neighborhoods. One of them, Highland Park, was seemingly plucked from a storybook page. I was agog at the enormity of some houses, the impeccably tailored landscapes, and streets so clean you could seemingly eat off them. If I moved to Dallas, surely this is where we would live. Unfortunately, this was before any state lotteries to make schools magnificent—and me wealthy—had been birthed, so financing an appropriate property would be problematic.

After touring Highland Park, Charlene drove us to a Dallas "icon" in the nearby downtown. With excitement, she was particularly pleased to introduce me to a department store called Neiman Marcus. I had never heard of it. Quickly, I extrapolated this paragon of paragons was a shopping shrine to the wealthy in Dallas. I considered crossing myself as we slowly passed the entrance to this high altar of retail—but Baptists don't do that. My parents shopped at J.C. Penney and Sears, for the most part, and Neiman Marcus didn't have a location anywhere near Jacksonville. Even if they did, it wouldn't have been within the WTPP (willing to pay price) for anything our family may have needed.

After parking, with the car pointed toward the eastern heavens, Charlene and I entered the golden gates of the Neiman Marcus "cathedral." Like GPS, my internal laser guided us to the "communion table," where a multitude of glorious edibles were beautifully displayed. As scrumptious as these offerings were, they were sufficiently priced to thwart any chance for my tightly-controlled wallet to be cracked open. After paying homage to Neiman Marcus, we left downtown for our next destination, Town East Mall. It was snazzy, new, and boasted two levels of impressive shopping opportunities. We had nothing so fancy in Jacksonville, yet the shopping temptations housed at Town East didn't pose any particular draw. No doubt, Charlene was attracted to shopping, and no doubt, I was not. Nonetheless, the city tour was enjoyable and the perfect diversion to the issues we were facing as a couple. We didn't have any deep discussions; however, the next day would prove to be a different story.

We returned to the Harrelsons' house later in the day, and Charlene's mother was interested in what we had seen.

"Did you see Neiman's? What about Sanger Harris (another department store)? Didn't you just love our wonderful city?"

I answered yes (of course) to all three queries. Truthfully, I was impressed with what I saw, and it was evident glitzy, oil-rich Dallas was a city on the move, particularly when compared to relatively sleepy Jacksonville.

The next morning greeted us with hot, sunny weather and a hazy blue sky. The agenda for the day included an outing to a large lake north of Dallas, followed by a visit to Charlene's grandmother's house in Farmersville, which was in the same general area. The drive to the lake—actually a reservoir—took less than an hour and traversed unremarkable countryside. On this excursion, there was no singing "over the river and through the woods," as neither geographical feature existed to any significant extent. There were few trees, and most of what I saw after exiting the last of many newly constructed cookie-cutter neighborhoods were fields of brown, water-starved grass. It occurred to me that Texas had the oil, but lacked the water gushing in the springs, lakes, and rivers in verdant Florida. Also, noticeably absent in the expansive north Texas landscape was an ocean. We had one of those in Jacksonville.

Charlene and I arrived at the lake around 11:00 a.m. and found our way to a mostly deserted park, dotted with a few trees on the water's edge. Charlene knew I loved the water, which is why the outing to the lake was included in the tour. I discovered that water-based activities near Dallas were indeed possible. What most astounded me, though, was that the general populace swam, no doubt urinated, and God only knows what else in this depository of drinking water. Never mind the purifying filtering systems and chlorine cleansers in place to prevent dysentery; it bugged the heck out of me.

We spread out a blanket on the mostly dead grass under a tree and unpacked the picnic lunch Charlene had prepared. A breeze off the water rustled the tree leaves and mitigated an otherwise sultry day. Charlene's porcelain-like skin glistened in the bright light as occasional rays of sun penetrated the tree canopy, illuminating the honey tones in her hair.

For some reason at that moment, my emotions nearly took charge as I gazed into her face, remembering the first time I saw her. I almost cried—the realities confronting us were inescapable, if not insurmountable. Could I really move to Texas? Could Charlene find happiness with me in Jacksonville? Even if she could, would she leave her parents? Should we just cut our losses and go our separate ways into the sunset? I loved Charlene, but at this juncture, concerns about my capacity to satisfy her sexually continued to be eclipsed by other obstacles.

Charlene was pensive the entire time we were in the car and even more so at the lake. My stomach was churning in response to her mood and my own quiet deliberations.

Tough Conversation at the Reservoir

We sat on the blanket, looking at each other, occasionally stealing glances at the lake. The lack of conversation was painful, although unpacking and eating lunch blunted the uncomfortable silence. As I ruminated, it was increasingly difficult for me to put my thoughts into words.

Charlene broke the ice and asked, "Seth, what are you thinking?"

All I could say was: "I wish things didn't have to be so complicated."

She said, "It doesn't have to be. It seems to me living in Dallas is the best solution for us. Seth, you can find a great job here. There is much more opportunity than what exists in Jacksonville. I understand you love growing plants for a living, but there are better and easier ways to make money—besides, your contentment at work is probably not going to last."

I cringed, wishing I could "delete" the statement I had made to her mother many months back regarding my dissatisfaction at work. Even though my job satisfaction was now much improved, it was evident my original statement was still gaining traction. Charlene was correct when stating I was not likely to remain satisfied in my job for an extended period. Nonetheless, her feelings about my career choice greatly dismayed me, and my initial response was to say nothing.

After a few moments, in an exasperated tone, I asked, "Would I be true to myself to abandon my career choice? Do you have any idea how difficult it was to obtain the degree and how specific it is?"

An uncomfortable silence ensued. Clearly, Charlene's position had hardened; she briefly hung her head and loudly sighed.

A few moments later she looked up with tears in her eyes and quietly replied, "If you truly loved me, I don't think we would be having this conversation."

Her declaration went through me like an arrow. If we married, I knew our lives would be on her terms, which I felt were her parents' terms.

I had to ask one question before it burned a hole in my throat: "Charlene, when you said yes to my marriage proposal, you never expressed any reservations about my job or residing in Jacksonville. Why did you not say anything then?"

Her initial response was evasive. "I didn't know we would be moving back to Dallas so soon. Now that we're out here, everything has changed."

I said, "This is what I don't understand. What has changed? Why was Jacksonville an acceptable place to live five months ago, and now it isn't?"

"My parents are here, and they really need me here."

Finally, an honest answer. She admitted what I knew in my gut. Bingo! Maybe this admission would cause her to come to terms with what the real debate was, and in my assessment, it wasn't my career choice and it wasn't Jacksonville. I also knew any considerations I had about moving to Dallas were quickly diminishing. Even so, I chose to remain quiet for the time being. Without question, Charlene's devotion to her parents overshadowed her love for me and, accordingly, she didn't want to displease or challenge them.

It was not a healthy formula for beginning a marriage—not to mention the gigantic problem with my own internal "formulation." I had no idea of the extent to which Charlene was at odds with her parents over our relationship, and would find out firsthand the night before leaving Dallas.

To Grandmother's House We Go

After spending not much more than an hour at the lake, we packed up and drove out of the park en route to Farmersville. Neither of us was in the best frame of mind for visiting her grandmother, but she was expecting us and Charlene really wanted me to meet her. It was a short distance to Farmersville and the conversation we had in the car was inconsequential. We held hands, occasionally smiling at each other.

We both knew we had reached an impasse unless one of us capitulated. I strongly felt it wouldn't be me and sensed it wouldn't be Charlene, either.

We arrived in Farmersville around 2:00 p.m. and easily found our way through the streets of the small country town, to her maternal grandmother's house. Farmersville was no different than most other small towns and, true to its name, was in a farming region. It was in another world compared to what existed in fast-paced, city-slicker Dallas. The house where Charlene's grandmother lived was a classic wood house that looked like someone's grandmother should be living there. It was modest, likely built in the 1920s, and had an inviting, y'all-come-inside appeal. It reminded me of my own grandparents' house in Palatka, Florida, and its simplicity resonated with me. I recall it was painted a light color and had a good-sized shade tree in the yard.

Charlene parked the car, and we walked up to the front door where Charlene's grandmother was already standing. She opened the door and gave Charlene a big hug and kiss. Charlene was adored by this gracious southern lady, who was a widow and lived alone in the house. Charlene introduced me to her grandmother, whose name was Blanche Collins. She seemed taller than average, had silver hair, and was probably in her early seventies.

She looked at me and said, "Seth, I can see why she likes you."

I probably blushed, which in itself was a source of embarrassment for me, and I thanked her for the compliment.

Our abbreviated visit with Mrs. Collins lasted about an hour and accomplished the original intent, for her to meet the man who was going to marry her granddaughter. Well, maybe not anymore. I remember nothing about our conversations during the visit, yet remember with fondness, meeting Mrs. Collins and the compliment she gave me. I also remember the warmth of her house, which was a page from an all but forgotten, sweet era. Charlene and I said our goodbyes to her grandmother, and we both hugged her as we left.

On the trip back to Dallas, Charlene said she could tell her grandmother liked me. It was ego boosting to hear the affirmation, yet did little to alleviate the cut-it-with-a-knife tension existing between Charlene and me.

I was getting increasingly distressed with each passing mile. Jumping out of the car was one consideration; however, this action was surely inadvisable. Even if I survived the leap, it would likely have left me wandering in a foreign pasture with no cell phone (they didn't exist) and nothing to eat. The nothing to eat part of the equation was the determining factor not to jump. Surely, I could never have done anything so inane, even though my feelings of desperation were consuming.

Toward the end of the drive back to her house, Charlene broke the silence permeating the car and asked me for the second time what I was thinking.

I lied. I told her I was thinking about the picnic at the lake and how much I enjoyed meeting her grandmother. In truth, I was thinking about how much I wanted to run home—like I did after the softball slammed me in the eye. In this case, there was no exit.

Charlene challenged my answer and inquired seriously, "Seth, you know what I'm asking. What are your thoughts about moving out here?"

I took a few moments to carefully construct an answer. "Charlene, I have closed no doors. I love you and want this to work."

The tension between us suddenly evaporated with my less than honest response to a legitimate question. I couldn't bring myself to tell Charlene it was highly unlikely I would be moving out there. Again, I had fallen into my predictable pattern of handling a challenging situation with a girl, by not handling it. I hated confrontation. By the time we returned to her house, Charlene's frame of mind was much improved. Not so for me.

That evening, Charlene and I went by ourselves to a nearby steak house for dinner. Her parents had been hands-off and never imposed themselves on any of our activities, which allowed us to maximize the limited time we had together. During dinner, our conversation was not relating to whether or not I would relocate to Dallas. Instead, we talked about Gail and Anthony. I assessed they were happy and appeared well suited to each other. They soon would be having a baby and life was going well for the fledgling family. No doubt, Charlene envisioned the same for us. I hungered for it as well, while facing the fact that there was no "Camelot" for us in Dallas.

My Last Day in Dallas

My last full day in Dallas, like all the others, was well planned by Charlene. The foremost activity of the day was to attend church services with the Harrelsons. We all went to church together, dressed in our "Sunday best," which meant dresses for the ladies and coats and ties for the guys. This was expected in 1973. Additionally, I construed Jesus (and His emissaries) would like me better if I was dressed up. (Many years later, I changed my opinion and decided Jesus would probably have worn jeans and sandals to church.)

We arrived a few minutes early for the 11:00 a.m. service at First Baptist Church in downtown Dallas. The building, constructed of red brick, was built in the late 1800s. We quickly found seats several rows back from the pulpit area. Charlene and her parents were proud of their home church, and were thrilled to be back after living away from Dallas for a number of years. If Southern Baptists had a national shrine, this "holy grail" church undoubtedly would have been it. It had the largest membership of any Southern Baptist church in the U.S. and had a legacy of celebrated pastors.

Upon entering the red-carpeted sanctuary, I was impressed by the beauty of the white-painted, almost icicle-like woodwork behind the choir loft which housed the organ pipes in a tall, broad arc. The windows in the church were arched, some stained, others not. I was captivated by the simple yet beautiful Victorian architecture. A large horseshoe balcony rimmed the sanctuary, and by the time the service started, the place was packed.

The service was unforgettable. The pipe organ sounded magical and the huge choir was superb. The music gave me goose bumps and brought tears to my eyes. The white-haired pastor was clearly a skilled orator with a spellbinding technique. He interspersed speaking softly with almost yelling, and did so with a quiver in his voice, which at times was like a vibrato. He preached with fervency, and congregants paid attention, whether they agreed or not. I am confident most agreed with what he said. I don't know why, but for some reason the lyrics to Neil Diamond's classic hit, "Brother Love's Traveling Salvation Show" popped into my mind. This church service was nothing like the tent revival described in Neil's song, yet somehow I found a parallel and chuckled to myself. While I don't remember the topic of the sermon, I well remember the preaching style of the pastor.

Following the service, I was complimentary of the church without being prompted or asked. I loved it, and could see why the Harrelsons were so homesick for it when they lived in Jacksonville.

The rest of the day was spent close to the house, and I can remember thinking I just wanted to go home. My inner voice was speaking loudly and, for once, I was listening. Mr. and Mrs. Harrelson had been cordial, but I could sense a degree of tension in the house. It was not the type of thing I could put a finger on; nonetheless, it was perceptible.

Before I went to my bedroom to pack for the next day's flight, Charlene and I had a discussion about my observations of Dallas. Truthfully, they were favorable, and I said so. Despite this, I knew a move out there even for a "temporary" period as Charlene had suggested, would be ill-advised. Where would I live? More than likely, not with the Harrelsons. Even if they extended such an invitation, which was a stretch, it would be a bad idea for a myriad of reasons.

I knew I loved Charlene, but the circumstances surrounding our engagement were plainly a disaster. And of course, the gay elephant on top of me continued to exert an agonizing load. My prayerful requests for "sexual healing" had still not been granted, and this was the looming thunderstorm refusing to dissipate. I had no real desire to have sexual relations with Charlene or, for that matter, with any other woman. I wondered why God was taking so much time to answer my prayers, yet knew (as I had been taught) God's timetable didn't necessarily correspond to mine. I rationalized: If I married Charlene, it would prove my faith and my prayer would be answered. It would be "all systems go" for a successful marital launch!

I surmise many lesbians and gay men who enter into marriage with an opposite-sex partner do so with the belief it will all work out—because they are following God's will (and the demands of society).

I didn't give Charlene any guarantees, assuring her I was prayerfully considering options. It was noncommittal. I kissed her, wished her a good night, and went into my bedroom.

Bam!

I finished packing, and crawled into bed a little before midnight. I languished there, awash in a tsunami of emotions crashing over me in an unrelenting fashion, wave after wave. Sleep was not on the agenda, even though the late hour mandated it should be. Not long after I settled in bed, I heard the unmistakable sound of a door slamming shut with a loud *bam*.

Being curious, I got out of bed and quietly cracked the bedroom door to investigate the commotion. I saw some faint light emanating from the hallway where the other bedrooms in the house were located, and other than that, couldn't make out anything. I nudged the door to the point where I could stick my head through the opening, and then heard a verbal altercation coming from either Charlene's or her parents' bedroom. There was not even a modicum of domestic tranquility and, as I had sensed earlier, there was indeed tension in the house. It had now reached the boiling point.

Most of what I heard was between Mr. and Mrs. Harrelson, but I could tell Charlene was in the room with them—and she was getting an earful. The argument was about me, as I heard my name being mentioned in the "conversation." I opened the door farther and tiptoed a few steps closer to the "war zone." I was able to discern the Harrelsons expected I wouldn't move to Dallas, and, if Charlene married me, she would be living in "hell" in Jacksonville. This was probably true—there was no Neiman Marcus.

At times, I couldn't hear well enough to distinguish exactly what was being said, but one unforgettable statement made its way to my wide-open ears.

In an audible outburst, Charlene's father stated, "It is bad enough to have raised one stupid ass, and it now looks like we have raised two."

The statement was a reference to Charlene's older sister, her only sibling, who had married a man to whom they strongly objected.

It was one of those infamous statements remaining with me through the years. Occasionally, I still recall it—and now with a laugh. That last night at the Harrelsons' house stands out as one of the most unforgettable, uncomfortable situations I have ever experienced.

Aftermath

Morning finally dawned after a sleepless night, and my flight back to Jacksonville couldn't depart soon enough. Any nervousness I had regarding the flight was overshadowed by my desire to leave. Mr. and Mrs. Harrelson were polite to me that morning, but, unmistakably, there was no levity in the house. Charlene was clearly a wreck—her eyes were swollen and red. We just looked at each other and neither of us initially said much of anything since her parents were circulating in the house.

When we managed to have a few moments alone, Charlene asked if I had heard anything the night before. I admitted to hearing the door slam and to some loud conversation. I didn't let on I heard as much as I actually did. She was horrified and apologized that I had been a witness to the exchange. She said she couldn't freely talk about it in the house and stated a lot went on.

Before Charlene took me to the airport, I expressed my gratitude to her parents for their hospitality and told them how much I enjoyed the visit. They were gracious and extended an invitation for me to return at some point in the future. I gathered my luggage and couldn't hightail it fast enough.

During a strained ride to the airport, Charlene shared many of the details of what had transpired in the middle of the night. There were no surprises. The Harrelsons wouldn't give their blessing to our marriage unless I agreed to move to Texas. They also didn't believe I could adequately support Charlene. Their assessment was Charlene would have to work the rest of her life in order to maintain an acceptable standard of living, and she would be expected to wash and reuse tinfoil.

By golly, that aforementioned piece of garbage was resurrected for a purpose I had never envisioned. Thank you, Reynolds Wrap!

I could tell Charlene gave a lot of credence to her parents' suppositions, even though she never acknowledged it.

Once we arrived at the airport and parked, Charlene walked with me to the gate. Before boarding the flight, I hugged her and we kissed each other goodbye. It was not a highly emotional scene, and I think we both were relieved the visit was over. However, much more to the story was yet to be written.

As I entered the Jetway, I glanced back at Charlene for what I figured would be the last time. She was still standing where I'd left her. She was teary-eyed and her arms were crossed in resignation. It was one of those "Norman Rockwell" moments, now painted in my memory.

The flight back home encountered some rough turbulence a few minutes after taking off from Dallas. How appropriate. It further unnerved my already unnerved state, when the jet shook hard enough to open a couple of unlatched overhead compartments and spill a few items of loose clothing. Lord, save us; we are going down! Of course we didn't, and I survived to write this. While the turbulence was short-lived, my memory of this incident has not been.

As soon as I arrived back home, I called Charlene to let her know Delta had safely delivered me to Jacksonville. We talked briefly, and there was little conversation regarding the disastrous ending to my visit.

After I hung up the phone, I realized the trip had accomplished two things. Number one, it confirmed to me how futile our situation was, and secondly, it signaled our engagement would likely be coming to an end.

Chapter 20

Last Gasps

A few short months prior, Charlene and I had exclaimed to the Langleys that we were engaged. The train had now derailed, although the screeches prior to its leaving the tracks were noticed by them.

I called Leona the day after returning from Dallas, to let her know I was back and to find out if Charlene had called her. Much to my surprise, she had not spoken to any of the Harrelsons. I didn't go into the trip's details, though I told her about Charlene's plea for me to move out there. I also told Leona about the heated confab occurring the night before I left.

Leona was genuinely interested and patiently listened without offering any judgments or giving any advice. She admitted she suspected the relationship was headed for rough waters as soon as the Harrelsons announced their move. I don't know how much Liz Harrelson had shared with Leona, particularly after the move was known, but believe Leona knew more than she ever alluded to. She and Burt had become confidants, and they also treasured their friendship with the Harrelsons. In my estimation, they never compromised the friendship on my behalf.

Unexpectedly, there would be another chapter to this narrative.

The Long-Distance Relationship Resumes

Our letter writing resumed and two days after I returned to Jacksonville, an airmail letter from Charlene arrived. It was principally a letter expressing how sorry she was my last night was marred by the clash I overheard in the middle of the night. She stated the altercation taking place was heated, and her parents asserted a marriage to me would be a huge mistake. My fiancée shared additional details my inquiring ears had not picked up that bizarre night. What stung most was a comparison her parents drew between the area where I grew up in Jacksonville and a similar area in Dallas they considered highly undesirable. They predicted Charlene would be living in an unacceptable neighborhood in Jacksonville, and eventually a divorce would ensue.

When I read the letter, it singed me. In my estimation, it was a personal attack from Charlene's parents and clearly revealed their lack of faith in my ability to provide for Charlene. It also served to confirm what I already knew; I was from the wrong side of the railroad tracks, as far as the Harrelsons were concerned. Moving to their side was not going to happen. More so, it was clear the Harrelsons couldn't deal with being separated from Charlene.

I never showed the letter to my parents, but told them what Charlene had written. I had already described the details of my last night in Dallas, so the letter's contents were not startling to them. From a parental perspective, my mother and dad understood the Harrelsons' actions were intended to protect Charlene. Nonetheless, they unequivocally didn't agree with their conclusions about me. My parents became concerned I would develop a perception of poor self-worth as a result of what the Harrelsons had said. They stressed that being true to myself and following my heart were the ultimate validations of self-worth. My parents were wise. They assured me I had no reason to feel ashamed, even though the Harrelsons' views were upsetting. In all truthfulness, I was hurt—but not to the degree my parents perceived. Without question, any feelings of negative self-worth were related to my sexuality, not to the failure of a relationship.

Before I went to Dallas, Charlene had stated in one of her letters that my trip there would answer a lot of questions; it surely did. Following my return to Jacksonville, her letters became less from the heart and more resigned. Mine were equally so, and I told Charlene that a move to Texas wouldn't be in my plans. It was increasingly apparent she was acquiescing to her parents' demands, which was no surprise. The inevitability of it was like holding an ice cream cone in 95-degree heat; it's going to drip over your hands no matter how quickly you can lick. We were both tired of licking.

I finally received a "Dear John" letter acknowledging it was over. She expressed sorrow about things turning out the way they did, and concluded that continuing our relationship was pointless. I agreed. The struggle between Charlene and me (and her parents) was over. I was relieved the book was closed, but as the saying goes, "It ain't over till the fat lady sings." Indeed, she was tuning up for an encore.

After the Dance Is Over

Following the breakup with Charlene, I began to do some soul-searching; I asked myself—and God—a litany of questions. Are things supposed to be this difficult? What about the sex thing? Was my lack of sexual desire for Charlene because we were not yet married? If I ever say "I do," will the dormant systems be activated? Would I have an erection as I exited the church with my bride? On a deeper level, the ultimate question reared its head: Am I really gay, and, if so, why? I went to church, prayed, sought God, read my Bible, and believed what it said. What did I do wrong?

I felt I had done everything required, and was becoming angry and even more inquiring. I began to consider maybe, just maybe, *if* I was gay, it was because God made me that way—but such a heretical notion had to be instantly dismissed before God struck me down. Yet, for me, three cups of sugar, three cups of flour, two sticks of butter, a cup of sour cream, and six eggs didn't equal a pound cake. No matter what I did, my cake simply wouldn't rise. I knew something was missing. As a result, the seeds of self-discovery I had so arduously tried to keep from hitting the ground were planted, one by one. My questioning served as drops of water eventually allowing them to sprout.

In the days following the announcement that Charlene and I were kaput, my parents confessed they were relieved Charlene and I wouldn't be getting married. They loved that she was Southern Baptist and had a temperament similar to mine; however, they were concerned my lack of interest in a country club lifestyle would be a problem. Charlene was used to having access to the best of things. Whereas, the best of things to me meant being outdoors in a state park and being attired in a pair of shorts and a T-shirt. My parents also knew Charlene and I would encounter problems if she exhibited buying habits counter to my nature of financial conservatism. In other words, my perspectives would likely be a challenge for Charlene and vice versa. Their assessments were dead-on.

And the Band Played On

In the weeks following my newfound unengaged "condition," there was a false perception among church and non-church friends alike that my seriously "available" status needed rectification. In other words, "poor Seth" was in dire need of rescue and, as a result, my well-intentioned friends lobbied to set me up with eligible young ladies. It was the absolute last thing I wanted or needed. I had the perfect excuse for declining all offers—it was way too early. Furthermore, it would be unfair for any girl to be the recipient of me on the rebound. This excuse was plausible and, accordingly, it worked beautifully. So I played the card for months, and even my parents bought into my rationale for not dating. I overheard my mother tell someone I was having a rough time and my recovery was proving more difficult than she would have hoped. Of course. In truth, I was satisfied with my girl-less existence and was enjoying my peaceful state.

In the meantime, like a broken record, my subconscious mind occasionally kept my "dating life" active during my dreams. This provided for a more unrestricted playground than what I ever would have permitted if awake. In keeping with the pattern established during puberty, these dreams were usually about guys who had caught my eye, were sexually based, and self-liberating up to a point. Unfortunately, they short-circuited before a sexual act was completed, resulting in a distressing scene where invariably someone would walk in and, in horror, discover my indiscretion. I would suddenly wake up, frustrated, guilt-laden, and unable to go back to sleep. I was twenty-four years old and still desperately fighting to deny my orientation, which is probably why the dreams wreaked such havoc on my psyche. Interestingly, Anthony Petrini—my ultimate fantasy—never appeared in these erotic dreams. Maybe this was because my subconscious mind considered him unattainable.

The angst these dreams created was exacerbated by the realization I had no control over them. Even more upsetting was my patent awareness that I had never had a sexual dream involving any woman, including Charlene. I hated my situation and thus hated myself, yet managed to play the hand I was dealt without sinking into depression. There were two lifelines giving me respite: working out, and my aforementioned physician, Dr. Hiram Edwards.

The lesson my dad taught me in high school regarding the link between the psyche and physical exercise was well remembered. I was a fit guy and by nature rather physically oriented, which my childhood friends would find shocking. Other than tennis matches, I was not physically competitive with other guys, but enjoyed challenging myself by lifting weights. Additionally, my work at the wholesale nursery was highly demanding physically. I was not a big guy, yet had packed 170 lean pounds on my 5' 10" frame. Girls wanted to feel my biceps, which was an unexpected—and unwelcome—outcome to my working out; I didn't like being touched by girls, although their interest confirmed my efforts had rendered positive results. I didn't object to this part of the equation.

My other lifeline, Dr. Edwards, had been our family physician since I was in my teens. Our fathers had been work associates in the insurance industry for many years, so the relationship between the families was well established. It was assumed Dr. Edwards was gay; he had never married, was an artist, and had a statue of the *Venus de Milo* in his house. Dr. Edwards' mother previously told my mother about the statue and, according to my mother, "homosexualists" liked statues and paintings. This pearl of wisdom imparted by her stuck with me and I have laughed about it for years. I also made sure not to have any such ornamentation in my house (when I finally had one). Actually, I preferred minimalistic, sleek interior design, so not having these items in my house had nothing to do with placating my mother.

Dr. Edwards had become a good friend and occasionally I went to his house just to talk. His circa 1920s house was located in Riverside, a beautiful, old, live oak–studded section of town bordering the west bank of the St. Johns River. In reality, my conversations with Dr. Edwards were counseling sessions, and since they were conducted in the privacy of his home, I knew it was a safe place. He was not a psychologist or psychiatrist, yet his insights were still laser sharp. I probably visited with Dr. Edwards several times a year.

My most memorable visit revolved around a frank discussion we had about my sexuality. It took place one evening while we were seated at opposite ends of his living room couch, and marked the first time in my life I had ever had an honest discussion about the subject with anyone.

He questioned me about my relationship with Charlene and asked if we ever had sexual relations. He also wanted to know if I was distressed about the breakup.

I answered with an honest no to both questions, and admitted I was in a generally unhappy condition; the breakup had amplified whatever was lurking in the background.

He asked if I had ever had sexual relations with any woman and, if not, was I eager to have them.

To those two questions, I also answered no. Through misty eyes, I said I just wanted to run away from Jacksonville.

What he asked next knocked me off the couch. "Seth, have you ever had thoughts about having sex with a man?"

Eureka! I admitted to it and felt an immense moment of relief I had never before experienced. I began to spill my guts. I talked in detail about my frequent sexual dreams involving men and couldn't ignore mentioning the erotic pool episode with Anthony. I acknowledged I instinctively eyeballed good-looking men and would frequently experience an erection when doing so.

He asked me at what age I could remember finding men attractive.

I answered, "When I was about five."

We talked about my religious upbringing and how those teachings were creating an overwhelming internal conflict. I expressed that my hopes and prayers for "healing" would still be answered.

With no emotion, he asked why I felt healing was needed if I was not sick.

My answer was: "Because God requires it, and my family and church will likely disown me if I don't change."

Dr. Edwards raised his eyebrows and asked, "Do you really think God would require you to change the way you were born?"

I had no answer, and truthfully, it was a question I had frequently asked myself.

Dr. Edwards then confided he was gay, and added he had never experienced the degree of guilt and anxiety plaguing me. The primary advice he gave was for me to continue to have conversations with him. He also said he hoped I could come to the point where I would accept who I was.

This visit was never forgotten, even though my struggles were far from over and a final chapter to the Charlene novel was yet to be written. As was the case when I was in high school, having access to Dr. Edwards as a confidant helped me survive a challenging period in my life.

My parents never knew Dr. Edwards and I had become good friends; and I can attest to one thing—their suspicions were right. Dr. Edwards was indeed a "homosexualist," with a house full of statues and a myriad of paintings. On one visit to Dr. Edwards' home, he invited me to look at some of his paintings, which were primarily housed in a separate artist studio in an old garage in his backyard. His passion was to paint impressionistic landscapes, primarily using oils. The characteristic smell of oil paint permeated the studio space where he painted prolifically. I was amazed at the number of completed and in-progress artworks. Paintings which testified to his talent were on the walls, on tripods, stacked on the floor, and piled on tables.

His artistic interests extended beyond landscapes. In one corner of the cramped room, I noticed a sketch he had drawn in pencil of a nude woman. He had other beautifully drawn sketches of both male and female figures. Before I left, he asked if I would be willing to pose seminude for his art class; a "grape leaf" would be provided. It would be about a two-hour gig and they would pay me for my time. I thought about it for a few seconds and agreed to do it. Funny realization: my religious hang-ups didn't extend into the realm of posing. Maybe because I had studied art appreciation in college and was awed at many masterful works depicting the human form (particularly male) in perfect detail. Perhaps I was a closet exhibitionist. I imagined my likeness being sketched, sculpted, or painted by a future Michelangelo, while recognizing the finished artwork would never find its way to the ceiling of any church. I was disappointed the class disbanded before I had the opportunity to pose.

Chapter 21

Unexpected Encore

In the months following the dissolution of my relationship with Charlene, I stayed in close contact with Burt and Leona Langley. I relished my connection with them. It was not like a parent-child relationship, as the age disparity may suggest, but a true friendship.

Burt and I loved ambling around their beautiful, highly-prized yard as we talked about certain specimen plants and the never-ending war with plant-gnawing bugs. He and I had a good time conversing, and I particularly enjoyed the entertaining interactions between Leona and him. They were devoted to each other, and both laughed frequently. Leona's frequently unfettered remarks were a draw. She also maintained contact with the Harrelsons and kept me apprised of what was going on with them when I asked. Hearing Charlene was dating and looking forward to graduation was heartening. Even so, I was told Charlene was still facing formidable challenges in dealing with the consequences of the move and adapting to life without me. This saddened me.

In the early fall of 1974, about fifteen months after the final curtain with Charlene came down, Leona called my mother (since I was still living at home) and asked her to have me drop by their house when I had a chance; she had something I may want. I was intrigued, so my curiosity compelled me to visit them that evening.

In a quick digression, my mother and Leona had become occasional phone buddies, which was no surprise; each shared a penchant to find humor in most situations.

When I got over to the Langleys, Leona said she had received a letter from Charlene—and was careful not to show it to me. She told me Charlene had graduated from the university, was living with her parents, and was teaching in a nearby elementary school. I had assumed as much, so this was not earth-shattering news.

Leona advised me, in a laughing manner: "You might want to sit down."

She had me entranced (as usual), so being her devoted pupil, I followed her directive and plopped onto the couch. She explained Charlene had enclosed something with the hope I would take it; if I didn't want it, she would understand. Leona handed me a recent picture of a forlorn-looking Charlene, sporting a short haircut and holding her small dog. She also gave me the address of the elementary school where Charlene taught.

Clearly, Charlene wanted me to contact her and, understandably, was reluctant to ask me directly. It didn't take much thinking to figure out that writing to her at her home address would be plain stupid. Regardless, I was stunned to receive the message from Charlene, as I considered the relationship dead. I never remotely considered an ember was still smoldering. Leona and Burt didn't give me any advice and acted as messengers. I thanked them for the picture, which I received with mixed emotions.

My parents were of course curious to know what Leona gave me. I showed them the picture of Charlene and told them she would welcome hearing from me if I were so inclined. They were astounded. Their advice was for me to be careful; they didn't want Charlene or me to end up getting hurt on the same "Tilt-A-Whirl" that had nearly spun both of us to death.

Charlene's request presented a real conundrum for me. If we resumed communicating, a huge problem was guaranteed if her parents somehow discovered it. The last thing I wanted was to become embroiled again with the Harrelsons. It was not an easy decision, and I came to the conclusion that writing Charlene to confirm receipt of the picture would be appropriate.

The Reconnect

The emotional and physical distance from Charlene for over a year had enabled me to reassess myself. I was a little older, smarter, and hopefully wiser. My conversations with Dr. Edwards had provided a small access to the portion of my mind housing clarity and freethinking.

To be honest, my hesitancy in writing Charlene was fear based. I didn't want another emotional upheaval or an entanglement with her parents. My much-improved employment situation also served to keep my feet firmly cemented in the Florida sand. They weren't going anywhere, at least not to Texas.

After looking at Charlene's picture for several days, I sat down and wrote her a letter. I don't remember what I said, but know I acknowledged receipt of her picture and was warm.

Within a few days, I received a letter from a rather crestfallen Charlene. She began by telling me she was thrilled to have heard from me and was in hopes we would continue to correspond. Her letter was written when she was not in a good place. It surprised me to hear her relationship with her parents remained strained after we broke up. They had become impatient with Charlene's seeming inability to recover from our broken relationship.

In a subsequent phone conversation, Charlene told me her mother made her tear up the picture of me I had given her for Christmas two years prior. Mrs. Harrelson couldn't understand why Charlene couldn't move forward and determined that ripping my picture apart would facilitate the process. While understanding Mrs. Harrelson's rationale, I felt Charlene should have been allowed to "flush me down the toilet" when she was ready. I hope the picture frame survived the carnage; it was worthy of housing future suitors.

Charlene recounted that her last year at the university was emotionally tough and her objective was just to get it over with and graduate. She disclosed she had dated some, but had been in no frame of mind to pursue a serious relationship with anyone. Interestingly, one of the guys she dated received her mother's initial seal of approval, yet he was not Christian. This was mitigated by his being wealthy, which overrode other considerations. Charlene was befuddled by her mother's surprising position; at the same time, she knew it was her way of saying there were bigger and better fish in the sea than me. Funny how money can pave an otherwise unacceptable highway.

Over the next few weeks, Charlene and I remained in close communication. Like two ducks on the outermost circle of a whirlpool, we were gradually getting sucked in again. Though getting involved again made me downright uncomfortable, I mistakenly rationalized it still may be God's will. My Sunday school teacher advised me if it was God's will for Charlene and me to reunite, we would know it. A couple of weeks later, the pastor's sermon topic was "Finding God's Will in Your Life." He mentioned things like being patient, being prayerful, listening to trusted advisors, listening to your inner voice, and not trying to force an outcome when an answer was not apparent. Or the answer may be apparent and for whatever reason can't be accepted. Methodically, I mentally placed the checkmarks in all the boxes, including what should have been the "red flag" boxes—the ones about the inner voice, not trying to force an outcome, and acceptance. No doubt my inner voice had spoken, but I refused to listen. I was given the answer the first time around with Charlene, and was now questioning it. It was insane!

If there was ever anyone in a state of denial, particularly when considering one's sexual orientation, it was me. I was determined my "latent heterosexuality" was begging to be uncovered from some hidden crevice.

Chattanooga Choo Choo

Charlene's sister and brother-in-law, Ilene and Jeff, lived in Chattanooga. In a stroke of serendipity, my parents and I had close friends who resided in nearby Ooltewah. What a perfect coincidence. Christmas was six weeks out, and I suggested to Charlene that she fly to Chattanooga at some point during the holidays, ostensibly to visit her sister. I would drive up there and stay with my friends, the Creightons. Of course, the true nature of this clandestine escapade could never be disclosed to Charlene's parents. Ilene would keep quiet, as her own relationship with her parents was still strained.

The Harrelsons had never gotten past the transgression of Ilene marrying the "wrong man," over their strong protests. In the Harrelsons' judgment, Jeff was guilty of three major sins: (1) he was a "Yankee," (2) he was Catholic, and (3) he and Ilene didn't live in Texas. All three sins were listed in the unpardonable category in their bible.

I never divulged I had some Yankee blood coursing through my veins. My Canadian-born grandmother was raised in Massachusetts, which was one of the states listed in the "Be Wary Of" section contained in the "Official Unwritten Manual of Southern Acceptableness." Lord, have mercy.

I was above board with my parents regarding the trip to Chattanooga to meet Charlene. They were not too thrilled about it. I understood their position. My own trepidations were in the forefront of my thoughts, as my inner voice was telling me, "Seth, this is not a good idea. Be true to who you are." The pastor's recent sermon advice about acceptance and not attempting to force an outcome kept ringing in my head. I didn't want to be responsible for creating a situation that ultimately could be horrific for Charlene and me. Without question, my spiritual hearing aids were tuned to the wrong frequency, and I charged forward.

After first checking with our respective hosts, Charlene and I decided the period after Christmas and before the New Year would be optimal. Accordingly, I made roundtrip reservations for Charlene on Delta Air Lines, purchased the ticket, and mailed it to her at the school. Wow, the ticket cost seemed sky-high; nonetheless, it was commensurate with travel provided at 600 mph and 30,000 feet.

The day after Christmas arrived, and I awakened with a gnawing apprehension about the trip. Even though I was looking forward to seeing Charlene, it didn't feel right. I was in the infancy of a personal evolution and attempting to face myself in the mirror honestly. I had reached the point where I considered Charlene may not be the culmination of a journey to find a wife, but rather, the impetus by which I would embark on an entirely new journey. In other words, she might be the springboard for growth—and acceptance—of whatever God had in store for me. Before leaving that morning for Chattanooga, I prayed, asking God for guidance and clarity. My parents cautioned me to not exceed the speed limit, and then prayed for my traveling safety—knowing the reality of my driving habits.

The eight-hour trip was uneventful and, miraculously, there were no traffic problems encountered in Atlanta. Anyone who has ever driven through the place knows this is cause for celebration. I arrived at the Creightons' house in Ooltewah a little after 5:00 p.m., as it was getting dark. It was a drizzly, cold evening—a stark contrast from the relative warmth I had left in Jacksonville. When I arrived, Mr. and Mrs. Creighton and their twenty-one-year-old daughter, Rebecca, warmly greeted me with a lovely dinner. We ate and talked, and talked some more, until about eleven, when we all turned in for the night. These were cherished friends, and I had not seen them in several years.

After a fitful night, I woke around seven to a cold, rainy, foggy morning. Perhaps it was a bad omen. My stomach was in knots, so I reached for the Mylanta my mother had insisted I pack. Thanks, Mom, for the meds. Breakfast smells emanating from the kitchen soon filled my nostrils, and my mood improved. The eggs, grits, toast, and bacon were a welcome way to greet the otherwise dismal day.

Charlene's flight was scheduled to arrive around noon. I went to the airport about an hour prior to her scheduled arrival, to watch the planes. As it turned out, there were no planes to watch that otherwise would have distracted me from me, so I reverted to another one of my diversionary tactics—pacing back and forth in the concourse. Charlene's flight landed right on schedule, and she soon entered the waiting area adjacent to the gate. I was standing off to the far side of the gate counter, which blocked her view of me. I let her walk by and followed her while she looked around for a few seconds.

I was several feet behind her when I asked, "Ma'am, do you need help with your bag?"

She turned around, dropped her bag, which was a small overnight case, and hugged me. I hugged her as well, and we briefly kissed. Charlene was all smiles and as cute as a button with her short haircut. It was good to see her and, clearly, we both still had strong emotional bonds.

The first day in Chattanooga was spent primarily at Ilene and Jeff's house; there was not much else to do on such a dreary, drizzly day. Most of the afternoon was spent talking. During one of our discussions about marriage in general, Ilene made a surprising comment. She said as difficult as her parents had been with respect to her marriage to Jeff, some of their perspectives had generally been right. I interpreted her statement as an acknowledgment that her marriage was less than ideal, although she didn't say it outright.

Ilene and Jeff were gracious to me while I was in Chattanooga. In fact, most of my non-sleeping time was spent in their home. They were supportive, and expressed concerns about how Charlene and I would handle the Harrelsons, should we decide to marry. Not surprisingly, we were cautioned to be prepared for a long-term battle.

Charlene and I had discussed eloping when in Chattanooga, but we both knew, in that part of our guts where complete honesty resides, we could never do it. The splash created from that cliff dive would have quickly overwhelmed us.

We had three full days together in Chattanooga, and the sun never came out. Chilly air accompanied by fog, drizzle, and occasional rain continued to hamper the fun things I had planned for us to do. Particularly, I wanted Charlene to experience sunset from the top of Lookout Mountain, which unfortunately was not in the playbook. It would have been spectacular: sunset's dusky light projecting from the western horizon would provide a beautiful silhouette of the distant mountains and ridges. It was also a full moon, which, when not obscured, bathes the undulating landscape with an intoxicating mix of eerie, dim shadows and bright night light. It is one of those natural spectacles occasionally provided by nature that was cancelled due to adverse weather. Rain or shine, Mother Nature does not charge an admission fee for her incredible displays.

There are two distinct memories associated with our Chattanooga rendezvous that have survived the forty-plus years now separating me from the actual events. One night while we were driving down a narrow, poorly lit two-lane country road, the left-rear tire suddenly went flat. It was colder than a "well digger's ass" and was raining lightly. There was no way to call anyone for help (this was before the advent of cell phones), so I had no choice; I had to change the tire, right then, right there. It took me about ten minutes to perform the task in mostly dark conditions, although the darkness was ameliorated by some indirect light from the raised trunk lid. I also had a flashlight, which was hard to negotiate without a third hand. Charlene offered to assist, and I advised her that due to insurance regulations, she was not allowed in the work area. I managed to keep her out of the rain, but the frigid dousing I received turned me into a human icicle.

The other memory is much more personal and poignant. One afternoon when Ilene and Jeff were away, Charlene and I got as close to having sexual relations as we ever had. We were lying on the bed, stripped down to our undergarments and were involved in heavy petting. I briefly obtained a semi-erection and quickly lost it. My failure didn't escape Charlene's attention, and she rationalized it was due to our not being married. This experience, as embarrassing as it was, gave me the signal I needed. I admitted to myself that getting married was not going to initiate a magic switch. Incidentally, we would have never had sexual intercourse outside of matrimony, even if my internal frequency had been tuned for straight activity.

The time came for Charlene and me to leave each other again, and I drove her to the airport for the flight back to Dallas. Our parting was not emotionally charged, even though Charlene knew I wouldn't consider moving to Texas. She still hoped we would marry, and talked about moving back to Jacksonville. I didn't discourage her because I knew she would never do it.

My plan was to let time take care of the situation; I expected the relationship to wither. I had prayed for guidance and clarity before I embarked on the journey to Chattanooga. As I drove back to Jacksonville, I knew I had gained the clarity I sought. This was a giant step toward self-acceptance and the first of more to follow.

Am I Really Surprised?

Charlene and I returned to an apparent destiny of continuing a hopeless relationship through our letter writing and phone calls. Nothing had changed, yet for me everything had changed; I had changed, which was reflected by my increasing detachment in letters to Charlene.

Not long after the Chattanooga trip, Charlene started making plans for a covert trip to Jacksonville—without her parents' knowledge. This made me uneasy, now knowing without hesitation that marrying her was wrong for every reason. I was in the first stages of coming to terms with my "gayness," and loved Charlene enough to prevent a counterfeit marriage that would destroy her life. It was apparent to me the relationship had to end (for good), and I didn't know how to put a stop to the runaway train. One thing was certain: I could never tell Charlene I was gay. The only person other than me who knew my truth was Dr. Edwards, and I had to keep it that way. Providentially, the Jacksonville trip would prove to be a feat Charlene couldn't engineer.

As fate would have it, Charlene's parents found out she and I had been in touch with each other. They confronted her with their suspicions, and she was forced to confirm their worst nightmare. Mr. and Mrs. Harrelson had suspected for some time something was going on. The Chattanooga trip was rather curious to them, and it had triggered their radar, particularly since they knew I had close friends there. I don't remember the details, and my recollection is after the Chattanooga trip, Mrs. Harrelson discovered the "smoking gun," which may have been a letter from me. Regardless, we were caught, and the civil war within the Harrelson household reignited. Even though I was the reason for the battle, the real war—as far as I was concerned—was being waged on my own secret battlefield.

Again, Charlene's life had become an emotional mess and she admitted in a phone conversation that the stress was more than she could bear. A few letters followed, and it was unmistakable she was in a state of near surrender. I knew the end was close, and the tone of her letters reflected it. In her last letter, written in early 1975, she said my inflexibility was evidence I didn't love her. She abruptly ended her terse letter with: "I wish you a happy life. Goodbye. Charlene." She was profoundly hurt, and I deeply hated my role in this chapter of our lives. I didn't answer the letter and never spoke with her again. Our odyssey from June 1972 to the second final curtain had spanned nearly three years. I have long regretted that I didn't at least write her back to accept closure, wish her well, and to apologize for the hurt I had caused.

Many times, I have thought about Charlene's parents and am grateful they were successful in stopping Charlene and me from getting married. The irony is their reasons for not wanting us to marry were unrelated to the true reason Charlene and I broke up—a reason not even Charlene knew.

Even though she did the breaking up, my refusal to move and the increasing detachment forced her to do what had to be done. In the final analysis, Charlene was the only woman I ever loved, yet my love for her was clearly not enough. No matter how much I tried to fit the mold, it just couldn't happen.

In the months and years following our courtship, I became increasingly grateful our paths had crossed. Charlene had unwittingly helped me to face the inescapable fact that I was gay. I frequently think of her and hope she married a handsome native son of Texas who's garbed in a Stetson hat, cowboy boots, and armed with a Neiman Marcus credit card. She deserved no less after everything I put her through.

Collateral Damage

Leona and Burt Langley remained my steadfast friends after Charlene and I sang sayonara. It greatly disappointed me to learn the Harrelsons discontinued all contact with them afterwards. Christmas cards and letters from the Langleys to the Harrelsons remained unanswered. Even Charlene didn't respond, which I considered insensitive and baffling. I knew the Langleys were hurt; however, they never displayed it nor did they often speak about it. It was evident the strong friendship between the two families had come to an unfortunate end, and I couldn't help but feel partially responsible. Leona, Burt, and I discussed it one evening, and we surmised Charlene had told her parents that Leona gave me Charlene's picture and school address. More than likely, the Harrelsons considered it unforgivable interference. Regrettably, the chasm was never bridged and contact between the families permanently ceased.

The Langleys occupy a special place in my life history. Memories of them warm my heart and bring a smile to my face. I stayed in close contact with them until they died. Burt passed away at the age of eighty-seven, in 2007, after a lingering illness and dementia. Toward the end of his life, he briefly had to be placed in a nursing facility in Orange Park, which was about twenty-five miles from his and Leona's home. Leona was uneasy about the drive, so I occasionally took her to visit Burt until he passed away. In 2013, at the age of ninety-one, Leona passed away at home in her sleep. Toward the end of her life, she was mostly confined to her home, never surrendering to her age-related maladies. It delighted me she never lost her feistiness, her wonderful sense of humor, or her down-home common sense. I loved Burt and Leona, and never shared with them that I was gay. In my estimation, it would have accomplished nothing.

Chapter 22

I Yield to the Wind Direction

Not long after my relationship with Charlene ended for the last time, a barrage of dating opportunities began from all quadrants. The prevailing thought and collective mission of the folks in the church was I needed some help in finding a wife. I didn't, and was terrified at the thought. The well-meaning and clueless church ladies were descending on me like bees, with opportunities to meet eligible girls. It was not my nature to ever be rude or unappreciative, so I usually politely turned down their overtures and thanked them for their concern.

My never-fail excuse that it was too early after the breakup with Charlene had long passed its expiration. When someone irritated me with their persistence, I attempted to defuse them by citing the Apostle Paul, who remained single and held the position that being so was better than being married. For anyone wishing to read his position on this, it is found in 1 Corinthians 7. Even with Paul's blessing to single people, I felt trapped in my overall predicament and desperately needed to find the escape hatch.

To compound the situation, I sensed I was about to spiral into another depressive episode, which frightened me even more than the "why are you not dating" questions. Major changes had to take place in my life; I was tired of playing games. There was no doubt I had to accept myself as God made me and learn to live a life of validity "off the heterosexual grid."

Adjusting to Reality

I had a rough time understanding why my prayers for "straightness" were not granted and, admittedly, felt abandoned by God. I floundered for about a year, during which time a mini personal crisis ensued that was deeply rooted in the church. I was dejected and repeatedly read two Scriptures that had been pounded into me as a child. For starters, Matthew 7:7 (KJV) says, "Ask, and it shall be given you; seek, and ye shall find; knock, and it shall be opened unto you." This is probably one of the most oft-quoted verses in the entire Bible. Similarly, Mark 11:24 (KJV) says, "Therefore I say unto you, what things soever ye desire, when ye pray, believe that ye receive them, and ye shall have them." I had asked, knocked, and prayed until my knees ached—but to no avail. Did God's "book of instructions" contain unwritten caveats? If so, they remained hidden while I searched.

I had been taught that all prayers should include the utterance, "according to God's will." This begs the following question: Why would God's will be other than to grant my request to be made straight, particularly if God finds gays to be an abomination, as the evangelical church preaches? If I prayed for my dark-brown hair to be made blonde, would it be in God's will to grant this? I think not, because my natural hair color was God's intent when I was conceived. Perhaps the same corollary applies to sexual orientation.

I started to seriously doubt what I had been taught by the church. My brain was waking up and I was thinking. I believed the Bible, but also began to consider some parts of it were subject to misinterpretation from the original language, resulting in misunderstanding. I looked at my own church, which proclaimed to be Bible-believing and Bible-practicing; however, I didn't see the poor being fed, the widows being cared for, or the sick being visited. I also didn't see "Love thy neighbor as thyself" or "Do unto others as you would have them do unto you," being practiced. What I did see were bigger buildings being built and elaborate renovations being completed. Priorities seemed misplaced, and my observations were that the folks throwing darts the hardest at people like me were the same ones who conveniently ignored the crux of Christ's message and the true mission of the church.

I Surrender

After years of prayer, mind games, angst, and anger at God, I at last walked out of the wilderness and into the realization that trying to force the "choice" to be straight was in vain—because God didn't give this "choice" as an option. My sexual orientation was no different than the spots on a leopard; the best eraser can't change either. This honest, once and for all, "thank God" acknowledgment set me free. The battle was over; I surrendered. Martin Luther King Jr., in his heart-wrenching quest for equality, said it best: "Free at last, free at last, thank God Almighty, I'm free at last." While my freedom was not related to the racial oppression he experienced, I understood what being free was all about. Free from guilt, free from a life of futility, free to be who I am. I felt born again. If I had ever been inclined to preach, this is when it would have happened.

It was late November 1975, and the "sexual revolution" was in full swing across the U.S. Gay rights were beginning to be championed, particularly in New York and California. In response, the evangelical churches came out swinging and have been ever since. In addition to the usual admonishments from the pulpit regarding premarital sex (which were largely ignored), condemnations of "homosexuals" were becoming commonplace. Even so, I could no longer allow the church—and the straight world—to dictate that I must force myself into the "one size fits all" mold which didn't correspond to God's personal specifications for me. This acknowledgment allowed me to dismiss the anti-gay "it's a choice" rhetoric spewing forth from many pulpits. For the time being, I remained active in my home church, continued to sing in the choir next to Anthony Petrini (such sweet torture), and stayed in the "closet" while I calibrated my course. The seeds I had so adamantly kept from sprouting had been nurtured by God and were now emerging as a flower garden of self-acceptance. Tough times would surely come; however, a new journey had begun, and amazingly, my church would prove to be the springboard.

As Fate Would Have It

One Sunday night, a young guy, probably in his early twenties, came into the church just ahead of me for the evening service. He sat alone in an unoccupied pew near the rear of the church. I concluded he was probably a first-time visitor, so I walked over to him, introduced myself, and welcomed him to the church. He seemed a little aloof, was tall, blonde, nice-looking but not too much so. We shook hands, and he told me his name was Leonard Brewer. I can't remember why I was not in the choir; for whatever reason, I wasn't. Call it providence. Leonard asked me if I would like to sit with him, which I did. (Why not? He was cute.) We chatted for a few minutes prior to the service, and he mentioned he was looking for a church with a good choir. He told me his church, a large Baptist congregation nearby, was in a decline due to a split in the congregation. My recollection is the pastor of his church had "suffered an indiscretion" with his secretary and was forced to resign.

Nevertheless, Leonard had landed in the right place. Our church had a growing and dynamic music program. During the hymn-singing portion of the service, it was apparent Leonard had a beautiful and well-trained voice. Afterwards, he told me he and his three brothers sang as a quartet and had done so for several years. I would soon discover all four of the Brewer brothers were equally loaded with the type of vocal ability causing church choir directors to salivate.

Leonard and I became instant friends, which was a curiosity to me since our personalities and demeanors were dissimilar. As I had originally guessed, he was indeed aloof—also sarcastic, serious, plainspoken, and comfortable in his skin. On the other hand, I was none of the above. Leonard soon joined the church and became a choir member. Two of his brothers followed him. Thus, the choir director hit the musical jackpot with these three guys. The brother who didn't join the ranks was Leonard's fraternal twin; he chose to remain in another church.

Over the course of the next couple of months, Leonard and I occasionally went out for a hamburger or pizza after choir practice. He was articulate, interesting, and nobody's fool. In one of our conversations, he asked if I was dating anyone. I told him I wasn't and recounted the abridged version of my recently ended relationship with Charlene.

My mini dissertation evoked some unexpected personal questions. He wanted to know if I was upset about the breakup, and if I was interested in dating any of the girls in the church.

I told him I was not upset and had no plans to begin dating.

Nonchalantly and without any preface, he asked, "Are you still a virgin?"

I surely didn't see that one coming and took a few seconds to consider my answer. I told him I was, and asked him the same question.

Without hesitation he answered, "No."

His answer surprised me; I had him pegged as a "toe-the-line" Baptist, particularly since he was raised in an even more fundamental church than mine. He surely projected an air of being straitlaced; evidently, his laces were not tied as tightly as I suspected.

Our conversation continued, and it was apparent his interest in my personal life was more than passing. I had no idea where this was headed, and went with it. Casually, Leonard mentioned he was told one of our fellow choir members was gay. I asked him who it was, but he wouldn't disclose the name or his source of information. I respected his discreetness, yet was itching to know who might be gay, right here in the seat of homophobia. Leonard made no judgment and didn't seem at all disturbed about this "deviant" individual being in the choir. He made no reference to Leviticus 20:13 (one of the oft-quoted "abomination" verses), which is usually the first place evangelicals go to support their anti-gay views. Curiously, he was most interested in knowing if I was uncomfortable knowing there may be a gay person in the choir. It was all I could do to keep from saying, "Take me to the altar. I confess!" I wondered if Leonard was referring to me, and at the least, I sensed he was on a fishing expedition. Was his mission to "out" me, befriend me, or figure me out?

After some brief thought, I carefully chose my words and told Leonard a person's sexual orientation was between them and God and therefore not for me to judge. I elaborated by saying gay people didn't make me uncomfortable, and I strongly believed being gay was inherent. This was not the approved evangelical answer. Without any expression, Leonard told me in confidence the person in the choir who was gay was him. I was surprised, but admittedly didn't have finely tuned "gaydar" (and still don't). Leonard didn't come across as being gay in any fashion (although he preferred designer clothing and liked antiques—a lethal mix).

The door was wide open, and I could either walk through it or close it like I had done in the past. I chose to take the chance; I told Leonard I was gay. He remained expressionless and said he had considered the possibility the first time we met. This distressed me—a lot. Had my muscularity from weightlifting not accomplished an appropriate smoke screen? Was I *that* obvious? Leonard said I wasn't, although he pointed out that like many gay men, I was rather demonstrative and friendly.

He was right in his assessment. In fact, the caption under my picture in the high school yearbook reads: "His friendly manner speaks his thoughtful mind." For whatever reason, I was embarrassed by the caption. Now I knew why.

Leonard and I developed an instant camaraderie, and it was superb to have a gay friend, particularly in the church. Other than Dr. Edwards, Leonard was the only gay person I knew (or so I thought).

Even though Leonard was four years younger than me, he had street smarts and was discreet. He was familiar with the gay establishments in the area and would serve as my "tour guide."

Chapter 23

Blake

Leonard and I were not attracted to each other, and even if we had been, nothing long-term could have developed between us. We were too different. It is true that opposites attract, but sometimes, as Rudyard Kipling wrote: "Oh, the East is East and the West is West, and Never the Twain shall Meet."

One Thursday night following choir practice, I drove Leonard home but can't remember why he was without a car. Like me, he was still living with his parents. The fifteen-minute drive went too quickly; I was bombarding him with more questions than he had time to answer. I was primarily interested in knowing how and where to meet gay men and if guys kissed on a first date. He was astonished at my innocence, lack of "gay awareness," and that I had never kissed a guy. In my defense, I was a fledgling in an unfamiliar maze and terrified to navigate it. To complicate matters, living at home was a huge problem. For this and many other reasons, staying "in the closet" was an absolute necessity. In fact, most gay folks, including Leonard, were in the same situation. In this respect, I had good company.

The Brewers lived on a dimly lit country road. I pulled in to the long, dark driveway, which was barely illuminated by a light near the front of the house. I stopped the car a good distance from the house. My curiosity about kissing a guy was driving me past the point of distraction and I desperately wanted to experience it—with Leonard.

Before he could escape from the car, I told him what was on my mind and asked if he would kiss me.

He started to lean toward me, then backed off a bit, and said, "You know we can go no further than a kiss."

I assured him it wouldn't be a problem. He kissed me, and without hesitation I kissed him back.

It was the kiss that unequivocally confirmed to me what was missing when Charlene and I had kissed. Leonard's lips were soft, almost like cotton—in fact, softer than Charlene's. The electricity of the kiss sent tingles up and down my spine—it was unlike anything I had ever experienced. I had indeed tasted of the "forbidden fruit." At the age of twenty-six, I understood for the first time in my life how powerful a kiss could be.

Only then did I understand what Leonard meant when he said we could go no further than a kiss; it was extremely difficult to stop. This brief exchange, lasting well less than a minute, instantly activated my "equipment." I was fully erect and pre-seminal fluid leaked into my underpants. I was speechless. This had *never* happened to me; however, the pool experience with Anthony may have rendered similar results in my wet bathing suit. Yep, the litmus test was positive. No matter how much I had tried to jettison the "sugar in my tanks," it wasn't successful.

Where Do I Go from Here?

My true self had been awakened and I was ready to meet other gay men. Even so, I would never go into a gay bar by myself, and, in fact, I had never been inside a bar of any type. This is an unbelievable admission for a twenty-six-year-old University of Florida graduate. Given Leonard's "helpfulness" with the kiss request, I decided to ask if I could go with him sometime to one of the local gay bars. Based on a previous conversation, I knew he was familiar with this component of gay life. We spoke later in the week, and he was open to my request; I would have to wait a month, when my parents would be out of town—the golden opportunity to stay out late without being subjected to unwanted scrutiny.

The month soon passed and on a Friday night in early January, I drove the two of us to a "den of iniquity" called Brothers, which was tucked away on a quiet side street in the Riverside section of town. By nature I was an early bird; however, I was soon educated to the unbelievable reality that the early bird gets nothing but a locked door at a gay bar. We arrived about 9:00 p.m., which was late for me and still on the early side for the bar crowd. Even so, there were a decent number of men and a few women in the establishment. I was excited, yet as tense as a cat in a dog park. The place was smoke-filled and dimly lit, with great dance music reverberating off the walls. A small dance floor was located in the center of the room, near the bar, and a pool table sat in a separate area off to the side.

Leonard suggested a couple of beers would "tranquilize" me, particularly if I drank the prescribed "dosage" fairly fast. As instructed, I gulped a draft beer, which was the first beer I had ever consumed. The taste was vile (still is), yet the brew was fast acting and within a few minutes I was feeling the initial effects of its "medicinal properties." Leonard and I ended up standing in a spot near the pool table where most of the guys were congregated. It offered a great vantage for guy-watching and taking in the gyrations beginning to take place on the dance floor. There were guys dancing with guys and girls dancing with girls; it was a lot to digest, yet seemed strangely normal.

Amazingly, no guys were drinking beer with a straw—and I knew the room was full of "homosexualists." My mother's belief that gay men typically drink with straws was clearly incorrect—however, I surely wouldn't be the one to educate her. I also noticed the hairstyles, which corresponded to no particular "tipoff" pattern. The guys looked no different than their straight counterparts in every aspect. The beer I guzzled surely had not dulled my soberness to the point where my observational skills were impaired—I saw what I saw.

I was still a little on edge, and the second dose of beer in my virgin stomach soon put me "over the fence." My cares began to evaporate and I landed in the "promised land." (I was feeling my first-ever sensory impairment—an appropriate degree of intoxication.) Leonard told me he had a surprise, but I would have to wait a few minutes for him to retrieve it. He left me standing there alone, holding onto my near-empty beer glass for dear life; I didn't budge.

A few moments later, an overly welcoming "lady" came up to me and was interested in feeling my biceps. Even in my semi-compromised state, it was easy to discern this curvy vision of heavy-duty makeup, haute couture, and piled-high platinum coiffure was a drag queen—the first one I had ever met. What a sight! She was dripping in rhinestones, and with dramatic flair, introduced herself as Anita Tampax. Even though usually slow on the uptake, I fielded that one and burst out laughing.

She said, "You gotta love it," and added a comment I won't repeat, before sauntering off to her next victim.

Leonard walked up, laughing, and said he had enjoyed observing the interaction between Anita and me. I found it hysterical and thanked him for the surprise. He said he had nothing to do with the "spectacle" I had just met—the timing of which was entirely coincidental. He insisted he had something in store for me and I'd need to wait a few more minutes. My curiosity was piqued. I was at a loss as to what his surprise might be.

More folks were beginning to filter into the area where Leonard and I were standing, and it was getting increasingly crowded. I noticed an adorable guy had slipped into the room, probably while Anita was keeping me entertained. There was an attraction and, in a quick surveillance, I assessed he was probably in his early twenties, was about my height, had broad shoulders, brown hair, greenish eyes, and was slender. He seemed to light up the room, and everyone appeared to know him.

Much to my amazement, he walked over to us and with a wide, gorgeous smile, he said, "You must be Seth."

I about melted.

He told me his name was Blake Sinclair. I found him disarming and was smitten by this self-assured guy from Alabama. He was the surprise Leonard had arranged. Blake was polite and seemed to be from superior breeding stock. Because Blake was an excellent conversationalist, we ended up talking (actually yelling above the bar noise) nonstop for about an hour. There was, without question, chemistry between us.

However, by 11:00 p.m. I was ready to leave. The place was elbow to elbow and the smoke was choking. My overview of the gay bar scene was less than positive. Still, meeting Blake made the excursion well worth the price of admission (free). Before we left, Blake gave me his phone number and specifically asked me to call him the next morning, but not before 10:00 a.m. I assured him I would call, and then left with Leonard.

During the drive back to our side of town, Leonard told me he had known Blake for a short time, and thought the two of us would enjoy knowing each other. He also had advised Blake I lived with my parents and was in a "discovery" phase in regards to my sexuality.

When I got home, I undressed in the garage and threw my clothes in the washer—they reeked with the smell of cigarette smoke. I did as well. A personal detoxification was in order, so I took a shower and washed my hair before going to bed.

The following morning I woke up around 8:00 a.m. with a feeling of excitement, despite having a dry, sour-tasting mouth and being slightly off-kilter. These hallmarks of my "initiation rites" the evening before seemed to dissipate after I ate breakfast. After pulling my clothes out of the washer, and drying and folding them, it was ten o'clock.

I didn't need to write or rehearse any "lines" prior to calling Blake. There was no state of high anxiety—just eagerness. After several rings, Blake answered the phone. Unmistakably, he was groggy. I knew I had awakened him when he asked me what time it was. How embarrassing for me. I gave him my phone number and asked him to call me back when he was ready to greet the day. The phone call came at 11:30 a.m., and Blake was as chipper and engaging as he had been the evening before. The conversation was brief, and the result was a date with Blake that night. We decided to meet at his apartment at seven and go to Victoria Station for dinner. Interestingly, Blake lived in the same general area where Charlene used to live, which meant the "bridge of death" would have to be crossed. I was willing to accept the risk.

Coincidentally, Georgi had called earlier in the morning "just to chat," which was not unusual; however, the conversation was a tad uncomfortable. Among other things, he was interested in knowing who I had been dating since Charlene and I broke up, and if I was getting serious with anyone. When I told him I was not yet ready to date, it made little sense to him, given a year had since passed. Georgi was a terminally girl-crazy guy and clearly was puzzled by my response. I didn't know what else to say. Even though we were close friends, I could never tell him I was gay. Fortunately, he didn't press further, though my lack of interest in girls seemed to disturb him.

First Date

I didn't need directions to find Blake's apartment complex, having passed it numerous times when Charlene and I were dating. I negotiated the maze of apartments and easily found Blake's second-floor unit at the end of his building. My heart was racing with excitement and anticipation—almost like Christmas morning when I was a kid. I skipped every other step, effortlessly scaling the stairway leading up to the door. I knocked several times before Blake opened the door. Damn, he had a winsome smile and dimples complementing a handsome face.

At the age of twenty-six, I was experiencing for the first time in my life what it was like to be in a state of "gaga" over a date. Admittedly, I was smitten with Anthony Petrini, while knowing my private attraction could not be anything other than that. With Blake, the possibility existed in the future ... a meaningful relationship could develop. This didn't frighten me in the least. Having an intimate level of association was a deep desire—and need—I no longer suppressed. What a fresh, natural, welcome, and electrifying feeling. My most intense relationship in the past, which of course was with Charlene, had given me considerable heartburn when sex was contemplated. Now, at long last, I was experiencing what all my friends likely experienced when they had their first dates as post-puberty teenagers. Better late than never!

Blake's apartment was comfortable, upscale, and, like Blake, immaculate. The door to his apartment was more than an entrance to a living space—it represented the portal which allowed me to leap across the chasm separating me from my true self. It was a moment of personal triumph. Blake uncorked a bottle of red wine, and we toasted to a new friendship. We talked effortlessly for about a half hour before walking to Victoria Station, which was nearby.

Blake and I had no pauses in conversation and continued to become better acquainted at the restaurant. The food was excellent—but truthfully, they could have served dog food and I probably would have liked it (we both had prime rib). I discovered Blake was bright, had a good sense of humor, and, as previously established, was easy on the eyes. He worked as an accountant for a large construction outfit, and like me, was raised in a Southern Baptist family. Unlike me, he didn't experience a huge degree of difficulty in accepting his gay "assignment" and was relaxed when talking about the subject. Blake put me at ease, and it was apparent he was as interested in me as I was in him.

At about nine o'clock, we concluded our dinner and went back to his apartment to watch TV. Blake invited me to sit on the couch, which was directly opposite the TV. He sat at one end of the couch and I sat at the other end. We settled in and tuned to *The Mary Tyler Moore Show*. Blake made the comment, "I don't bite," which was my cue to move closer to him. He put his hand on my knee, and without any forethought I placed my hand on top of his hand. It seemed so natural, so unrehearsed, and so easy. Neither of us was paying much attention to the TV program, so it primarily provided background noise. We looked into each other's eyes for longer than if it were just innocent visual contact. Blake asked if listening to the stereo would be preferable to the babble on TV. Absolutely! I sensed with eagerness a romantic interlude may be the evening's next course.

I was right. Blake stood up and walked to the stereo. He chose a station that played "mood enhancing" music and then sat close to me. We instantly wrapped ourselves in a tight embrace and feverishly began to exchange kisses. "The First Time Ever I Saw Your Face," sung by Roberta Flack, was playing. If this song doesn't thrust one over the precipice of passion, nothing will. Well, it did, and I yielded to years of pent-up passions. All of my repressed desires and frustrations were released like fireworks on the Fourth of July. My first-ever sexual experience was deeply visceral and opened the floodgates for a long-overdue spiritual and physical fulfillment. I had indeed been "knocked off my feet," just as my mother predicted would happen some years back—although her crystal ball clearly didn't impart some pertinent details.

Blake and I cuddled and talked until a little past 1:00 a.m. I could have "danced all night"; however, church obligations awaiting later in the morning dictated that I go home for some sleep. Plus, my parents were expected to return later in the day, and I needed to do a little house cleaning. When I fell into my bed, the faint scent of Blake's cologne caressed me. The scent invited me to relive the evening's events, although drowsiness overtook me just as my passions had done earlier.

I awoke around 8:00 a.m. with a never-before-experienced feeling of what it was like to be freely enthralled with someone. It was marvelous. After showering, I went to Sunday school and was greeted by a friend who wanted to set me up with a "super nice girl" she knew at her place of employment. This had to stop; I responded with a half smile and a rather stern "No, thank you." Several other people were standing nearby and they got the message. This perfunctory style of answer was not my usual method of communication. It accomplished my goal. The setup opportunities, at least from this group, ceased.

Guess Who Shows Up at Church

Just after entering the choir loft and as the organ prelude was being played, I noticed Blake walking in. We made eye contact and smiled at each other. I had no idea he was going to attend church. While I was thrilled to see him, it made me uneasy. During the course of the entire service, we kept looking at each other, exchanging grins. I didn't hear a single word of the sermon; my distraction was in full command of my senses and I anxiously anticipated the conclusion of the service. Finally, the last verse of "Just As I Am" was sung, and it mercifully ended.

Stepping down from the choir loft, I walked toward Blake to welcome him. It was all I could do to keep from giving him a kiss—probably the wrong place for such a display of carnality. We walked back behind the choir loft, where I had him wait at the base of the stairs leading up to the choir room. I bolted up the stairs to return my music and hang my choir robe, attempting a fast exit—all in an effort to avoid answering questions from anyone about Blake. My ultimate fear was some "well-intentioned" magpie would mention Blake to my parents. I was already mulling over my response in case something came up. I spirited Blake out of the church and, remarkably, was able to do so without anyone asking me who he was.

Back home, I changed into casual clothes and subsequently drove to Blake's apartment, where we ate hamburgers he had picked up. We spent the next couple of hours cuddled up on his couch.

Blake asked if I was going to tell my parents I was gay.

I screeched, "Definitely not! I could never do that. It would devastate them."

My secret would have to remain. Blake understood my viewpoint, but was of the opinion my parents and I would be much better off with the truth. We then discussed how I was going to handle gay dating while still living at home under the scope of my parents. The simple fact was it would be virtually impossible.

Fortunately, I had already taken first steps to achieve "self-emancipation" (for the second time in my life). Several weeks earlier, I had contacted my confidant and physician, Dr. Edwards, who owned a six-unit apartment building in Riverside. He mentioned a vacancy was possible in early February; however, I hadn't had any conversation with him since my initial inquiry. The sparks between Blake and me were undeniable and we wanted to continue dating each other. It was not easy to leave Blake that afternoon. Obligations dictated I head back home at about three. I made a pledge to follow up with Dr. Edwards on Monday morning.

My Parents Return

When I returned home from Blake's apartment, I took a shower to rid myself of any residual cologne scent, which my mother's finely tuned nostrils would have detected like a bloodhound. I knew in order for Blake and me to be able to date, I would have to plan our escapades carefully. I hated the idea of living in a continual lie, but felt no other choice was viable. This wouldn't be easy. My hope was to move out in the near future.

My parents got back around 4:00 p.m. and, as expected, they inquired about my weekend. I was nonchalant, and mentioned Georgi and I did some catching up on the phone Saturday morning. There was no further discussion, and later we went to the evening church service as usual.

Much to my relief, no one said anything to either of my parents regarding Blake. However, Blake's presence didn't go unnoticed by Anthony; he wanted to know who was with me after the morning church service. I told him the guy's name was Blake and he was a friend of Leonard Brewer. I also mentioned he was a first-time visitor to the church and I had just met him. This was the spiel I had rehearsed in case my parents asked questions about Blake. Nonetheless, Anthony's question—while innocent—unnerved me because everything unnerved me.

I Make Plans to Move Out

Meeting Blake gave me another reason to look for my own place; however, leaving home had more to do with "it was way past time" than anything else. In retrospect, it amazes me I lived at home for over three years after returning to Jacksonville from Naples, particularly when it was expected to be a temporary arrangement. It did allow me to stash a little money. My situation now was drastically different, and the cost to my personal freedom could no longer be justified.

As it turned out, the unfurnished apartment in Dr. Edwards' building would be available on February 15, 1976, and I grabbed it. My parents were surprised yet pleased at my strike for independence. They were not too happy I would be renting from Dr. Edwards, given his "reputation." They also didn't like the idea of my living in Riverside, which had the connotation of being a "haven for gays." Never mind the apartment was at most, ten minutes from my work. There was no question my parents' antennas were up.

Blake was ecstatic when I told him the apartment was available and I would be moving in a few weeks. Since the two-bedroom apartment was unfurnished, I had a pressing need to buy furniture. Actually, I already had furnishings for the second bedroom—my dumbbells, barbells, and weight bench.

One Saturday, Blake helped me scout out various furniture stores, looking for bargains and sales. For the kitchen, I bought a small, garden-style, glass-topped wrought-iron table that was round and painted white. Four matching chairs with bright green vinyl seats completed the set. It was a half-price feature in one of the store's back rooms. There was no dining room in the apartment, and the living room was large enough to accommodate a matching sofa and love seat, with coordinating tables. This entire floor sample vignette was offered at "never seen before" pricing, which was an opportunity I snapped up. The last furniture item purchased was a dark-stained, rustic-themed, pine bedroom suite I found at Sears. It was offered at "seen before" pricing—I still bought it. Miscellaneous items such as curtains, towels, pots, pans, dishes, and such were the last things I bought. Setting up housekeeping was much more involved than I had expected. Nonetheless, it was an exciting time.

He Sure Is Pretty

Prior to the time I moved into my apartment, Blake and I managed to surreptitiously see each other a good bit. I couldn't hide him from my parents, and I could never share with them the true nature of our relationship. We planned our time together cautiously. My excursions "to the mall" were in fact trips to Blake's apartment, and "tennis matches" with Blake didn't take place on the courts. Blake started attending church regularly, and, believe it or not, he joined it. This made it much easier to "pal around" with him since he was part of the church flock. I casually introduced Blake to my parents at church one Sunday when he, Leonard Brewer, and I were chatting. My parents knew Blake was becoming a good friend, but they didn't know he and I had met prior to the time he came to the church. Our friendship was now plausible since it appeared to be church related.

We were just good friends, as far as the church folks were concerned; however, Blake's friendship with me didn't escape the attention of the pastor. One Sunday, he made the snarky comment to my mother that Blake was sure a "pretty boy." There was no doubt as to the inference, and my mother fielded the pastor's comment exactly the way it was thrown. She of course relayed it to me and, unmistakably, was not pleased. She was insistent on knowing if Blake liked girls. My answer was yes. It was the answer she wanted to hear, so I delivered it. And it was a truthful answer since Blake did like girls; he just had no sexual interest in them—something we had in common. Unquestionably, my mother's real concerns were about me, not Blake.

Beware of Church Ladies

The girls at church were all over Blake like ants on sugar, and hallelujah, they had given up on me (the girls, not the ants). Blake came up with the enterprising idea that he and I could "double date" one night with two seemingly reserved girls—or should I say, young women—at the church who were roommates. We could all go to a movie, then take the girls home and leave. It made sense to me because it would be great for our image and should be sufficiently newsworthy to warrant headliner status on the church's active grapevine. We put the plan into action and approached the two girls with our proposal, which was accepted.

The following Friday night, Blake drove the two of us in his new Ford LTD coupe over to the Riverside apartment where Yvonne and Cheryl lived. The thought had previously crossed our minds they could be lesbians, given the address. We arrived at the old, gray-painted, two-story house where the girls resided, and rang the doorbell to their downstairs apartment. They came to the door promptly, and we left for the movie without going inside their apartment. I have no recollection of what movie we saw, and it was over around 9:00 p.m. or so. We offered to take the girls to a hamburger spot in the area, but they declined. This was going well.

When we brought the girls back to their apartment, Yvonne invited us to come in for a minute to see how they had furnished and decorated their space. I was hesitant to go inside, while Blake was curious to see what the girls had done. His curiosity nearly killed two cats! We went in and before I knew it, Cheryl pressed a glass of chardonnay into my hand.

I thought, *Hey, wait a minute. You girls are Baptists, and besides, chardonnay tastes like cat piss to me.* I graciously accepted the wine and made all efforts not to gag on it while "admiring" their not-to-my-liking decorating style.

Blake had also received a complimentary refreshment from Yvonne and was generous in his appraisal of the apartment. We sat and yakked about inessential subjects for an endless time—probably twenty or thirty minutes. I was about to crawl out of my skin and could tell Blake was in the same crucible. I couldn't take another second of this charade, so thanked the ladies for the wine and stood up to leave.

Cheryl walked over to where I was standing and plainly wanted me to give her a good-night kiss. So I did. It was a brief peck on her lips, although it might as well have been a call to mate. She latched onto me, slithered her wine-infused tongue down my throat, and pulled me down to the couch. Cheryl proceeded to make out with me as if we were long-lost lovers. She tried to unbutton my shirt. Before I could call 911, she grabbed my hand and placed it squarely on her breast. No interpretation was needed. She wanted me to unbutton her blouse, and all I wanted was to "unbutton" the lock on the front door. I was being accosted—by a church woman! I don't know what was in her chardonnay, but she sure put the "fear of God" in mine.

Meanwhile, Yvonne had tried to entice Blake into some sort of lovey-dovey on the love seat. Fortunately for him, her methods were less ravenous than those drawn from Cheryl's arsenal. Never before had any girl come on to me like the freight train that had hit me. Blake and I managed to squirm out of the lions' den with our clothes disheveled, yet otherwise unscathed. No doubt, Cheryl's and Yvonne's behavior could be partially attributable to their being wine-fueled. More important, we deduced they were not lesbians. This incident ended any future double-dating.

I Occupy My Man Cave

The apartment was ready for occupancy a day early and Dr. Edwards allowed me to move in on Saturday, February 14. It was an exciting day and a noteworthy road marker on my journey toward significant personal growth and freedom. The affordable apartment allowed me to save a portion of my salary, which was important to me.

The residents in the apartment building were wonderful. Most were longtime tenants and in their senior years. Before long, this loving group of fellow apartment-dwellers had embraced me. Most notable was a sixty-year-old woman named Gladys Muller, who was a major in the Salvation Army. She had never married and devoted her life's work to helping the disadvantaged. I could easily include several chapters about this wonderful, nonjudgmental lady, whom I grew to love during my seven-year residence in the building. She frequently brought me home-cooked meals, and since she had no vehicle, I occasionally took her shopping.

Major Muller lived in the building until she was in her early eighties, at which point she moved into an assisted living facility near her brother and sister-in-law in Tallahassee. She cried when I surprised her in Tallahassee for her eighty-fifth birthday. I found her to be frail, yet in great spirits and not at all diminished mentally. It was the last time I saw her, although we continued to correspond until just before her passing, two years later.

Cupid's Arrow Finds Me

I settled into apartment life quickly. Blake and I became inseparable, although we didn't move in together. The pangs of love couldn't be ignored, and before I knew it I had fallen head over heels in love with Blake.

One night, we went to an upscale neighborhood restaurant for dinner and, while there, split a bottle of Louis Jadot Beaujolais-Villages, which was a good red wine. Unlike my experience with Cheryl's chardonnay, it paired well with my taste buds and the chicken cordon bleu I ordered. In this romantic setting, we stayed in the restaurant for almost two hours. The wine enhanced my already amorous mood, which made it easy for me to express my feelings. Blake and I continually exchanged gazes while playing footsie under the table.

I asked Blake how he felt our relationship was going and he said, "Great."

I agreed and admitted to having strong feelings for him. In fact, before I had a chance to change my mind, I told Blake I had fallen in love with him.

Blake broke into a huge smile and said he was wonderfully surprised.

When asked if he shared similar feelings for me, he responded by saying, "Couldn't you tell?" He stated he recognized a couple of weeks earlier we were getting serious. Blake admitted to having concerns about developing a relationship with me because I had never dated any guys before we met.

In the meantime, Cupid had other ideas and pierced our hearts with his love arrow.

A Most Uncomfortable Conversation

No matter how much I tried to hide my feelings about Blake, they evidently were more apparent than I thought. I usually had Sunday lunch with my parents and, at my mother's invitation, Blake had joined us on a couple of occasions.

On one Sunday afternoon when Blake was not with us for lunch, my mother stated she was uncomfortable with me becoming good friends with Blake; she felt he was not a good influence. I asked her why, and with no hesitation she spelled it out—she thought Blake might be gay.

Yikes! Undoubtedly, this had been fermenting in her mind since the pastor so graciously served his comment about Blake being "pretty."

My mother said she was concerned that my being "jilted" by Charlene had turned me away from girls. My mother's logic tied right in to the commonly-held belief that being gay is a choice and can be flipped on and off like a switch.

In an upset and elevated voice, she blurted, "You are not becoming gay, are you?"

I knew darn well I'd better say no, and that was exactly what I said. I *wanted* to say I was taking lessons so I could determine whether or not to sign up.

Nonetheless, my mother seemed relieved to hear what she wanted to hear, and reiterated my need to be dating girls. She ended the discussion with: "I don't want people in the church to start talking about you."

I was aghast by what had just transpired, and knew my move to Riverside had occurred none too soon.

This was the only time my mother ever asked me "the question," and I never regretted my dishonest answer. I knew I couldn't handle being responsible for dealing my parents such a "body blow." Nor could I cope with the guaranteed religious lecturing and inevitable estrangement resulting from such an admission. I am well aware many folks would disagree with my handling of the situation. But I couldn't tell the truth—to anyone—about my sexuality. From a professional perspective, "coming out" would likely have been career suicide in my field of agricultural work. Remember, this was in the mid-1970s and, as hostile as some groups are toward LGBTQ people today, it was much worse back then.

The Honeymoon Period

In the months following my move, Blake and I started building a relationship and a life together. Blake moved from his apartment to a cute two-bedroom bungalow in Riverside, about five minutes from my apartment. We maintained separate residences, and saw each other about every day. I was happier than I had ever been, as far as my personal life was concerned, and I felt complete. Occasionally, I reflected on how close I had come to getting married to Charlene and what a travesty it would have been. It was, and still is a frightening memory.

As wonderful as my personal life had become, my situation at work was the opposite. The recession in the middle 1970s had a negative consequence on the wholesale nursery business, which was largely tied to a plummeting construction industry. As a result, I was not able to sell our containerized landscape plants as quickly as projected and had significant unsold inventory sitting in the field. Since containerized plants are difficult to maintain for extended periods in peak condition, they become perishable. We lost a lot. Understandably, I didn't receive the promised salary increases, and continued to plod along—glad to be employed.

I was itching to go into my own wholesale nursery business, of which Blake was aware. He had a strong entrepreneurial spirit and was interested in the two of us starting a venture together. I knew how to build and operate a wholesale nursery, but lacked the confidence to strike out alone. What I lacked, Blake had, and what Blake lacked, I had. We believed the winning combination for a successful business partnership was in our hands.

Over my parents' trepidations, Blake and I forged ahead and filed papers of incorporation. It was late 1976 and the recession was abating; things were looking up in Florida. We began to comb property in rural areas suitable for a wholesale nursery operation. We settled on ten acres of land in a neighboring county exploding with growth. Neither of us had the money to buy the land outright, although we each were able to put a substantial amount down. We obtained a five-year mortgage to finance the outstanding amount. In addition, Blake and I obtained a small business loan with a local bank, which was enough to cover our startup costs. We continued to work in our regular jobs and in our spare time prepared the nursery site, which involved a good bit of hard labor. I expected it would take two to three years for us to start turning a profit, so it was imperative we remain employed at least until then.

I told a few trusted friends about our venture and no one else. I couldn't risk my employer finding out I would be a competitor in a couple of years. My looming conflict of interest was a concern, and it was resolved in a few months when I found employment in a non-related industry.

The Devastating End of a Close Friendship

Georgi called one evening and was exuberant in telling me he and a young lady he had been dating were engaged. His news was awesome and I was overjoyed to hear he would soon be getting married. If any man ever wanted—and needed—to get married, it was Georgi. This extremely hardworking and enterprising guy would no doubt be a terrific husband and provider. He asked me to be a groomsman in the wedding, which would take place in a few months. I agreed.

About six weeks prior to the wedding, Georgi dropped by my apartment for a visit. It was the first time we had seen each other in a while, so I expected we would have a lot to chat about. As chance would have it, Blake was at my apartment when Georgi arrived. It was the first time the two had met, although Georgi knew Blake and I were in business together. Surprisingly, Georgi stayed less than ten minutes; the visit was pleasant, even if short.

A couple of days later, I received a terse phone call from him that jolted me like no other I had ever received. In a brief and to the point tirade, Georgi insisted Blake appeared to be gay, and he couldn't imagine I would associate with him unless I also was gay.

I asserted that we were business partners and neither of us was gay.

He didn't buy it. Georgi then "cut me to the knees" by saying he couldn't have someone "like me" as a groomsman in the wedding. As if this was not enough, he finished the insult with the statement: "Since you have already been sent the invitation, I can't stop you from attending the wedding." He closed his diatribe by saying he would never understand how I could choose such a disgusting way of life when I could probably have any girl I wanted. He abruptly ended the call.

It was unquestionably the most hurtful barrage ever leveled against me. It seared my core, and the reality that one of my best friends conveyed it with such vehemence magnified the blow. If ever I was in a state of bewilderment, this was the time. (I didn't attend the wedding.) It took months for me to recover—even now, I recall the stinging phone call in disbelief.

Georgi and I never spoke again, nor did he send an acknowledgment for the wedding gift I sent. Unfortunately, this experience drove me into an unhealthy state of introspection and caused repressed feelings of inferiority to surface. One thing, though, wouldn't change—my sexual orientation was inescapable and fixed. While I have long forgiven Georgi, I will never forget the hurt he dealt.

The Rose Wilts

The ensuing months were arduous in the nursery, as we purchased seeds, started plants from cuttings, and began growing our stock. By the late spring of 1977, the nursery was shaping up. Even so, increasing time requirements and the physical work under the broiling Florida sun were grueling. The nursery began to take a toll on our personal relationship and it became apparent Blake's patience was growing thin. He was an excellent bookkeeper and administrator, yet not as physically inclined or persevering as I was. We began to grow apart as we disagreed on how to run the nursery operation while still maintaining our respective employments. Blake wanted to hire some help to lessen the physical requirements burdening us. Although he had a valid point, it was premature. This luxury was at least two years out, when adequate cash flow was projected. I wouldn't agree to procure another loan, which was a major bone of contention. We saw each other less, and I worked alone at the nursery more often. Accordingly, we decided to dissolve the business partnership while still attempting to maintain our painfully strained personal relationship.

The dissolution of the business partnership was amicable; Blake was as eager as I was to cut the rope. I didn't have the money to buy him out, instead devising a mutually beneficial solution. I proposed we divide the land in half, with me assuming sole ownership of the back half where the fledgling nursery was located. In return, I would assume all debt and he would take sole ownership of the unencumbered front half, which he could sell. He agreed to the proposal and, within a year, doubled his money when he sold his five-acre parcel.

Our relationship was like a roman candle; it burned hot and fast and then came crashing down. Unfortunately, by late 1977 our relationship succumbed to the ordeal as well as to other issues. Even though we lasted less than eighteen months, I will remember Blake for being my first consummated love. Without him, I may never have gone into my own nursery business, which in time became a successful venture. Blake eventually left Jacksonville for North Carolina and ultimately returned to his home in Alabama.

Astrological Road Trip

Prior to the implosion of my relationship with Blake, we met a guy named Lou Roberts, as the result of a chance encounter at the home of my friend and physician, Dr. Edwards. We developed a quick rapport and became lifelong friends. Our personalities were similar, and he had an infectious, off-the-wall sense of humor. Lou could have been on stage; he had a nonstop wit and a penchant for storytelling that had people in stitches. He was naturally a comedian, even though he didn't seem to be aware of how entertaining he was.

Lou was four years older than me, street-smart, well educated, an experienced traveler, and was gifted with a broad-spectrum innate intelligence enabling him to give me (and many others) advice on anything. Whether it be direction in investing, real estate, ferreting out shopping bargains, or even the appropriate use of tools (my challenges in this department are well documented), he became my trusted confidant.

When Lou was twelve years old, his father passed away, leaving him, his mother, and his sister to fend for themselves. The three surviving family members struggled for a number of years with no outside support, yet managed to hold things together with little glue. Undoubtedly, the experience provided Lou with survivor skills which prepared him for adulthood; much of his knowledge was acquired as a consequence of family hardships.

One of Lou's outstanding "skills" was his ability to calm me down when I got worked up about "emergencies" most clear-thinking individuals would instantly dismiss. One of the funniest of these occurrences transpired in the wake of my eavesdropping. While at work one morning, I overheard two women quietly discussing physical symptoms one of them was experiencing. The diagnosis indicated that a dreaded surgical procedure was possible, which was reflected on their worried countenances. I couldn't ascertain everything said, but clearly heard the part about lower back pain, cramping, discomfort during a bowel movement, and the name of the disease. I was experiencing identical symptoms, which is what stimulated my attention. Naturally, I promptly deduced I had the same affliction. (These were the days before instant online "self-diagnosis.") Obviously, medical intervention was needed, and, as soon as I could get to a phone I called my personal 911 consultant, Lou. It didn't take him long to conclude my symptoms were likely attributable to gas and constipation—particularly after I shared my perceived malady was called endometriosis. He assured me it was impossible for me to have the condition since it was exclusively reserved for women. Boy, was I relieved.

One other noteworthy story involving Lou had to do with a short road trip. One Saturday evening, he loaded up his "land yacht"—which was akin to a limousine—and hauled a group of us to South Daytona Beach, which was a little over an hour down I-95. Our destination was an "institution" called the Zodiac Lounge, a legend in our general region of the state for its female impersonator shows. I had never been to one of these productions prior to this excursion. We arrived at the tabernacle of debauchery early—we had to. Not only were the needs of the local populace served, it also attracted pilgrims from Orlando and Jacksonville—so it filled up fast. This was surely not on my list of Southern Baptist–recommended businesses, and I sort of freaked out when we arrived. Lou had to circle the parking lot twice while I perused the crowd to make sure everything looked "safe." It made little sense then and makes less sense now. I was reluctant to go inside; he assured me it was a "respectable" establishment and advised me to get a grip. He parked the car.

Once we found our way through the entry door, we strategically positioned ourselves adjacent to the stage, which was an engineering marvel fully equipped with runways. And after what seemed to be a long wait, another marvel was unleashed.

The room lights dimmed, and an explosion of fantasy began. Multicolored lights suddenly swirled and the glow of runway lights announced something *fab-u-lusss* was about to happen. With an intensifying sense of wonder, my wide eyes were transfixed. The music cranked up and, like magic, a parade of "beauties" flew out of the backstage darkness—on roller skates! Flowing, sequin-embellished gowns wafted in the drafts created by these circling wonders on wheels. Everything was over the top. Hair creations that must have been erected by mechanical engineers were not to be outdone by layers of makeup paint, likely provided by the magicians at Sherwin-Williams. Highly glossed lips and meticulously applied eye glitter gloriously complemented the final piece of supreme womanliness—copiously cultivated busts. All components together created an unbelievable, yet believable symphony of illusion.

One illusion in particular I will never forget was a vision in lilac, named Latese Chevron. This mixed-race beauty nearly scared me out of the place when she leaned down and tried to put her hand through my hair. When I jumped back, she said, "Oh, we have a shy one." Although she toyed with me for a few seconds, this "fright" didn't diminish my attraction to the place—so much, in fact, that a second trek to the Zodiac Lounge with Lou and his entourage would occur.

The Zodiac Lounge was eventually demolished. Gladly, my memories of it (and Latese) steadfastly remain.

Chapter 24

Up, Up, and Away

The year 1977 was laced with personal heartbreak, although the joy of watching the plants in the nursery respond to meticulous nurturing mitigated the disappointments. I desperately needed to find a conflict-of-interest-free job to provide a decent income until the time when the nursery could pay me a salary. I calculated it would take two more years before I had sufficient quantities of saleable plants to allow for this.

I mentioned to Gail Petrini (Anthony's wife) that I was looking for a job, and she told me Delta Air Lines was hiring reservation sales agents at their regional office near downtown Jacksonville. Millicent Baker worked there and had recently told Gail that Delta was hiring, thinking she may be interested. She wasn't, but I surely was. I obtained an application and submitted it along with a personal letter to Mr. Harry Williamson, the local manager. My opening sentence was: "If you are looking for a dependable, hardworking, self-starting individual, you can end your search with this one application."

I was called for an interview the day my letter was received by Mr. Williamson. Millicent advised me if the interview went well, I would be required to take a typing test on an electric typewriter. Yes, such an advanced communication device really did exist, and Delta required a minimum passing score of thirty correct words per minute. Fortuitously, I had taken typing in high school, but had not typed to any degree since graduating from UF, five years prior. Furthermore, I had never typed on an electric model. To ameliorate the situation, I rented an electric typewriter and spent the next several evenings practicing.

The interview was conducted a week later, and it went well; a few minutes later I was ushered into a room where the hallowed electric typewriter was enthroned, awaiting its next victim—me. I took the test and was told to wait while Mr. Williamson's secretary graded it. Soon I was cheerfully greeted with the news that I had typed fifty-five correct words per minute. My reward was a plane ticket to Atlanta, where a final interview would take place. "Mr. Vicarson, will you be able to participate in a final interview in Atlanta on Thursday at 11:00 a.m.?"

Wow, this was two days out—two days! I said yes and took the ticket, and within seconds my insides transformed into a cauldron of "upsetness." This was my body's usual response to stress, real or imagined. Surely, I was excited to be invited for a final interview, but was unnerved by the prospect of flying, even though I had survived flying to Dallas four years prior. Admittedly, this made no sense for someone applying to work for an airline.

I decided the best way to handle my dilemma was to drive five and a half hours to Atlanta for the interview and then drive back. It would indeed be a grueling day; however, the idea yielded a sense of calm. I discussed my intention with Millicent, who strongly advised against this course of action for a number of reasons. More important, she insisted it would send the wrong message to Delta. She told me Delta encouraged employees to experience firsthand the product they sell, and I might even be asked during the interview about my flight to Atlanta. I mulled it over and decided to "man up" and take the jet. Interestingly, I loved airplanes and was amazed at the wonder of flight. I was well aware my fear was an irrational holdover from the time, when as a six-year-old kid, I had witnessed the aftermath of the aforementioned Eastern Airlines crash.

"Delta Is Ready When You Are"

For me, this long-running slogan—which was impossible to miss—was never more fitting. As instructed, I reported for my 8:30 a.m. flight to Atlanta forty minutes in advance. Though I was on a standby basis, I was not worried about getting bumped since ample seats were available. Much to my delight, I was boarded in first class and, shortly after takeoff, was served a hot breakfast. By the time we landed in Atlanta, I was already in love with Delta Air Lines and enthusiastic about the possibility of being an employee.

The interview took place without incident, and a few days later I received a congratulatory letter. My training had been approved, and I was advised my class would commence in ten days. I was energized with a resurgent confidence in my future, and composed a letter of resignation to Mr. Halverson, my employer. Unfortunately, I was not able to give a two-week notice. He seemed surprised I was resigning to go to work for Delta Air Lines and predicted I wouldn't like it. This time, he made no attempt to persuade me to remain in his employment. While my reasons for leaving were not related to compensation, Delta's pay and benefits package were "sky miles" ahead of what I had.

As requested, I reported for a three-week training class at Delta's Jacksonville Reservations Sales Center. The office had about 200 employees, most of whom were college graduates and all well-dressed. Thirteen people were in my training class, and we quickly became a close-knit group.

The work environment was collegial; however, being confined to a telephone was a challenge. Even so, I excelled in class, and in a relatively short time was my team's leader in sales production. I worked a late-afternoon shift, which gave me the daylight hours to work in my nursery. My goal was to be able to quit Delta in 1980, to work exclusively in my nursery. This goal was shared with no one.

Floor Exercises

Shortly after beginning my employment at Delta, one of the supervisors called me into her office "just to chat" for a few minutes. She took the opportunity to welcome me to the office, which I thought was strange since she was not my supervisor. I was in for a surprise.

She said, "Seth, you will find you are among many friends here at Delta, and in fact, you and I have a mutual friend."

I had no clue who she was talking about, and when she said it was Dr. Edwards, I must have turned white. I thought, *Oh Lord, she knows I'm gay.*

She reacted to my astonishment by saying, "You are not alone and your secret is safe. Pick yourself up off the floor."

She was reassuring, and I thanked her profusely for putting me at ease.

In time, I discovered many other gay and lesbian folks worked in our office. Most of us were closeted, although several pioneers amazingly made no efforts to hide their sexuality. Fortunately, Delta management didn't seem to care. Even so, it was assumed that moving up the corporate ladder would be difficult for anyone who was gay. This was not a concern since my ambitions were more tied to the nursery than to Delta.

If ever there was anyone paranoid about being "found out," it was me. Other than my gay colleagues, no one in the office knew my secret—as far as I knew. However, there was one incident that tripped my high-alert alarms. One afternoon, I arrived at work to find a sealed note lying on my desk. I opened it. It was short and to the point—and the point surely made an impression.

"Dear Seth, we know you will never seek us out, but we want you to know we are here for you." It was signed, "Your Admiring Ladies."

It freaked me out (everything did), and I assumed the note was a reference to my sexual orientation, which I had made all efforts to hide. I was concerned that Millicent, who knew many people in my church, would find out I was gay. I remained uneasy for weeks. I feared Pandora's box was about to spill its contents. This didn't happen, and I never found out who wrote the note.

At Delta, I made many friends. We worked together, partied together, and traveled the world together. It was here I learned about the horrors of endometriosis. Delta was my magic carpet and I took advantage of many opportunities to navigate the globe. My fear of flying vanished, and I fell in love with my colleagues and my employer. It was the most cohesive, caring group of people I have ever known. The collegial atmosphere was directly attributable to how well Delta matched personalities to the job. My tenure at Delta was life changing.

Since my position required I work every other weekend and at night, I could no longer remain in the church choir. This was a positive tradeoff. I was surrounded by individuals with backgrounds and experiences different than mine. This was largely because Delta embraced diversity long before the term was in vogue or even valued. My previously myopic perspectives were shattered and I soon developed a much more open world view. The changes in me were exciting, as my expanding mind created a desire to embrace this new world of diversity. What a gift!

I continued to work at my flourishing nursery during the mornings and on my days off. Demands at the nursery were the least in the winter months and, accordingly, I took advantage of Delta-related opportunities during this time. I discovered the joy of skiing at numerous locations out West and even in Europe. My many friendships at Delta had become deep, and, in fact, I had more close friends there (both straight and gay) than I ever imagined possible. It was indeed an extremely happy time in my life; I experienced true joy.

Chapter 25

Where the Boys Are

It was late 1979, just before the AIDS explosion, and the sexual revolution which began in the 1960s was in full swing. I was dumbfounded to discover sex among some in the gay community could be a free-for-all. Being conservative by nature and basically unaware, I was not prepared for this aspect of gay life.

Gay acceptance in mainstream society was still generally nonexistent, particularly in ultra-resistant Jacksonville. Consequently, secrecy was the rule for many of us. Unquestionably, I fell into the secretive lot and rarely went to bars. When I did go, it was when accompanied by a group of friends. Besides, I didn't think the kind of men interesting to me would be found in a smoke-filled bar. I was looking for an individual who was well-educated, a nonsmoker, gainfully employed, understated, not into alcohol (social drinkers were not a problem), and into fitness. Religious affiliation was not particularly important. Admittedly, my "specifications" narrowed the field.

I was not as active in church as I had been prior to my Delta employment, yet still attended services often enough. One afternoon, I was having a conversation with my good friend Leonard, and expressed frustration that the only place to meet gay men seemed to be in gay bars. He informed me I was wrong and said he had recently discovered something I would find shocking. He whispered that there were four other gay men in the choir, whom he initially wouldn't identify. I couldn't believe it. I had never considered anyone in the choir (other than Leonard) could be gay, particularly in a Baptist church—in my Baptist church! There were gay Christians other than Leonard and me? Five gay choir members (including Leonard) represented about a third of the men in the choir, which was an astounding percentage, considering the percentage of gays in the general population was reportedly much less. Had I still been in the choir, the number would have been six. Leonard invited me to join this rather "special" subset of choir members, who would be getting together following the next choir practice—and luckily, I was scheduled to be off work.

When Connie Francis sang her iconic song, "Where the Boys Are," it never occurred to me she was referring to my church choir.

Thursday night came, and boy, was my curiosity ever aroused. I drove to the church, cruised around the block several times while waiting for the choir crowd to disperse, and then parked the car in the back lot.

Soon, Leonard came out of the building and hopped into his car, which was my cue to join him. When I opened the door of his car, he requested I sit in the back since one other person was going to ride with us. While we waited, Leonard told me two additional choir members would be meeting us at a predetermined location. The destination was Brothers, the gay bar in Riverside. Even with my urging, Leonard still had not told me who would be joining us, so an air of drama added to the suspense. No doubt, Leonard was having fun, keeping me dangling.

I had not noticed someone had walked up to the car, and before I could say "Holy Saint Anthony," he opened the door and ducked in—it was Anthony Petrini! I about fainted. Fortunately, I was already sitting down and therefore able to avoid any embarrassing theatrics.

When Anthony saw me, he initially seemed perturbed and gasped to Leonard, "What is he doing in the car?"

I didn't wait for Leonard to answer and advised Anthony we had a lot in common.

His mouth dropped open; he was flabbergasted. So was I.

Even though Brothers was close to my apartment, I stayed in Leonard's car for the ride rather than driving my own, and in doing so I found out who would be meeting us. The disclosure was anticlimactic, given the "pièce de résistance" had been served first—and sat within inches of me.

When I walked into the near-empty bar with Leonard and Anthony, we spotted the two other choir buddies, and wow, did we ever have a confab. We were in amazement that we had all flown into the same church choir nest. We compared notes as to who else in the church we thought could be gay. The "who-do-you-think-might-be-gay game" is an interesting gay pastime. Funny thing: it's usually not who you think. We broke up for the evening around ten. Oh, what a night. Never did I remotely consider Anthony Petrini could be gay, even though I had fantasized about him since we first met in 1972. Not surprisingly, this narrative was just beginning. I had some questions and wondered if Gail (Anthony's wife) did.

It Was Inevitable

After going to work at Delta and starting my nursery business, I had seen Anthony infrequently. He and Gail were busy with their own careers as well, and recently had an addition to their family—a little boy. With the revelation that Anthony and I had way more in common than either of us ever realized, we were bound to become much closer friends.

Not long after Anthony and I shocked each other in Leonard's car, we had the chance for a quick chat in the men's room at church. It was one of those "we need to talk" types of exchanges. The two of us genuinely wanted to have an honest conversation and decided to meet at my apartment one afternoon when we were both off work. Since we each frequently had time off in the middle of the week, it was not difficult to arrange. We didn't waste any time getting the huddle scheduled, and a few days later Anthony knocked on my door.

Admittedly, I had "visions of sugar plums" whenever I saw him; I also knew any progression of our friendship had the potential to blow up the universe. We both knew it. My lifelong friendship with Gail and her family, our families' prominence in the church, and Anthony's importance as a deacon in the church were huge deterrents.

As soon as Anthony stepped inside my apartment, we embraced each other in a tight bear hug, and then sat at my small kitchen table. We talked for probably two hours, maybe more. I had a barrage of questions for Anthony, and he had a few for me as well. First, I was curious to learn if he knew he was gay when he married Gail, and, secondly, how he was able to maintain a sexual relationship with her. After all, they had two kids. He was straightforward—he knew he was gay well before he married Gail. Without my asking, he explained that getting married was a family expectation and he wanted kids; marrying Gail seemed appropriate. He added that he loved Gail and had believed once he was married, his same-sex desires could be sublimated. Indeed, his theory resurrected a still-raw chord within me. When I asked if this had happened, his answer was a short "Not at all."

I expressed to Anthony that I didn't understand how he could have sex with Gail if he was gay. Before he answered, he questioned whether or not Charlene and I had ever had sexual relations. He seemed surprised when I told him we had not, particularly considering our long-term relationship. Anthony said having sex with Gail was a mind-over-matter exercise. Even so, he shared that he knew the infrequency of their having sex was not normal for a young couple. He suspected Gail couldn't be happy with their sex life, and acknowledged he was in a growing predicament. He said his love for Gail had not prevented him from ignoring his natural sexual impulses.

Even though surprised, I understood, being painfully aware that guys come fully equipped with hard-to-control sex drives. I can't imagine most men—gay or straight—can put a throttle on natural urges for any significant duration. Undoubtedly, this is why marriage is such a popular contract. For a gay man who is married to a woman (or vice versa), it is even more problematic; the effectiveness of mind games to "play straight" is inevitably going to sputter, if not cease. Anthony had reached this point at around age thirty; he admitted to having had same-sex encounters for several years, primarily in New York City where he occasionally worked. I asked him if Gail suspected he might be gay, and he nonchalantly said he didn't know.

There was no conversation about the two of us pursuing anything sexual. However, there was now a bond between us that heretofore didn't exist. More conversations would follow in the weeks to come, and we became close. Anthony's experience in marriage served to further confirm my marriage to Charlene would have ended in a personal catastrophe. Thank God, this didn't occur. My dread was Anthony and Gail were unavoidably headed for some rough times.

Bitter Honey

During one of our tête-à-têtes, probably about a month after our initial "discovery session," Anthony and I were sitting on the couch in his and Gail's living room. Anthony and I were drinking beer (God forbid), sitting fairly close. My recollection is Gail was at work and the kids were probably in daycare. The physical proximity to him and my slightly dulled inhibitions amplified my yearnings.

I could no longer resist the temptation, and asked Anthony if I could kiss him.

Without hesitation he said, "I didn't think you were ever going to ask."

I laughed and replied, "Why didn't *you* ask me?"

He responded, "Because I have never had to ask. Guys have always come to me."

Gee. I received a teasing dose of his ego, but didn't care. We exchanged one heck of a kiss, and I was transported back seven years to our romp in the pool at Millicent's apartment complex. This time, I didn't have to fake a pulled back muscle to hide the excitement evident in my shorts. Neither did Anthony. We were passionate for a few minutes, at which point we stopped. Nothing beyond heavy kissing transpired. Even so, I knew we had waded into forbidden waters.

For days, I was preoccupied with Anthony's kiss of honey and couldn't stop tasting it. There was no denying I wanted more—while knowing how wrong it would be for every reason. Nonetheless, my newly-lit "pilot light" was a flickering ember, and I was eminently aware the slightest passionate overture would be like throwing gasoline on it. Anthony and I started talking to each other more frequently. It didn't take long for us to meet at my apartment one morning.

Initially, Anthony's visit seemed casual, yet the sparks between us were flying as we stood inches apart, barely inside the front door of the living room. Before we had the chance to sit down, he stated how much he'd enjoyed our interlude of brief passion during our last get-together. My heart was already pounding, and my sensibilities were blown to smithereens by his comment. Neither of us uttered another word. We embraced each other and kissed for what seemed like an hour—certainly it was much less. Thus, the foundation was laid for a torrid but short affair.

In the weeks to come, Anthony and I saw each other several times, which was not difficult with our odd work schedules. We were careful in planning our rendezvous and met at my apartment. It was apparent our emotional involvement was increasing—too much so—and I became uneasy. My primary apprehension was that somehow Gail was going to "smell smoke," if she hadn't already. Anthony seemed less concerned; however, my cautionary nature—and guilt—began to erode the excitement that initially had heralded our mutual infatuation. Anthony clearly wanted a committed relationship with me and at the same time wanted to maintain his family life.

Without question, this had the makings of a barnyard mess, and, accordingly, I wouldn't give Anthony such a commitment. I believed what little love life Gail and Anthony had would unavoidably be eliminated by his distraction with me. I feared Gail would become disillusioned with their loveless marriage, which would exacerbate an already tenuous relationship. My ultimate nightmare was that I could be implicated in a hugely embarrassing, high-profile exposure and divorce. We backed off and returned to being good friends.

Jimmy Carter Made Me Do It

Matthew 5:27–28 (NIV) says, "You have heard that it was said, you shall not commit adultery. But I tell you that anyone who looks at a woman lustfully has already committed adultery with her in his heart." Certainly, Anthony was not a woman, yet I considered this Scripture to still be applicable to me. I will venture to say few people who have walked this earth haven't lusted in their heart. Former president Jimmy Carter grappled with this, according to his well-documented admission in a November 1976 *Playboy* magazine interview. I extrapolated that since I harbored lustful desires for Anthony and thus was already deemed guilty, then I might as well commit the act. This was my initial justification—albeit a seriously erroneous one—for my affair with Anthony. The affair was a blatant betrayal of my good friend Gail, of Anthony, of their two children—and also a betrayal of myself. I trust God has forgiven me, but I still think about those days with tremendous remorse. Of all the "trespasses" I have committed in my life, the Anthony indiscretion is at the top of the list and the one for which I am most ashamed.

In the months following my affair with Anthony, I saw him and Gail in church fairly often. From all outward appearances, they seemed to be the perfect family. Both had great jobs, were good-looking, and they had two precious children. I knew the ugly truth. It was all I could do to even look at Gail, knowing what I had done. Even so, Anthony and I remained friends and occasionally had some frank discussions about his marriage, among other things. How he managed to keep his extracurricular life concealed was a wonder. "Wonders never cease," but this particular wonder eventually did.

Chapter 26

Out of the Blue

My good friend Leonard Brewer had a medical need requiring professional attention, so I introduced him to Dr. Edwards (my friend, physician, and landlord). Within a few months they became partners. Stranger matchups have occurred, but this arrangement was unlikely. The affable Dr. Edwards was as laid-back as a beach blanket; Leonard was the opposite. There was an age gap of about twenty-five years between them, yet they shared a keen interest in antiques and fine art. As fate would have it, Dr. Edwards owned an antique store, which was right next door to the apartment building where I lived. Not surprisingly, Leonard ended up managing the store. The antique store would also serve as the headquarters of Leonard's "matchmaking avocation," at which he was skilled.

My dating life had slipped back into "quiet mode," and Leonard was determined to give me a "system reboot." He thought I was incapable of finding datable guys on my own, which was a correct assumption since I didn't go to bars. I was much more comfortable working from "referrals."

One early fall afternoon in 1981, as I was about to leave my apartment to go to work at Delta, Leonard called and asked me to come over to the antique shop. Ostensibly, he needed me to help him and a friend reposition a piece of furniture. I obliged, and when I entered the shop, Leonard introduced me to a guy named Barry Cardine. An item in which Barry was interested was squeezed behind a large couch.

Clearly, there was no real need for me to help them move the couch, but I assisted nonetheless—with an eye fixed on Barry. It was impossible not to notice he was handsome and probably about five years younger than me. He was slightly taller than average, had big Mediterranean-blue eyes, thick brown hair, and arrow-straight teeth. He looked a little like Ricky Nelson, who was a popular singer-actor in the late 1950s and 1960s.

Leonard, Barry, and I talked for about five minutes, at which point I had to leave. In this short time span, I found out Barry had recently split with his partner of several years, lived in an apartment around the corner, and worked in his father's construction business. It would never have occurred to me he was gay. I was interested in getting better acquainted with Barry, which was Leonard's supposition when he had asked me to help them move the couch.

When I got home from work a little after midnight, there was a note taped on my kitchen door from Leonard, asking me to call him when I had a chance. I made sure the chance presented itself at a more reasonable morning hour. I called Leonard around nine o'clock, before going out to the nursery. Much to my elation, I was told Barry would welcome a call from me if I was so inclined. *Inclined* was hardly the word to describe my enthusiasm. It had been well over a year since I had dated anyone. Since Barry was already at a jobsite with no phone access, the phone call would have to wait until later.

The opportunity came at 8:00 p.m., and I made the call to Barry from the Delta employee lounge. I apologized for not getting back to him sooner; Leonard had already apprised Barry of my wacky schedule. The call was short. The result was a date on my next off day, which was a couple of days out, on Thursday.

Thursday evening came and we decided to keep it simple and not go out anywhere. After eating a quick dinner at home, I walked over to Barry's apartment, which took every bit of two minutes. His apartment was one of several units in a 1930s-era, two-story brick building with a green barrel-tiled roof. A neighborhood grocery occupied the bottom floor of the building and the apartments were perched directly above. Each apartment had white multipaned French doors opening to balconies facing the street below. Like Juliet, Barry was on his balcony when I was walking across the street toward his building. I waved to him, and he directed me to use the stairs in the back. He met me at the door and ushered me into the apartment, which was a surprising departure from the building's exterior. It was sleek, minimally decorated, uncluttered, and equipped with high-tech lighting. He had an affinity for pop art, with two Andy Warhol prints hanging on the walls. The space was reminiscent of loft apartments in New York, which Barry frequently visited.

We made a fast, warm connection and talked until the wee hours of the night. We both had an appreciation for plants, were into fitness, shared a love for New York (where I had recently worked on a temporary assignment), and neither of us smoked. We started dating, and within a few short weeks I had become deeply and intensely invested in Barry. My relationship with him was different than what I'd experienced with Blake. I was physically attracted to both, yet the emotional attraction I had for Barry far surpassed what I had felt for Blake. Barry was worldly, grounded, continually looking to improve himself, and he exceeded my basic "requisites." The rapidity in which I became so attached to him defied all logic, and even now I don't understand why, from a psychological perspective, I fell so hard so fast.

About two months into the relationship, I could sense Barry was becoming less affectionate and a little distant. When questioned, he dismissed my concerns and attributed his detachment to being stressed out at work, which I knew was an ongoing problem for him. In a short time, I knew something else was wrong, as he increasingly pushed back. Finally, after much prodding, he admitted his ex-partner, Scott, was pressing for a reconciliation, and they had recently seen each other several times. Barry assured me there would be no reconciliation, although he needed some time to help Scott work through it. I believed Barry, probably because I couldn't stand the thought of losing him. Things were destined to become bizarre.

One morning, I saw Barry walking up the driveway to my apartment building and rushed out to meet him, thinking he was coming to see me. Much to my disappointment, he was discernably not interested in engaging in any substantive conversation. He was squirmy, elusive, and seemed generally uncomfortable with my presence. A few seconds later, Leonard showed up with a ring of keys in his hand. Only then did Barry tell me Leonard was showing him the recently vacated apartment directly above mine. In a shocked tone, all I could say was "What?" Barry mumbled that he was interested in renting it because his apartment—which I knew he loved—was too small. I was speechless. He offered no further elaboration, and I could sense any questions I would like to have asked were unwelcome. Barry took Leonard upstairs to see the unit, and I took the cue to retreat to my own apartment. About fifteen minutes later, they came back downstairs, noticeably without stopping by my apartment. I was perplexed, and suspected there was much more to this story.

Christmas was about a week out, and I had not spoken to Barry since our brief encounter in the driveway several days before. One night, I discovered a beautifully wrapped gift propped against my back door, which Barry knew I used exclusively to access my apartment. A brief generic note was attached: "Merry Christmas from Barry." Upon opening the package, I found an expensive, burgundy-and-white-striped Calvin Klein shirt. It was beautiful, and I was buoyed.

My World Shatters

I called Barry the next day to thank him. He was distant, yet seemed open to my suggestion of seeing each other soon. Well, the bizarre turned into the unbelievable.

The next morning, Barry, with the assistance of a friend whom I didn't know, starting moving into the apartment directly above me. This was not a total surprise, as I knew Barry had rented the apartment. An amalgam of excitement and curiosity was burning in my stomach, so I decided to go upstairs, ostensibly to offer help. Of course my mission was for fact-finding purposes and any help I could offer was a peripheral consideration.

I was greeted at the open door of the apartment by the friend who was helping Barry move in. I introduced myself and asked if there was anything I could do to assist. He had little personality and didn't introduce himself. In a speedy estimation, I judged he was devoid of social graces.

He was coolly appreciative of my offer and said, "Thanks, we don't need any help. Sorry for the noise. We expect to be settled into our apartment later tonight."

The word *our* screamed in my head. Barry never came to the door, which was consistent with his recent behavior. The chimes then rang: he was moving into the apartment with someone else—more than likely, Scott, his "ex-partner."

In a state of disbelief, I retreated to my apartment downstairs and called Leonard. He had previously said nothing to me about this unfolding apartment drama, which was no surprise, given his nature to be tight-lipped. In his usual matter-of-fact manner, he confirmed my assumption; the "mystery man" I had met was undoubtedly Barry's "ex-partner," Scott. Boy, was Barry ever pulling out all the stops in his effort to help Scott "come to terms with them breaking up!" I was astounded. Scott was average-looking at best and not personable (at least, not to me). He did have the "redeeming factor" of a nice build. I couldn't reconcile the in-my-face reality that Barry was attracted to Scott and still harbored affection for him. Why else would they be setting up housekeeping together? It was eating me up. I painfully acknowledged Barry was probably keeping me on the string while he figured out what he wanted. Still, I couldn't exercise a modicum of dignity by severing the string Barry held. I was possessed by him and had never been in such a fog of bewilderment over any relationship.

The Love Nest Is Occupied

Clanging sounds of dishes, pots and pans, and silverware were followed by annoying floor screeches from the positioning and repositioning of furniture. With each passing minute, my increasing irritation yielded to anger, although my anger had little to do with the noise. Finally, at about 11:00 p.m., the noise mercifully ended, and I went to bed. I tossed there, wide awake, in an inescapable, all-encompassing quietness that had become a prison. My own internal circuitry, which was already on high alert, prevented me from going to sleep. The unsettling silence was soon interrupted by the more unsettling sounds of unintelligible conversation and occasional giggling from upstairs. It got louder. The lack of soundproofing in the 1940s-era building and the state of my heightened senses forced me to listen to the unmistakable sounds of bouncing bedsprings from their lair directly above me. There were accompanying moans, gasps, and squeals confirming the reality of a reconciled couple.

Immersed in my emotions, I was reduced to a state of abject distress—like no other I had ever experienced. All the "road signs" that should have warned me to step back—weeks prior—had gone largely unheeded.

I was unable to sleep the entire night, and crawled out of bed in the morning looking like a mentally disturbed individual—and in reality, I was. My eyes were swollen, with distinct circles underneath, and my naturally heavy, nearly-black beard was rather pronounced since I had not shaved the day before. My ego was laid to waste and my heart broken. With the ultimate rejection slammed in my face, I ambled around the apartment in a trancelike state of disbelief. I found myself repeating out loud, "I can't believe this," over and over and over. For lack of a better term, I was in some sort of psychological concussion and consumed by a feeling of crashing desolation. Fortunately, I had two days off from work leading up to Christmas and had planned to work in the nursery during this time. I couldn't bring myself to leave the house and—instead of going to the nursery—I chose to simmer in my emotional cesspool.

The "reconciliation" of Barry and Scott, magnified by Barry's lack of honesty about it, spiraled me into the abyss of depression. I didn't want to see anyone, speak to anyone, or participate in any holiday activities. This depression was noticeably different than what I had experienced in high school. The onset was sudden, and the intensity reduced me to a pile of rubble. Unlike my high school despair, the causal mechanism of this near-collapse was clearly apparent.

My parents would be hosting a big Christmas dinner at noon on Christmas Day, which was two days away. I had to go. Christmas came, and I dragged myself out of my self-imposed apartment incarceration and went to my parents' house. I ate little, which was highly unusual for me—the human garbage can, as my brother frequently described me. I insisted I had an upset stomach, and everyone seemed to believe me. I stayed until about two, and then left. My personal problems had me engrossed, and all I desired was to find a cave and hibernate. Nevertheless, I went to work, which forced me to temporarily divert my entire focus from myself.

The days following Christmas were a living hell. I desperately wanted to talk to Barry and couldn't find the right opportunity; I knew it was inevitable our paths would soon cross. Nights continued to be long and restless, with no diversions to dull my misery. At least the bedroom antics upstairs diminished. I had excessive time to dwell on being heartsick. It was the first time in my life I had experienced significant personal anguish as a result of being enraptured with someone who didn't share the same feelings. It was all the more reason to reflect on my relationship with Charlene and to fully comprehend her devastation when we broke up. I hated the thought.

Several days after Christmas, Barry and I took our trash-laden garbage cans out to the street within seconds of each other. It was too late for him to find an escape route around me; he was semi-cordial, and we exchanged the usual "good mornings." I tried to start a conversation, and it was clear Barry didn't want to talk—he tersely stated he needed to go to work. Determined, I was not going to allow him to slip by so easily.

As he started to walk off, I grabbed him by the arm and, with pent-up anger, said, "Not so fast. You can spare me a damn minute."

He jerked his arm back and shrieked, "What do you want!"

I replied, "Honesty about your relationship with Scott."

Unbelievably, he insisted they were primarily roommates.

Without thinking, I blurted, "So this is why I heard the two of you banging your brains out right above my head at eleven o'clock the night you moved in?"

My incendiary comment infuriated Barry, and I was promptly informed his sex life was none of my business. He was right, but it didn't stop me from disputing it was my business when their ruckus kept me from being able to sleep. Truthfully, I was already wide awake and probably would have heard a roach crawling on the floor upstairs.

Nonetheless, this unpleasant exchange with Barry killed any vestige of affection he may have felt for me. No matter how much I had tried to make it work, it was not going to happen.

Barry and I had no substantive communication for two years.

Recovery

The months following the Barry fiasco were overwhelmingly challenging, as my heartache persisted. Every time I heard Sheena Easton singing "You Could Have Been with Me" on the radio, I cried like a baby. Gosh, did that song ever resurrect easy-to-tap emotions—emotions that stayed raw for an inordinately long time. I continued to muddle through life and worked through my depression without any outside assistance—which surely would have helped. Physical work at the nursery, jogging, and working out in the gym were hugely cathartic, as was my job at Delta.

In about six months, the light at the end of the tunnel was visible, and I emerged from it a much wiser man. Even so, my emotional attraction to Barry was unlike anything I had ever experienced; I continued to long for him, even after my depression abated. My reaction to the failed, relatively short-term relationship with Barry defied all logic, and even now it puzzles me as to why I was so besotted. One takeaway for me is that the length of a relationship can't be used to measure intensity of affection.

Several long months after Barry and Scott moved into the apartment above me, the sound of bouncing bedsprings was replaced by the raised voices of two not-so-in-love-anymore individuals. I couldn't ascertain the exact content of their heated exchanges, though I did my best to listen. At last, the saga ended, with Barry and Scott moving out and going their separate ways. A couple of years later, Barry moved to Atlanta, but not before our lives would intersect again.

Of my failed relationships, the one with Barry evoked the most intense emotion. Occasionally I think of him and have a different perspective than I had during that painfully crippling time in 1981. Barry had valid reasons to give his relationship with Scott another try; I probably would have done no less, had I been in his shoes.

Believe it or not, the Calvin Klein dress shirt Barry gave me has held up beautifully through the years, and I still occasionally wear it.

Chapter 27

A House of Cards Comes Tumbling Down

Anthony and Gail's marriage had miraculously continued to percolate right along until early 1982, when Gail made a shocking discovery that turned her world—and Anthony's—upside down. Anthony called me soon after he returned from a trip to New York City and had a decidedly serious tone to his voice. My first thought was he was being transferred to New York, or even worse, something had happened between Gail and him. It was the latter.

Without any emotion, he told me that prior to his trip, Gail had inadvertently discovered a directory to New York City gay bars that he had packed in his suitcase. She opened the suitcase to place something in it and saw the directory. She confronted Anthony, who was caught red-handed and defenseless; he admitted to Gail he was gay.

All I can remember saying was an emphatic, "Oh, no!" The resulting "emotional shrapnel" blasting me after hearing such horrific news left me numb—I just about dropped to the floor. Even though shocked, I was not surprised Gail had finally uncovered his other life. What I had long feared would happen, had indeed happened. I didn't ask Anthony many questions, and listened intently as he discussed the unfolding family tragedy. He confided that Gail was justifiably mortified and he expected she would file for divorce. Anthony bemoaned the humiliation this would create for him, Gail, and their respective families. Fortunately, their kids were too young to fully understand the morass surrounding them.

Gail soon filed for divorce. The news of their marriage dissolution hit the church airwaves and spread like an epidemic. A few people initially knew the true reason for their split. My mother questioned me as to why the "golden couple" was getting a divorce; I played dumb and told no one what I knew—especially my mother. Inevitably, the revelation of Anthony's "unthinkable sin" found its way to a few additional folks. And the extreme gossip-worthiness of this breaking news propelled it throughout the congregation. I hated it more than I can describe and my heart ached for all parties involved. Fortunately, I was not implicated. Nevertheless, for many years I was haunted by the disintegration of Gail and Anthony's marriage.

No doubt, rumors about my sexuality were circulating around the church. I had never married, was thirty-three years old, didn't date, and Anthony was a close friend. As a result, I became paranoid about Gail eventually connecting the dots between Anthony and me. To my knowledge, she never did. Gail eventually remarried and moved to another state where she and her husband raised the kids.

Not surprisingly, Anthony left Jacksonville after the divorce; he moved to Atlanta, which has long been the destination of choice for gay escapees living in the South. There, he found a partner and a new work life in the burgeoning communications industry. Through the ensuing years, we occasionally talked—but only when I called him. Anthony seemed pleased to hear from me; however, I wondered if I was too much a reminder of the excruciating circumstances he had left behind.

Ironically, there was a groundbreaking movie, called *Making Love*, which was released about the time Anthony and Gail divorced. The movie revolves around a young, beautiful, superstar married couple who start experiencing marital problems eight years into their marriage. The husband, Zack, played by Michael Ontkean, is at a point in his life where he can no longer ignore the overwhelming tug of his gay sexual orientation. He starts experimenting with his sexuality, initially having brief encounters with other men. Claire, his wife, played by Kate Jackson, can't understand why Zack has become increasingly distant and unaffectionate. In time, Zack has a full-blown affair with a guy named Bart, played by Harry Hamlin. Eventually, amidst insurmountable emotional turmoil, Zack admits to Claire he is gay, can no longer live a life of divided affections, and wants to be free. No doubt, there are many deeply conflicted gay men like Anthony, whose real-life stories closely mirror Zack's representation in *Making Love*.

It was particularly gratifying to see the male characters in the movie played by athletic, masculine men, and not the stereotypical effeminate caricatures frequently portrayed. Beyond that, the storyline contained uncanny parallels to the still-fresh Anthony and Gail saga. Because of this, the film was believable, personal, and poignant.

Chapter 28

More Bad Karma Upstairs

After Barry and Scott vacated the apartment above mine, Dr. Edwards began renovations, which took several months. At about the time renovations were complete, I started dating a guy who was a friend of Leonard's (who else?). In retrospect, I should have paid Leonard matchmaking fees for his continuing efforts to get me into a relationship—particularly a stable one.

This relationship was initially a breath of fresh air, but it would prove to be short-lived and underscored by a dramatic conclusion. It all began with a phone call one evening around 9:00 p.m. from a guy named Aaron, whom I didn't know. He introduced himself as a friend of Leonard's, and stated he and I had something in common—Barry Cardine. My curiosity was piqued, and we talked for about a half hour. As it turned out, Aaron's experience with Barry was eerily similar to mine. Fortunately for Aaron, being jilted by Barry didn't carry a crippling emotional reaction. Unlike me, he was able to brush it off and move forward. Aaron asked if he could come over to my apartment to continue the conversation, and I suggested another time would be better since it was getting late. We agreed to reconnect the next day and concluded the phone call.

A few minutes later, there was a knock at my door, which startled me because it was almost 10:00 p.m. Through the front door peephole, I could see a guy about my age, standing in the well-lit foyer. He was dressed in a dark suit, white shirt, and red necktie. I had enough street smarts not to automatically open the door. I did so when the caller identified himself as Aaron. He apologized for his uninvited late visit and asked if he could come in. I reluctantly let him in and mentioned it would need to be a short visit since I was about ready to hit the sack. Aaron was engaging, articulate, and, not surprisingly, a salesperson. He had good looks—not to the point of distraction—and was an excellent conversationalist. It was easy to like him. His "short" visit turned into a little over an hour as we compared notes about Barry and life in general. We met for dinner the following evening and developed an easy rapport.

We started dating and the relationship was going fairly well, even though Aaron's controlling personality was concerning. After dating for two months, and against my better judgment, Aaron and I decided to set up housekeeping together in the newly renovated apartment upstairs. It was the wrong thing to do at the wrong time, and with insufficient thought I agreed to do it. I was still awash in the emotional wake left over from my association with Barry, and my relationship with Aaron was undoubtedly a rebound situation. Secondly, it was the first time since having roommates in college that I had shared an apartment with anyone. Such a huge commitment would suggest Aaron and I were deeply involved; in actuality, I was not. The true extent of Aaron's involvement was also a question mark. Additionally, explaining my new living arrangements to friends and family would prove to be a challenge.

When I announced my intention to set up housekeeping with a roommate, my parents were uncomfortable with the idea.

My mother's response was: "It does not look good for you to be living with another man. It's time for you to find the right girl and get married."

My dad agreed. Their reaction was no surprise and, true to form, my mother bombarded me with a series of questions: "Where did you meet Aaron? Where is he from? What does he do for a living? How old is he? What church does he attend?" And the clincher: "Does he have a girlfriend?" This particular question was expected. Also, I knew it was the one mattering most.

I had already planned my defense well before the barrage began and did what I had learned to do best—fabricate a pile of baloney. Several of the questions, I could and did answer truthfully since they were relatively benign. Aaron was Catholic, he grew up in Tampa, was employed in sales, and was the same age as me. Easy questions, easy answers.

The other questions, perceptibly the red flag variety, required some invention. The most outrageous baloney I served was that Aaron was the tennis partner of a close female friend at work named Verna. My parents had previously heard me speak of Verna and knew she and I had played tennis in the past. I continued to weave the story and painted Verna and Aaron as a couple. The two, in fact, had never met. Nonetheless, I continued the "embroidery" and described meeting Aaron at the tennis courts during a doubles game with Verna and another friend. I explained that during one of our tennis matches, Aaron mentioned he was looking for a suitable roommate to share living expenses. Coincidentally, the renovated apartment upstairs had become available; so we looked at it and decided to take it. I would save money and be in more comfortable surroundings. Voila! The baloney appeared to be palatable (I know it really wasn't), and no further questions were shot from my mother's auto-reloading cannon.

My parents eventually met Aaron. It didn't hurt that he was masculine and muscular—he looked like he fit the straight-guy role I had represented. As a side note, it is curious to me that much of the world still subscribes to the belief that most gay men are easily identified by effeminate mannerisms. Some of us are—which is perfectly fine (God makes us in all shapes and sizes)—and many of us are not. Besides, I have met some straight men with effeminate characteristics. Although not grammatically correct, a former work colleague said it best by exclaiming, "You don't *never* know for sure!"

Without any fanfare, Aaron and I moved into the new apartment and were happy for several months—then things began to unravel. It was apparent we had little in common and were not well suited to each other. Aaron knew I was miserable and made futile attempts to mend the relationship; undeniably, it was over. I selfishly asked him to consider looking for alternative living arrangements. The comment fell on deaf ears. It didn't occur to me that I should have been willing to look for a new place to live, even though all the furniture was mine.

With the Anthony calamity still weighing on my mind and a desire to distance myself from Aaron, I seized a golden opportunity affording a temporary respite from both situations. In early December 1982, Delta presented me with the chance to work in Washington, DC, for several weeks. The timing was perfect; it was during a traditionally slow period at the nursery. With one day's notice to prepare for the trip, I packed my bags and went.

The venture turned out to be one of the most superb experiences of my life. I fell in love with Washington and the Delta reservations office in Rosslyn where I worked. Through a work associate there, I was introduced to a host of new friends including a polished, brown-haired, blue-eyed gentleman named Ted Petersen, who hailed from Minnesota. He was three years younger than me and worked on Capitol Hill in the office of a well-respected congressman. Additionally, I discovered Ted was an accomplished church organist, wonderful cook, and consummately erudite. We established a natural connection since I enjoyed listening to pipe organs and was fascinated with the mechanics of the instrument. We started dating, and soon a world of new horizons opened up as we attended concerts, went to parties, and explored museums. Before I knew it, my tour of duty came to an unwelcome end and I had to leave Washington. I returned to Jacksonville with new perspectives under my belt and a renewed zip in my step.

I had not spoken with Aaron while in Washington and had no idea what to expect upon my return. When I walked into the apartment, Aaron was there and in a hostile mood. By nature, he was basically a sweet guy, so his demeanor was out of the ordinary. Aaron said he had lost his job and would be returning to Tampa. He accused me of abandoning him; in reality, he was right. My trip to Washington was an abandonment of sorts. His anger was understandable; nonetheless, I was relieved he would be leaving. Within a few days, Aaron seemed to be in a better frame of mind, and he moved out. By all appearances, his anger had waned, and I expected we would remain friendly. As it turned out, Aaron was not done with me—he had a parting shot in store.

Several days after Aaron moved out, he called me in the late afternoon and had a decidedly upbeat tone in his voice. Initially, I was glad to hear from him and expected he would tell me he had landed a new job in Tampa. Not so. He went straight to "the jugular," and in a matter-of-fact tone, advised me he was back in Jacksonville with the sole purpose of going to my parents' house—to tell them I was gay. He knew this was my ultimate fear and mercilessly played me to the hilt. I went into panic mode and begged him not to do it. I pleaded that my parents were older, and telling them would be devastating. He insisted they needed to know who their son was and he was going to introduce them to the real Seth. I continued to plead, and the more I begged, the more belligerent Aaron became. Finally, the conversation ended with my telling him in total resignation to go do what he had to do, and I hung up the phone.

I waited for hours in a state of extreme anxiety, expecting to receive a phone call from my dad. A miserable night followed as I alternated pacing the floor, with lying in bed.

The next morning, there was an unexpected knock on the kitchen door and I assumed my parents were on the other side. Without asking who was there, I popped the door open and, much to my astonishment, the visitor was Aaron. I was speechless.

Aaron stood there and said, "Seth, I am sorry for what I put you through. I never had any intention of telling your parents. I wanted to punish you for ending the relationship. The game was over when you told me to go do what I had to do. That deflated me."

He had actually made the threatening phone call from Tampa and drove to Jacksonville to apologize. My relief was overwhelming, but I have never forgotten the details of that nail-biting experience. We parted as friends, eventually losing touch with each other.

My Delta flight benefits made it relatively easy to make frequent visits to Washington to visit Ted. Occasionally he came down to Jacksonville, although the cost of plane tickets made repeated visits impractical. The difficulty associated with being separated by hundreds of miles eventually took its toll, and we stopped dating after about a year. Had it not been for my nursery business, which by then was thriving, I would have considered a transfer to Washington. Even though Ted and I discontinued the long-distance dating, we remained good friends and occasionally visited each other from time to time. Years later, fate dictated that we would become much closer again.

Chapter 29

Major Changes

The time had come for me to take another significant step toward assuming bona fide adulthood, which chronologically had occurred years prior. It was mid-1983, I was thirty-four years old, and had been living in bachelor-pad apartments for a little over seven years.

Lou Roberts had been urging me to invest in real estate for a couple of years—it was past time to buy a house. In a stroke of serendipity, a fellow Delta employee was getting married and consequently was selling her house in the San Marco area of town. It was perfect for me and located less than five minutes from the Delta office. After Lou and my dad put their stamps of approval on the property, the transaction was signed, sealed, and delivered in a whirlwind without the house ever being listed with a realtor. The seller and her new husband moved to the "burbs," and I assumed residence in my unique 1939-vintage brick bungalow.

The house was in an excellent but outdated condition when I bought it. Naturally, I wanted to put my mark on the property. Soon, a renovation was completed, including a glitzy new kitchen and the addition of a large screened porch in the back. The "icing on the cake" was a relandscaped, magazine-worthy yard, which I designed and installed in stages. Most of the plants were from my own nursery, which added a layer of pride to the finished product. What a joy! When the house renovation and landscaping were complete, my little "pride and joy" house was a gem on the street. Someone told me once to watch out when gays and lesbians move into a neighborhood—house values will go up.

I was not exactly a celebrated interior decorator (this hasn't changed), and remembered how much I liked Barry Cardine's New York–inspired apartment décor; I wanted to create the same type of unexpected interior design in my house—minimal, sleek, and with clean lines. Oddly, the house provided an unanticipated avenue for Barry and me to reconnect. A mutual friend shared with him that I had bought a house and was in the renovation process. Barry dumbfounded me one morning when he came over—unannounced—to see the house. He surprised me further by staying an hour or two to help me paint the living room. It was the first time we had conversed with each other in more than two years. What a way to mend a previously shattered relationship—one I had considered dead forever. Interestingly, during this unexpected yet welcome visit, we spoke little about our troubled past; we focused on talking about my house and the future. I have to confess this relatively brief encounter with Barry resurrected my yearnings for him. Even so, there was no hint from him that he wanted anything more, and I surely didn't pursue him a second time.

In our conversation, Barry said he was making plans to leave Jacksonville and would more than likely move to Atlanta. He eventually followed through with his goal and, like Anthony, found a new and exciting life there. Barry and I never resumed regular contact. Still, it was heartwarming that this previously painful and unresolved chapter in my life was finally footnoted with reconciliation.

"Gay Cancer"

Just before the time Anthony and Gail divorced, national news media began to report a "gay cancer" was affecting a number of gay men in California and New York. Two rare, life-threatening conditions—*Pneumocystis carinii* pneumonia, and Kaposi's sarcoma (skin cancer)—had popped up in young and otherwise healthy individuals. Initial reports suggesting that the outbreaks were isolated soon proved false, as the number of cases—primarily in New York City, Los Angeles, and San Francisco—began to skyrocket. The name AIDS (acquired immune deficiency syndrome) was given to the disease, which was also affecting hemophiliacs and some heterosexual people. I didn't know anyone in Jacksonville with the disease, and most of the local gay community initially felt it wouldn't be a major concern in our little outpost. Time would prove this assumption false.

A community meeting was held to allow anyone with concerns about AIDS to obtain information about the prevalence and progression of the disease. I didn't attend, and the topic came up when Barry and I were painting my living room. He had recently attended a meeting where a physician advised against the use of poppers; it was believed that disease contraction might be linked to their use. I didn't know what poppers were, so Barry enlightened me. They were inhaled stimulants many guys used to heighten sexual experience. He also told me there was a belief the disease was sexually transmitted, and if so, the risk of contracting AIDS was likely proportional to the number of sexual encounters. I listened intently and vowed to never have sex again. In reality, my sexual contact with other guys had been limited; nonetheless, I was plenty frightened, since all that was necessary to become infected was one encounter with a diseased individual.

A Day That Changed Everything

For close to two years, purely out of self-preservation, I didn't date. Being immersed in my job at Delta, coupled with managing my wholesale nursery, made it fairly easy to overlook dating. Besides, Leonard had resigned as my personal matchmaker—given my track record of failed relationships. During this period, the AIDS epidemic continued to mushroom amid hopes for cures that never materialized. In actuality, considerably more people were healthy than sick; however, it was difficult to focus on this. I had developed a wonderful circle of gay friends and we frequently got together. Most of them were partnered and there were a few straggler "old maids" like me.

Two of my close friends who were partnered to each other, Charlie and Brock, frequently orchestrated get-togethers at their home or any other suitable location. On one occasion, they were rather insistent I meet them and a few other guys at a new seafood restaurant near the Intracoastal Waterway. It was mentioned that a few people whom I didn't know would also be joining the group. I readily accepted the invitation for the outing, which would take place on the next Saturday.

Nothing suggested this invitation was anything other than an opportunity for good food and fun. On Saturday evening, I drove to the restaurant, expecting to meet a few new people. To my surprise, I knew everyone there—except for one individual. In a quick assessment, I guessed the "mystery man" was probably of Mediterranean descent, perhaps of Greek or maybe Italian extraction. He was a good bit younger than me, had dark hair, dark eyes, and was slender. No doubt, he was eye candy. Charlie and Brock wasted no time introducing us and made sure we sat next to each other. It was a setup! I had no prior notion Charlie and Brock were attempting to practice some matchmaking—particularly with me as the subject of their designs.

For the next two hours, I enjoyed getting to know my next-chair table mate. His name was Thomas Marinos, and he was originally from Louisiana. This southern gentleman was polished, conversant, and getting started in his career as an attorney. Not at all a surprise, he was of Middle Eastern ethnicity. We didn't seem to have much in common, and I was not overly interested—mainly because he was ten years younger than me. I could tell Thomas had an impish side, which I liked; he somehow detected I had on purplish socks and playfully ribbed me about them. Admittedly, my trousers were probably a tad short, which served to accentuate my neon feet. In retrospect, the socks were awful, yet sort of matched—in dim light—a horizontal burgundy stripe in my otherwise tan-colored knit shirt. Those socks clearly announced my challenges when attempting to coordinate personal apparel. Thomas didn't suffer from this unfortunate deficiency; he had gained "mix and match ability" while working in his parents' department store specializing in men's and women's clothing. Undaunted, I wore the socks for several more years until the point was reached where a sufficient number of holes rendered them unworthy of further wear. I wish I had framed them.

When I Was Least Expecting It

As unlikely as the matchup between Thomas and me seemed, we went out on a second date … then a third … and a fourth. We enjoyed each other's company—a lot. Even though the ten-year age difference was a concern for me, it wasn't for him. After a period of several months, it was increasingly apparent our friendship had slowly matured into something more substantial; I was "growing in love" with Thomas, and he with me. This was unlike any other relationship I had ever experienced. There was never a head-over-heels period or an initial can't-stand-to-be-away-from-him emotion, as was the case with my previous serious relationships. Maybe I was older, wiser, and more together.

Thomas was intensely focused and in some respects more mature than me, even though he was twenty-six and I was thirty-six. We complemented each other well and seldom argued about anything. He was gifted with extraordinary artistic talent. He painted landscapes and abstracts, played the piano, had a beautiful baritone singing voice, and had outstanding writing ability. Our friend Charlie labeled him a renaissance man, which was the perfect description. Amazingly, Thomas also knew how to operate a screwdriver and a variety of other tools. His genetic makeup would not have suggested this competence to me. I had believed an individual couldn't be artistic *and* mechanically inclined. Thomas proved me wrong. Just goes to demonstrate how assumptions are frequently incorrect. There was nothing he couldn't do—and do well.

Before I knew it, we had been together for a year and were true partners, committed to each other. Neither of us would have ever predicted it. We were together constantly and usually spent nights together, either at my house or his. We knew we had to be discreet. Being gay in Jacksonville was a challenge; thus, living together as an "out" couple was not a consideration. Additionally, Thomas had purchased a new patio home prior to the time we met, and I had been in my home for a slightly longer time. For many reasons, we felt compelled to maintain separate residences.

One commonality we shared was that neither of us had ever apprised our respective families of our sexual orientation. Crossing this "bridge of acknowledgment," to become embroiled in what could be nasty family situations, was something we wanted to avoid. Thomas was raised in a devout Orthodox Catholic family, with strongly-held beliefs pertaining to the "wrongfulness" of same-sex relationships.

In addition to family considerations, our careers (particularly his) could be in serious jeopardy should it be confirmed we were a cohabitating gay couple. When Aaron and I briefly shared the apartment in Riverside, our living arrangements as renters were more easily explained. The situation between Thomas and me was vastly different; there was no reasonable explanation (which we could freely divulge) to account for our living together.

During the course of our first year together, I dropped hints to my parents that I had a friend named Thomas. I never elaborated to any significant degree and downplayed the relationship. I did share that I dog-sat his Pekingese on occasion. In time, they met Thomas and seemed comfortable being around him. I found it curious: they asked few questions.

Thomas had mentioned me to his parents on occasion and wanted to bring them over to see my impeccably landscaped backyard when they visited from Louisiana. Interestingly, his mother—an avid gardener and admirer of beautiful landscapes—was disinclined and even questioned Thomas as to why she needed to see what I had done. More than likely, her reticence was attributable to a general discomfort in meeting me. Thomas' parents had their suspicions and likely didn't want to have them confirmed. Had I been a young lady, they probably would have been excited to come over. Nonetheless, Thomas prevailed.

I remember being nervous about their visit and made every effort to "appear straight." To this end, my *Gentlemen's Quarterly* (*GQ*) and *Food & Wine* magazines were put away. This action may seem odd, but none of my straight male friends (I still had a few) subscribed to either, whereas many of my gay friends did. In addition to those two periodicals, I also had copies of *International Male*, a small mail-order catalog composed primarily of avant-garde men's fashions. The men's underwear offerings were probably the most viewed portion of the catalog and, to any gay man, a titillating experience. Scantily-clad, well-built male models were unmistakably demonstrating more than the semblance of underwear they were selling. My estimation is this sales catalog commanded an inordinate amount of window-shopping among gay men, prior to the point where a buying decision (if there was one) could be made. Any observer of this compendium of eye candy could easily suppose it was a gay-slanted "soft goods" repository. Therefore, I felt it prudent to hide my prized copies of *GQ*, *Food & Wine*, and, absolutely, *International Male* before the Marinos arrived. This action would eliminate the possibility of their connecting any dots—at least through literary associations.

So, Thomas brought his parents to my house. Gratefully, no dots were connected, the visit went well, and we all survived unscathed.

It Was Bound to Happen

Thomas and I were as careful as reasonably possible without becoming hermits. In most respects, we were living together—in two houses. I spent more time at his house than he did at mine, which was an agreeable arrangement. Thomas' patio home was nestled at the end of a fairly short street on a quiet cul-de-sac. He had a single-car garage, which meant my car was frequently parked in his driveway; it was easily visible. Thomas had a friend whom I had met, who lived in the same development, on a different street. She had noticed my car on numerous occasions being parked in Thomas' driveway—frequently at night—and mentioned it to her mother. To add a few superfluous details, Thomas had a large number of relatives living in Jacksonville, not the least of which was his dad's sister. The city had (and still has) a good number of Middle Eastern people—all with nonstop interconnections. Think *My Big Fat Greek Wedding* to picture the correct perspective. Fatefully, Thomas' aunt was a good friend of the mother of his neighbor who had spied my car parked at his house. There were *no* secrets held for long in this community, fully equipped for communication. I found out what "instant messaging" was all about, long before it was invented. In the bat of a hornet's eyelash, my car had become the "smoking gun," eventually resulting in Thomas and me being found out.

Thomas' aunt telephoned his dad with the information regarding my car's whereabouts—along with associated inferences. Questions were asked, and Thomas didn't lie to his parents, nor did he back down. His calm focus during this time was a good lesson for me; I was not nearly so calm—at least not internally. What if, through some "six degrees of separation" stroke of misfortune, the true nature of my relationship with Thomas were to find its way to my parents? This unrelenting fear was something Thomas no longer had to worry about with his family.

Cost-Benefit Analysis

Franklin D. Roosevelt famously stated during his first inaugural presidential address: "… the only thing we have to fear is fear itself …." This statement is one I have frequently thought about through the years. It was impossible not to notice that Thomas' admission—even though forced—had a positive effect on his psyche. His fear of being "outed" had been realized, resulting in his no longer living in fear. He had been set free. However, this freedom didn't guarantee that the ensuing period with his family was utopia. It wasn't.

Thomas' family didn't reject him, and they assured him of their continued love. Still, they were not pleased to learn he was gay and didn't approve of it. Thomas received a straight-from-the-heart letter from one of his three sisters, expressing sorrow he wouldn't be in heaven with the rest of the family. Another one of his sisters commented that if I gave AIDS to Thomas, she would kill me. Gratefully, neither of us had the AIDS virus, but the hysteria surrounding the disease did little to blunt the fact. In time, their attitudes changed, resulting in a wonderful relationship with his parents, his sisters, his brother, and their respective families.

Thomas had been extraordinarily close to his aunt, uncle, and cousins in Jacksonville. In fact, they were a major reason he had relocated to Jacksonville following his graduation from law school. Unfortunately, the fallout from Thomas' forced disclosure persisted for many years and they had much less contact with him. This was a major shift in the dynamic previously existing. Consequently, it was a bitter pill for Thomas. Although deeply hurt, Thomas adjusted to the situation. Occasionally he would visit with them, although his welcome was overshadowed by their disapproval of his sexual orientation. Even so, he held out hope for normalization of the relationship; this wouldn't occur for more than twenty years—when Thomas' father unexpectedly passed away. By then it was apparent the long years of detachment were not going to render the desired result of Thomas "changing his mind and deciding to be straight." That light switch was permanently fixed in the off position, and Thomas was powerless to flip it on. Regardless of the reason for the thaw, Thomas was grateful to see the previous chill suddenly warming, even though a heartbreaking occasion seemed to have been the impetus for the change of heart.

This narrative indeed had a positive upshot. Minds and hearts opened as Thomas and I began to spend time with this branch of his family. While I feel fairly sure his aunt, uncle, and cousins don't understand—or approve—of same-sex relationships (including ours), their warmth toward Thomas and me is unmistakable.

Chapter 30

Two Confessions

Dr. Benjamin Portman (my much-beloved former professor at UF) and I remained in contact through the years. Occasionally, I visited with him and his wife (of whom I also was fond) in Gainesville, and in Jacksonville where they later moved. It is funny how certain associations persist through the years and this one I could never let go. We had long been on a first-name basis, and I had tremendous respect for Benjamin. I loved him like a brother—even though he was twenty-two years older than me.

The prowess he possessed intellectually was equaled by an astounding musical ability. A Steinway concert grand piano graced the living room of their home. I witnessed firsthand how formidable his keyboard skills were, as I observed his fingers fly across the piano with precision and aplomb—he was a master. I can't ignore Benjamin's wife, a professor of English at UF and a darling of a lady. Many years prior, she had taught me how to make fork-tender roast beef after I raved about her cooking. This was as a result of being one of several students who were dinner guests at their home one evening.

Through the years as we became closer, Benjamin and I shared total honesty. I admitted to him I was gay, not long before Thomas and I met.

Benjamin's response was a rather matter-of-fact, "Well, I figured as much, so am not stunned to hear this. Incidentally, so am I."

My ears did an about-face. I can't say I was shocked to hear Benjamin's confession—but still was surprised.

The clues were there. His classroom lectures were a stage performance, he was a concert pianist and church organist, and he had that "I-can't-put-a-finger-on-it-quality" setting him apart. Of course, these types of "stamps" frequently suggesting someone may be gay, don't ensure "gayness" in any particular individual. With him, they were accurate indications.

Having acknowledged our "dark secrets" to each other, we began having deep, heart-to-heart conversations. As it turned out, Benjamin's wife was aware he was gay and gave him considerable latitude to connect with other professional gay men. Benjamin shared with me that these connections were nonsexual in nature and they fulfilled a need he had to establish emotional links with like-minded gentlemen. He was in his mid-fifties and experiencing internal conflict, which was not overwhelming to him. I had the chance to "counsel" him, even though he didn't specifically ask for my advice. Undeniably, Benjamin loved his wife and she loved him. Benjamin had toyed with the idea of separating from his wife to pursue living a gay life, which I discouraged him from doing. This may seem counterintuitive for me, a gay man, to suggest to another gay man to remain married. However, Benjamin's situation was unique, and I strongly felt the relationship he and his wife enjoyed was far better than what they both might find should he journey to "the other side." They remained happily married, which I firmly believe was the right decision, given their circumstances.

I was deeply saddened when Benjamin passed away in 2011 at the age of eighty-three. I am pleased to write that his wife is still living, and we remain in contact with each other.

When Love Trumps Fear

In 1987, about a year after Thomas' family found out he was gay, my brother and sister-in-law (Max and Ann) separated after twenty-one years of marriage. Max and I were like night and day in just about every aspect. I had dark hair, dark eyes, and was artistically inclined. He had lighter hair, blue eyes, and his idea of artistry was a car's curved water hose. He was much into mechanics and had an incredible ability to fully understand the "bowels" of a broad spectrum of complex technology. He was proficient in troubleshooting and reviving just about anything considered unfixable. From cars to house air conditioners, to our mother's recently malfunctioning, fifty-year-old toaster oven, he saved them from the wrecking ball. It didn't stop there. He was a whiz with electronics, avionics (his profession), and installed his own solar heating system, burglar alarm system, marine pilings, and dock. Our dad had the same brainpower, so it was apparent where Max obtained the talent. Without question, any such DNA available to be passed from our dad was surely exhausted with the first offspring—Max. Consequently, I was the recipient of less practical and undeniably different DNA strands producing results that are still the subject of analysis. The proof is in the pudding—I had zero interest in anything mechanical and could fix nothing other than breakfast, lunch, and dinner.

The bottom line is: Max and I spoke different "languages" and had almost nothing in common other than we were the products of the same set of parents (we think). Not surprisingly, he and I were not particularly close and seldom talked to each other. Even so, I offered to let him find refuge in my "house of deviancy"—with my full knowledge that he was a raging evangelical. Possibly, my own sanity should have been in question when I offered Max the house key, yet my lapse in rationality was overridden by my love for him—my only sibling. Even though he was my "big" brother, I knew he was not well equipped to hibernate in a lonely motel room. What now? My proposed arrangement presented an elephant-in-the-room dilemma—Max didn't know I was gay. I had no choice but to tell him, if he accepted my invitation.

Max didn't take long to deliberate. The next day he arrived with his worldly possessions packed in his suitcase, along with a load of emotional baggage. I was apprehensive about my imminent confession, and wasted no time in corralling him into the kitchen, where we sat opposite each other on two bar stools. He looked perplexed when I told him there was something he needed to know and he might find it disturbing. I advised him he would essentially be living alone in the house, and explained I would be there briefly, twice a day. While stammering around, I advised him that I spent the majority of time at Thomas' house.

Then I found my courage and said it: "I am gay and Thomas is my partner."

It was liberating! While I had long ago experienced liberation when admitting to myself the truth regarding my sexuality, this liberation was magnified when I *spoke* the truth. It was similar to the feeling I had experienced when first admitting to Dr. Edwards of my attraction to men—but this was much more risky. Nonetheless, I expected Max to brandish his King James Bible and pummel me with the usually cited condemning Scriptures. I was wrong.

Max responded by saying he was not surprised to learn I was gay.

What? After all, I worked out with weights and sure thought I acted straight. Well, not straight enough; my smoke screen did little to obscure the truth.

Max didn't condemn me; he acknowledged he didn't understand same-sex desires and would pray for my "deliverance." Of course, in my view, my "deliverance" had already occurred—when I accepted the truth. In time, Max adjusted to the reality of having a brother with a "skewed" sexual perspective and he never displayed anything toward me other than love.

My brother stayed at my house for several months, at which point he and Ann reconciled. An unexpected outcome of his marital "sabbatical"—and my soul-baring admission—was that he and I drew closer. Through this experience, we discovered much shared commonality, despite our conspicuous differences. My temporary role as my older brother's protector also served to bring a new understanding of the bond that can exist between brothers who otherwise seem to have little in common.

Through the years, our relationship continued to deepen. Our thought processes and views on life and living were actually much in sync. Max exemplified true Christian perspectives of love, compassion, understanding, and acceptance. He eventually distanced himself from the evangelical church and the myopic views many evangelicals exhibit. He, too, found his own liberation.

Max and Ann remained married until her death in 1997. He married again a year later, to Lois, who is his current wife.

Chapter 31

AIDS Becomes Rampant in My Town

By the late 1980s, the AIDS epidemic and its associated impacts began to penetrate our little corner of Florida. Like in the rest of America, panic was now becoming widespread in the local gay community as the disease spread, with no panaceas and no real hope. It was evident that being diagnosed with AIDS was an automatic sentence to a horrific death. A few "mainstream" Christian denominations brought relief and comfort to the suffering—at least to the degree in which they were able.

On the other hand, the evangelical church preached damnation and condemnation to the gay community. Their pronouncements, such as, "AIDS is God's judgment on homosexuals," didn't accomplish anything other than proliferate additional hate and fear of the gay population. And there was an inherent flaw in their dogma: "God's judgment" didn't extend into the lesbian sector since the epidemic seemed to skip this group.

This made me wonder if God could actually be a woman.

Nonetheless, the lesbian component of the equation should have induced any logically thinking individual to question "God's judgment" pronouncements. With the evangelical element, it didn't.

My close friend Brock made a statement about judgment that resonated. He said, "Being gay is not the sin. If God is rendering retribution, it's because of promiscuity, which is not exclusive to any group."

How true.

Inevitable Epiphany

As the AIDS epidemic grew exponentially, many evangelicals continued to pounce with hate-filled declarations, adding fuel to the rapidly escalating hysteria surrounding people who had AIDS. I was still a member of my much-loved home church, which unfortunately was morphing into a fundamentalist congregation. On the occasions when I attended services, my distaste was amplified by rants of condemnation directed at "unacceptables" like me, as well as anyone else who was not of like mind. My discomfort turned into ire and reached an intolerable point, leaving me with an overwhelming feeling of alienation.

The result was a long-overdue personal epiphany. I didn't choose to be gay, and indeed had another choice—to no longer remain emotionally entrapped by the brick-and-mortar cage my church represented. I had the keys to the lock in my grasp and was ready to open it. Resolute and no longer guilt ridden, at the better-late-than-never age of thirty-eight, I allowed my God-given intellect and internal compass to guide me right out the now-unlocked door. It was a one-way, never-look-back exit from the denomination in which I had been active my entire life. I gave superficial reasons to my longtime friends in the church as to why I left, but I felt the church had left me. I was still largely silent about my sexual orientation, and only my gay friends knew the true drivers behind my parting. My decision to no longer affiliate was deeply private. Was it difficult? Indeed. Much of my life history and a piece of my heart would remain in my home church. Did I ever regret leaving? Indeed not.

In my heart I knew the evangelical response to the AIDS epidemic was not reasonable, not Christian, and not responsible. I didn't believe the rhetoric decreeing God was rendering retribution to gay people—or for whatever reason to hemophiliacs who also had a high disease incidence. This simplistic "God's retribution" pronouncement fit right in to the overall evangelical mindset that being gay is a choice and through concerted church-approved tutelage and prayer, heterosexual desires will supplant "homosexual deviancy." From personal exposure to this flawed "voila" doctrine—which previously led me to severe depression—I knew better. Religious zealots also conveniently ignored the truth that in some other parts of the world, the highest incidence of AIDS occurred in the heterosexual community. Homosexuals couldn't be blamed for this!

I considered myself a Christian even though my church thought otherwise. There had never been a time in my life when I was without a church home, so I began to search. Thankfully, I found my answer in a "mainline" Presbyterian church that preached and seemed to practice God's love. Charlie and Brock (the guys who set me up with Thomas) were active members of this church, and it was three blocks from my house. I never heard any anti-gay venom spewing from the pulpit, nor did I hear derogatory comments hurled at other churches. After visiting on numerous occasions, I joined the church and, soon after, the choir. What a wonderful freedom this change in venue provided. My new church home was a fresh wind where I learned more about trust than distrust, and felt acceptance rather than rejection. Much of the membership probably assumed I was gay since I was single, never married, and was close friends with Charlie and Brock—who didn't hide who they were.

Lightning Strikes Close to Home

The first person I knew who contracted AIDS was a guy who worked closely with me at Delta Air Lines. He went by his initials rather than his first name, so I will refer to him as R.T. He was originally from Miami, and had moved to Jacksonville some years prior to accept a position as an officer with the local police department. R.T. looked like a policeman and exhibited the stereotypical persona associated with the profession. He was sort of gruff, not overly friendly, and looked like he spent a lot of time in the gym; he was about six feet tall and extraordinarily muscular. My suspicion was he may have been on steroids, although this was never confirmed. R.T. had a ruddy complexion, was not particularly handsome, and had beautiful sky-blue eyes. Unfortunately, the Jacksonville Police Department found out he was gay and forced him to resign. He was later hired by Delta, and had worked with me for several years prior to the time his health went into free fall. My association with R.T. was limited to work; however, there was a time, shortly after he started working for Delta, when I wanted to date him. This never occurred—he was not interested. Much to my chagrin, R.T. was much attracted to Barry Cardine (who wasn't?), and they became an item for a while.

In 1987, R.T. started to miss work, ostensibly due to a series of infections attributed to tonsillitis. Eventually he took a medical leave of absence and never returned to work. A mutual friend who saw him a few weeks after he went on medical leave, told me R.T. had lost a lot of weight, was feeble, and required the use of a walking cane. Huh?

When I questioned how infected tonsils could cause such drastic deterioration, he asked me incredulously, "Didn't you know R.T. has AIDS?"

The words hit me like a cannonball. Stunned, I couldn't believe what I was hearing; a few weeks prior, R.T. had looked fine, even though he had "throat issues." In a daze, I went for a walk. I dwelled on what had previously been unthinkable—AIDS had become a reality to someone I knew. It was no longer limited to what I read in the newspaper or heard on TV.

R.T. lived for a few more months, and died in 1988. He was thirty-seven years old.

In a short span of time, more people whom I knew became ill and died, including another work associate at Delta. If there ever was a living nightmare, this was it, and it worsened. Ashamed to admit it, I became numb to the AIDS catastrophe, as an assembly line of young men continued to die in increasing numbers across America.

My numbness quickened to unforgiving reality in 1991 when, during a telephone conversation, Anthony Petrini shared that he had been sick—he too had AIDS. The news flattened me, even though it had been several years since we last saw each other. The years had not diminished my fondness for him; consequently, the revelation was particularly difficult to assimilate. I also was deeply troubled about the emotional percussion Gail (his ex-wife) and their two children would experience, even though nine years had passed since the divorce. Thankfully, there was no physical consequence to Gail.

During the months following Anthony's disclosure, we spoke a few times. He endured the repeating cycles of the disease, with some encouraging times when a few weeks were reasonably good, only to be struck by the crush of symptoms heralding yet another onslaught of abject torture. Sadly, Anthony succumbed to AIDS during the spring of 1992, when he was forty-two years old. Even though I knew he had been sick before his death, seeing his obituary in the newspaper was an inconceivable sting; it just about ripped my heart out.

My hope for his children, whom I haven't seen since they were toddlers, is that they understand their dad loved them, and he didn't choose to be gay. I hope they understand when their dad married their mother, he did what he felt he had to do by conforming to the societally-dictated expectation of getting married and having children. He thought he could pull it off. I knew I couldn't.

Fall 1992 – My World Continues to Shatter

A few months after Anthony's death, I was scanning the newspaper obituaries, which back in those days was a routine activity for members of the gay community. My eyes nearly popped out of my head when I came across Barry Cardine's name. I had not heard of him being sick and initially wondered if his death was possibly accidental. Once again, I was rendered to a state of disbelief. In hindsight, I shouldn't have been.

Several months prior, Barry dropped by my house when he was visiting from Atlanta. Unfortunately, I was away and found his business card lodged in a crack of the front door when I arrived home. There was nothing handwritten on the card and the phone number on it was his Atlanta number. I assumed Barry wanted to see the changes I had made to the house, and I was greatly disappointed to have missed his visit. I never heard further from him and hoped to see him the next time he was in town. Not long after Barry's visit, I ran into one of his close friends, and in conversation he mentioned Barry had put on weight and looked great. I thought the comment was strange, given Barry's propensity to being slightly heavy, and assumed he had bulked up from weightlifting. It didn't register anything could be wrong.

As soon as I finished reading the obituary, I threw down the paper and, in a state of near panic, telephoned Lou Roberts (of course). This is the same Lou who had introduced me to the Zodiac Lounge in South Daytona many years before. Predictably, he picked up the phone on the first ring. Lou was like a switchboard operator and, accordingly, had a myriad of contacts who continually kept him informed on just about anything of importance. He was (and still is) my personal "oracle."

I dispensed with the usual phone etiquette and, in an upset voice, blurted that Barry's obituary was in the newspaper. Without giving him a chance to respond, I implored him to find out what happened to Barry. I assumed through some inexplicable, how-in-the-world-could-he-not-know quirk, he wasn't aware of Barry's demise.

Lou stopped me in the middle of my excited jabber. "Seth, calm down. I am aware of Barry's obituary and have known for some time he was sick. Barry had AIDS, and I didn't have the heart to tell you."

It then occurred to me that when I found Barry's business card stuck in my front door, he had probably stopped by to inform me of his illness. I had been "out to lunch" when clues were dangled in front of my nose. Being hit with the news of his death from AIDS was akin to being rocked by an earthquake, and it continued to reverberate for months. He was thirty-six years old when he died.

I have forever regretted not calling Barry after I missed his visit.

Chapter 32

When It Rains, It Pours

About the same time Barry died, Delta announced the closure of the Jacksonville office where I worked. Rumors—although denied—had been circulating for several years, so the announcement was not shocking. Nonetheless, receiving such life-changing news was a most unwelcome bolt of lightning.

The closure was scheduled to take place in about a year, which was a generous advance notice. Even so, my life would drastically change all too soon. My options were to accept a transfer to another city or take a semi-decent severance package. It put me in a highly problematic position—heartache and hassle were guaranteed, no matter what option I chose. There was a lot to consider and reconsider. Fortunately, Thomas was at my side to help me maintain objectivity and preserve my equilibrium. My decision would have to be made in a few months.

The chilly north winds during the second week of December were an unwelcome harbinger of yet another blow: my eighty-one-year-old father passed away after a protracted illness. It was a relief to see him released from his misery and my mother released from the burden of caring for him; but it was tough to lose him.

This was the man who had taught me how to ride a bicycle, taught me multiplication tables (prehistoric, still-useful mathematics all baby boomers had to learn), taught me to drive a car (and tried but couldn't teach me how to fix it), and made breakfast for the family every morning.

He encouraged me when I made mistakes and pointed out how to avoid repeating them. Other lessons were learned by observing the example he set as he lived his life. He was a consummate gentleman, polite almost to a fault, was firm without being offensive, was never late for anything (he would "break his neck" in order to be on time), and he honored his commitments. He lived by the time-honored principles of honesty and integrity. He loved his church, though he quietly questioned some of the positions taken by it. He *never* judged people and was quick to correct me when I appointed myself as a magistrate. My dad firmly believed an individual's faith was a personal matter and pounding folks over the head with a Bible was counterproductive. He understood the example he set in living his faith on a day-to-day basis was the best way to influence others. I agree.

Thank God I had Thomas for emotional support. During my grieving, it was poignantly apparent how fortunate I was to be able to shed tears over my dad's passing. He was a wonderful provider, an excellent father, and was devoted to his family. What more of a blessing could anyone receive? I pity individuals who don't feel a sense of loss when they lose a parent—maybe they didn't have parents like mine. When we buried my dad, I recognized a part of him would continue to live within me. I feel his influence every day. Thank you, Dad!

By early 1993, Thomas and I had been together for over seven years, with our living arrangements basically unchanged—we still owned and maintained separate houses. Thomas had moved into a lovely home across the street from the St. Johns River, in the same area where my house was located. We seldom stayed at my house, although I maintained the yard, collected mail, and checked messages on my telephone answering machine. My parents had no idea Thomas and I had been living together for years. With my dad now gone, I continued to live the lie.

I suspect many of my gay brothers and lesbian sisters today are dumbfounded at my inability to "air out the laundry." Others, particularly those coming from evangelical or religiously fundamental families, likely understand that doing so may render more negatives than positives. To my defense, confirming my sexual orientation to my mother would have been crippling to her. I didn't want to be responsible for upending her life by delivering news she would view as horrendous in this world and even worse in the next. Many years later, the confirmation of my sexual orientation would come to my mother—and not in a manner I would have expected.

Dusting Off the Crystal Ball

In the late spring of 1993, I was required to notify Delta of my intent to either accept a transfer to another city or accept the severance. It was the most gut-wrenching decision I had ever made up to that point. Misery loves company, and I had plenty; everyone else in the Jacksonville office was dealing with the same dilemma. My relationship with Thomas was strong, and the thought of leaving him was analogous to being adrift at sea, bobbing in unknown currents. I was forty-four years old (not ideal for job seeking) and had sixteen years vested with the company—leaving Delta would mean losing a lot. Thomas and I briefly discussed the possibility of us both moving to Atlanta. The final analysis proved that such a move was less than prudent; his practice was thriving and he was a partner in the law firm. For him to give it all up and start over in Atlanta would be ill-advised. Leaving Jacksonville was not the question; however, leaving our respective careers was huge—particularly for two card-carrying pragmatists.

After many nights of fitful sleep and months to hash and rehash options, I gazed into my cost-effective and reliable crystal ball (the one producing flying snow when shaken). I closed my eyes, held my nose, and in a leap of faith, jumped into the dark water—I accepted the company-paid transfer to Atlanta, where Delta was headquartered. It was a counterintuitive move, given Delta's financial tailspin. Knowingly, it was a calculated risk. Nonetheless, I would be eligible for retirement in eight years (should Delta still be around) and could walk out at that time with my flight benefits and pension intact. One mitigating factor was my ability to commute home on the weekends via the Delta flying carpet. Once the decision had been made, we had until September to prepare for the hard reality of living separated lives during the week.

Not the least of my considerations was how to manage the wholesale nursery while living in Atlanta. It would be difficult at best. The operation had grown and couldn't be successfully managed on short weekends, even with the part-time help I had hired. Moreover, it would be unfair to Thomas for me to spend what precious free time we had at the farm. The time had come for me to sell it. And to be honest, I was weary of managing two careers. Surprisingly, I sold the nursery quickly—too quickly, as it turned out. Unfortunately, the buyer was an unscrupulous sort and soon started to miss payments. Fortunately for me, Thomas had little patience for the con artist and legally "hung him out to dry." Miraculously, the buyer coughed up the money and paid the note off to avoid foreclosure. Surprising to me, he found some unsuspecting entity to front him the money.

Several years later, I rode out to the nursery to peer at it from a neighbor's property and was saddened to see it looking like Sherman had marched through it. Overgrown with weeds, my once-proud establishment had been reduced to an eyesore.

September Arrives in July

About a month after I signed the letter of intent to accept the transfer, I was offered a position with Delta Group Sales in Atlanta. While there was no salary increase involved, it would allow me to focus on an area of the business in which I was experienced and greatly enjoyed. There was a catch—I had to report on Monday, July 19, two months earlier than originally planned.

My experience in this highly specialized sales field was solely due to the insistence of a farsighted supervisor who, against my protests, pushed me into it. About two years prior to the time the office closed, she presented me with the opportunity to be trained in Group Sales—a prized area in which to work. I will never forget the conversation that ensued when I initially "advised" her I had no interest. My disinterest was mostly because my current job responsibilities, even though mundane, offered many midweek days off and a quitting time of three thirty in the afternoon. (Several years prior, I had ditched the late-afternoon shift for early morning.) Consequently, this schedule afforded me considerable freedom to operate the nursery, particularly during the daylight saving time months. On the other hand, Group Sales was a straight Monday through Friday schedule, with the requirement I work until five thirty each afternoon. It was a no-brainer—this was not for me. My supervisor was an understanding lady who never appeared flustered, rarely displayed emotion, and had the best interests of her "flock" at heart.

In me, however, she found a challenge. My expressed disinterest in Group Sales flustered her to such a degree that she became visibly perturbed. She sternly told me, much like a parent would (she was a few years older than me), "Seth, I am insisting you submit a request for the next Group Sales training opportunity here in Jacksonville. You can't continue to box yourself into one area of the company, and you can't assume your nursery is always going to be there for you. This is for your benefit." She then put the training request form in front of me and chirped, "Your move."

In my gut I knew she was right, and considered ways I could still operate the nursery. Without any further argument, I filled out the training request and slid it back across the table to her. I have thought about this for years. Along with several other people in the office, I was soon selected for the training.

I had no idea how critical this would be, even years later. I owe a world of gratitude to this wise and caring woman and have continued to thank her through the years.

Sunday, July 18, 1993

The day arrived much sooner than either Thomas or I wanted. We knew it was coming; of course, we tried not to think about it. Emotionally we were not ready, nor would we ever have been.

At about 1:00 p.m., the time had come for me to begin the journey. Thomas and I tightly embraced before I had to leave. The word *leave* had a sense of finality particularly unsettling on that impossible-to-forget day. Last attempts were made to prop each other up with encouraging comments such as, "The week will go quickly. I will be home on Friday." And "It will all work out. We will survive this." But this was different than leaving for a planned trip, which usually has a definite end date and a brief, temporary separation. This was a move, and eight years to reach retirement seemed like a lifetime. Thomas and I trudged out to my car, and neither of us said much of anything. We hugged each other again, and I slipped into my 1989 Acura and drove off.

Tears were pouring before I reached the end of the block. In a flashback moment, I was transported to a gut-wrenching day in December 1972—the day I drove off from Charlene's house, leaving her sobbing on the front porch. That was a poignant memory; this was eerily parallel, although this time the hurt was exponentially greater for me (and, no doubt, Thomas).

The trip to Atlanta seemed to take forever, although it was just under six hours. During the 356-mile drive, I couldn't hide from the consuming aloneness traveling with me. The white numbers on the green roadside mile markers increased incrementally as I traveled deeper into Georgia; each one was like the prick of a sandspur on a bare foot. I surfed the radio, finding options limited to an assortment of screaming preachers, who occasionally were interrupted by agricultural reports featuring pig futures (don't ask), expected peanut yields, and cotton prices. Even so, the offerings on the various radio frequencies were better alternatives to the stark solitude that otherwise permeated the car.

The drive provided excessive time to reflect on my decision to move to Atlanta, and even in my somber mood I knew it was right. It was difficult to leave my seventy-five-year-old recently widowed mother. Fortunately, she was youthful, vigorous, and highly independent. My brother lived nearby and was available should anything transpire whereby she needed help. My mother was supportive of my decision to transfer to Atlanta, which made the situation less worrisome than it could have been.

Settling In

One of my closest friends at work, Joe Sanchez, had been offered a position in Atlanta also requiring a late-July report date. We had a lot in common. Joe didn't advertise he was gay, had a partner who was a good bit younger, and they had been together for many years. Joe's partner, Randall Parker, was a crackerjack registered nurse, and he decided to move to Atlanta when Joe did. It was a gutsy move for Randall, having been established with one of Jacksonville's top hospitals for years. Without question, his skills would transfer well, but finding a comparable position would at least require a diligent search.

The three of us brainstormed and decided to live together initially. With this in mind, we spent two days in Atlanta, prior to the move, looking at apartments. While there, we signed a one-year lease on a three-bedroom apartment in a new, beautifully landscaped complex on Atlanta Road, near the headquarters for The Home Depot. Joe and Randall moved shortly after I did, and our transition to "communal" living was much easier than I had expected. The downside was a twenty-two-mile commute to work (which turned out to be not so bad), although the location's amenities overrode this detail.

My new life had begun; I soon established new routines and made many friends. Joe, Randall, and I were compatible and we respected each other's space. It helped that our work hours were divergent and we were not together frequently. The days were much easier than I had anticipated; I loved my work at Delta Group Sales in Atlanta and enjoyed excellent working relationships with my new colleagues. Many of my colleagues in the Atlanta office were "refugees" from other cities where Delta had closed offices. We enjoyed instant commonality, which resulted in the development of strong bonds, all due to the unfortunate circumstances placing us in the same corral. It was the best work situation I had ever experienced.

I would be negligent not to mention the gay population was well represented in the office, and they were less uptight than their counterparts in Jacksonville had been. I, too, became more relaxed, which was an unexpected personal byproduct. Atlanta provided the path for me to more comfortably celebrate my uniqueness, since I no longer felt the need to remain in hiding to the extent I did in Jacksonville.

This journey was proving to have many positives, not only for me, but also for Joe and Randall. Joe was happy with his new position, and Randall quickly landed a position at Emory University Hospital where he furthered his education and became a physician's assistant.

While my work situation was better than I ever envisioned, the separation from Thomas was tough. I missed him immensely and highly anticipated the weekends when we would be together. I commuted home every Friday evening and returned to Atlanta on Sunday nights. My vestige-from-the-nursery pickup truck was my ready transport that "lived" at the Jacksonville airport employee parking lot during the week. Since my flying was on a standby basis, difficulties were the norm. I was frequently bumped, which meant I lumbered home late Friday night or during the wee hours Saturday morning. Returning to Atlanta on Sunday nights was equally problematic, including the emotional upheaval Thomas and I endured when I had to leave. Occasionally, I had to fly into or out of Gainesville, which meant Thomas had to drive sixty-five miles each way to pick me up or drop me off. He never complained and remained a nonstop source of support and encouragement. The weekends provided a much-looked-forward-to respite, but were marred by the logistics of the commute. At least I had several friends in the same commuting situation and we kept each other buttressed.

One other immense source of support was my treasured friend, Ilene. This Georgia-born southern belle of the highest order had worked with me in Jacksonville, and we became extraordinarily close as a result of our continued working relationship in Atlanta Group Sales. She served as my chief confidant and "psychologist," providing wise counsel during some excruciatingly difficult times when I allowed myself to become immersed in a meltdown. Her understanding of my personal situation, unconditional acceptance, and heartfelt concern for Thomas and me was beyond measure. It is not an understatement to say she was my salvation in Atlanta.

Living in Atlanta took a huge financial toll; my ability to continue saving toward retirement was severely restricted. As a comparison, my little house in Jacksonville was paid for; now I was paying hefty rent. Florida had no state income tax, but fear not—Georgia had its wanting hand out in this department. My yearly car registration fee jumped from $35 to $400. The most significant blow was dealt by Delta itself—in the form of a 5 percent pay cut imposed on almost all employees. I was saving a pittance and this greatly troubled me. It also gave me a much greater appreciation for individuals who had not had the advantages and good fortune I had previously enjoyed. The painful and humbling experience compelled me to rent out my house in Jacksonville for extra income.

Up to this point, my mother assumed I had been staying in my house on the weekends, which of course was not the case—I was staying with Thomas. Renting out my house gave me a reasonable explanation for staying with Thomas when I came home. Additionally, he had moved again—this time into a much larger house. As a bonus to both of us, there was ample room for much of my furniture, which he could use to occupy empty space. It turned out to be a win-win; the benefits were mutual. Also, leasing out my house proved to be a fortuitous decision. My mother didn't say much about my open living arrangement with Thomas, although she was not overjoyed with it.

Even though my interrupted life seemed littered with negatives, it offered significant positives I couldn't ignore. I have briefly mentioned that my work experience in Atlanta was excellent—in fact, it proved to be life changing. About six months after beginning work in Atlanta, a work colleague and I were asked to troubleshoot some cumbersome processes killing our ability to effectively serve our clients. We were losing planeloads of group business to competitors, not because we didn't have an equal or better product, but because of the inordinate amount of time required to process our work. Our processes were duplicitous, unnecessary, and demanded time-consuming manual handling. Quickly, the two of us proposed solutions we believed would remove clogs and streamline our work without compromising quality. Those practical solutions were presented to management and soon were approved. I assumed my task was complete, yet surprisingly, the project served as a springboard for a paradigm shift in my job responsibilities.

Much to my surprise, I was asked to write a training program and then teach our newly adopted business methods to my colleagues in Atlanta. What? Me? I had never written anything along these lines, nor presented a training program to any audience—small or large. I was terrified. Nonetheless, the manager of our department instilled the confidence I needed to proceed, by assuring me he knew I could do what needed to be done.

This was huge for two reasons. Number one: I had zero experience, yet he trusted me. Number two: the manager was a devout Mormon, and he knew I was gay. Delta didn't have a nondiscrimination policy including sexual orientation, yet my manager saw beyond this. No doubt, his personal views (which I assume were in lockstep with the church) didn't interfere with his ability to manage objectively.

As it turned out, the initiatives were successfully implemented in Atlanta. Also, I was given the opportunity to train the other major offices where Delta maintained a Group Sales area. Before the project was concluded, we took the "show" to Cincinnati, Los Angeles, Dallas, Salt Lake City, New York City, and Miami—quite a departure from what I had envisioned when my BS in agriculture from UF was awarded.

The entire experience was pivotal and gave me confidence to be who I was as a gay man. It also prepared me for other opportunities I had not yet imagined. None of this would have been possible, had it not been for a forward-thinking supervisor in Jacksonville who put a form in front of me and said, "Your move."

Chapter 33

Rumors, Rumors, Rumors

About a year after moving to Atlanta, Joe and Randall bought a condo together—the first place they had ever jointly owned. Our living arrangements had been highly satisfactory. Inconveniently for me, it was time to find another place to live.

Fortunately, Rich Krause, a gay work associate, needed to move from his apartment at about the same time and was seeking a roommate to share expenses. Our association was work related and we had never spent any time together outside the office. Nevertheless, we enjoyed an excellent working relationship and decided to take the chance; we signed a one-year lease and soon occupied a two-bedroom apartment in the same complex where Joe, Randall, and I had lived. As anticipated, Rich and I were well-matched roommates and enjoyed each other's company. We were both on the quiet side, neither of us smoked, and we respected each other's space. Rich was tall, blonde, a good-looking guy, and easy to like. He was unattached, and undoubtedly a catch. Not surprisingly, destiny worked its magic on Rich; he became starry eyed when his Prince Charming emerged from the forest not long after we leased the apartment.

A few months after Rich and I moved into the apartment, rumors began to circulate: Delta was considering incentives to encourage higher-seniority people to leave the company. The corporate gossip was entertaining to consider, even though categorically denied by company hierarchy. Nonetheless, the fodder was excellent grazing material for someone as eager as me to chew on it. Delta's denials proved to be true; nothing transpired, and another year of tough commuting to Jacksonville slowly passed. Two years down, six to go before I would be eligible for early retirement at age fifty-two. My work at Delta was going better than I ever imagined, which made the remaining six years of my "sentence" seem attainable—still a lifetime away. Notwithstanding, I was heartsick living apart from Thomas.

Several months before the lease on our apartment was up, Rich advised me he and Prince Charming were getting serious—serious enough for them to move in together when our lease terminated. This was not a complete surprise, and I was happy for Rich, who was an all-around delight. Still, I didn't look forward to yet another hassle surrounding living arrangements. Rich soon came to my rescue. In a stroke of serendipitous planet alignment, he had a close friend—a gay Delta flight attendant—who had just renovated his house in Collier Hills, which was a close-in, tree-canopied neighborhood. Included in the renovation was a private downstairs bedroom and bath, soon available for rent. Within the week, the owner arranged to show me the space, and I agreed to rent it. Less than a month later, I moved in—and this tailor-made solution didn't require the signing of a long-term lease.

As Delta continued to fly into increasingly stiff financial headwinds, rumors of employee buyouts resurfaced and quickly reached a fever pitch not long after I moved. There was no hiding the painful reality that our once proud, previously cash abundant, and much beloved airline was desperately seeking a field to attempt a soft landing. This time there were no denials from upper management to the persistent rumors. Of course, this was interpreted as a silent confirmation. Again, I was an eager eater of any morsel ripe for picking on the Delta grapevine. I had to prepare, and, being true to myself, started to play the "What if" game. My favorite what-ifs included: If the company offered an incentive, would it be prudent to take it when I am relatively close (under six years) to getting the "full meal deal"? If Delta offered an incentive and I turned it down, would my employment last long enough for me to retire? Would I be old enough to qualify for an incentive? If so, how difficult would it be to find comparable employment back in Jacksonville—particularly at my "advanced age" of forty-six? My mind was in overdrive playing this futile no-win game, which was fanned by the contagion of many colleagues who were engaged in the same chase. It was the same type of fantasy many of us have enjoyed when playing the lottery with a group. Wow, if the group wins a gazillion dollars in the lottery, we can all quit at the same time! As is usually the case with lotteries, there was no winning ticket drawn at Delta either. Much to my chagrin, the rumors soon ceased.

Where There Is Smoke

Just when things were beginning to settle down—yet again—I arrived at work one morning and was greeted with a buzz saw of fresh "intelligence" straight from our finely-tuned rumor mill. It was almost a carnival-like atmosphere, and I feasted on the banquet along with everyone else. A phone call from a "highly-reliable source" to an unidentified individual in our division started this most recent beehive of activity. Anyone who has ever worked in corporate America knows grapevine communications, valid or not, *always* precede anything official. I didn't know "Highly Reliable" or "Unidentified"; of course, this was of little consideration when something of such supreme deliciousness was dangling. Nonetheless, it was imparted that Delta was going to announce incentives later in the day, for high-seniority employees. This "prophecy" was too specific not to be true.

And behold, it was! Within hours of the initial foretelling and with palpable excitement in the air, we the people were huddled into meetings with our managers. With great fanfare, the drumrolls and trumpets announced the reading of the greatly anticipated proclamation. "The Gospel According to Delta"—on official teletype parchment—was read. Indeed it was confirmed—at last. The company was announcing incentives for high-seniority employees to separate from Delta. Glory, hallelujah! The fine print was then read, and the drumrolls suddenly ceased. Our division was excluded. After we stopped slobbering over ourselves, we were advised our division and a few others were considered "essential." Therefore we were ineligible to participate. Cancel the "glory, hallelujahs," pop the balloons, and throw the infernal trumpets into the Chattahoochee River. The merry-go-round came to an abrupt halt and we were thrown headfirst off our high horses. The festival was indeed over.

Dejected, I shuffled back to my desk and begrudgingly placed my "What-if" game in idle mode. By early afternoon, specific details of the incentive offer became available for anyone in the company to peruse. Without question, I scrutinized "the deal," and it was a good one. Delta offered eligible employees the option to take a leave of absence for a duration of either three or five years. During this period, pension benefits would continue to accrue, just as they would if the employee were still working. Even though no company-paid insurance was provided, flight benefits would continue. At the end of the leave, the employee would be guaranteed the right to return to work at Delta or go directly into retirement if old enough. What a deal—sadly, not available to me. Even if it had been offered, the five-year leave of absence would have left me six months short of retirement.

As soon as I got home from work, I called Thomas. Downhearted, I explained the details of the day's events, and he predicted the announced incentives were probably just the beginning. He anticipated more incentives could be forthcoming, particularly if in-progress initiatives proved inadequate to stop the flow of red ink. He was encouraging; nonetheless, my expectation was another five years, six months, and three days in Atlanta would be in my future.

Waiting for an Encore

Many colleagues in my division were in situations like mine—tired of commuting, too young to retire, yet old enough that continuing to stick around seemed the best option. In my particular office, there were folks commuting to Detroit, New Orleans, Memphis, Knoxville, Jacksonville, and even Seattle—the worst possible commute. We were all hoping for the same miracle, which was to be able to go home and resume normal lives with family and friends.

Within a couple of months after Delta's initial announcement, more incentives trickled out—still none for my division. Nonetheless, the latest official communication stated that other areas of the company were being considered for inclusion in the future. It was a ray of hope. The management in our office had no knowledge of what areas might be next and couldn't prognosticate. It seemed possible an incentive might be in my future; we were a large division with many high-seniority people in a number of cities. I also considered that employees previously deemed essential could become dispensable as cash flow and cash on hand continued to diminish.

Days turned into weeks, with nothing but eerie silence from the incentive-granting gods residing in the Delta General Office (corporate headquarters), which was down the street from where I worked. Nonetheless, the modus operandi of our managerial staff had noticeably changed. They were constantly in planning meetings and much less visible than usual. The corporate culture at Delta was one of deep camaraderie across all areas and generally open communication. When the usual managerial response of "I don't know" to some questions was replaced with "I can't comment," my internal antennas buzzed. There is indeed a difference in the two responses. I began to believe the sweet scents of orange blossoms may soon be replacing the distinct odor of jet fuel.

Early Orange Blossoms

In the fall of 1995, the "piñata" was finally delivered to our division, replete with the incentive goodies that had been so elusive. The particulars were unchanged from the original offering, which included the option to take a three- or five-year leave of absence. Not surprisingly, Thomas and I were ecstatic my "sentence" was about to be commuted. When the incentive details unfolded, there were two unexpected strings attached. The most eye-catching was a non-compete clause specifying I couldn't work for another airline for five years. This was a zinger—changing careers was a formidable prospect. Secondly, the latest possible exit date, March 15, 1996, was a little too soon. I would be six weeks short of retirement at the end of the leave and, accordingly, would be required to return to work in order to retire. Delta gave several weeks for me to consider the offer. Thomas was my biggest cheerleader, and with his encouragement I decided to accept it. I signed the papers with a dose—a big dose—of trepidation, while hoping time would substantiate my decision.

Before my leave of absence began, I took advantage of Delta-sponsored career coaching sessions. The sessions included assistance in résumé writing, interviewing techniques, and networking. It became uncomfortably apparent: finding unrelated employment was not going to be easy—my life was immersed in Delta. As excited as I was to be going home, this excitement was tempered by having to leave cherished friends (some had been workmates for nearly twenty years) and a company I loved. I also had concerns regarding gay intolerance among employers in Jacksonville. However, my guiding light was Thomas, and employment apprehensions were secondary to my desire to be with him.

Being the consummate worrier, I was five-years-in-advance fretting about having to return to Atlanta for six weeks in order to retire. By then, I should be established in another career, and being able to take a six-week "vacation" to complete my Delta employment would be hugely problematic.

The unbelievable happened. About a month or so before my leave of absence was scheduled to begin, Delta management solicited volunteers who would be willing to delay leave commencement. Clearly, droves of exiting employees were leaving the remaining crew with an overwhelming workload; service levels were dropping in response. There were not many takers on the request to delay emancipation. Even so, I needed no more than a millisecond to answer the call. My hand catapulted to the ceiling, and Delta allowed me to choose a delayed exit of April 26, 1996. I would be retirement eligible *three days prior to* the end of my leave in 2001. I would be able to retire without having to return to Atlanta!

On-Time Departure

The weeks leading up to my leave commencement passed faster than I would have expected, as if I were in some sort of time warp. During this time, I reflected on my experience in Atlanta and recognized it had been a period of professional transformation and personal growth. I discovered previously hidden talents and became more comfortable in my own skin. My appraisal is this "exile" in Atlanta, as difficult as it was, provided a necessary path adjustment for me to continue my life exploration and celebrate new discoveries.

My last day at work was emotional and supplied the ultimate taste of bittersweet; I made frequent trips to the men's room, where I would find a private stall and secretly cry. The tears were reminiscent of those I had shed in July 1993, when I left Thomas in Jacksonville to move to Atlanta. In both instances, I was leaving something I loved. This time, my sadness was overshadowed by the joy of returning home—something I had dreamed about every day since landing in Atlanta in 1993.

I had snacked on bananas every day at 10:00 a.m., which was a ritual my colleagues at work couldn't ignore. Deservedly, I was ribbed about this never-to-be-missed, high-priority personal requirement. As a surprise, I was given a twenty-one–banana salute on my last day at work. My colleagues had written various messages on each banana in bright blue ink, which easily contrasted against the yellow outer peels. Some expressions were heartfelt, some funny, some encouraging, and all emotional to me. Knowing the messages would disappear when the bananas turned brown, I wrote each one on a piece of paper so I would never lose the sentiments expressed. I had developed deep friendships with my colleagues, and cutting the Delta umbilical cord was probably the hardest decision I ever had to make. Had it not been for Thomas' support, I probably wouldn't have found the courage to make such a life-changing call.

As I walked out of the building for the last time—thankfully, alone—the tears were again streaming down my face. The familiar scent of jet fuel wafted in the air and assumed an appropriate sweetness as I reflected on unforgettable times when I was magically propelled through the skies to discover the world. It also was a reminder of the uncertain prospects Delta faced. I waded through the wall of water blurring my eyes and located my car, parked in its usual spot. Once I managed to get situated in the car, I just sat there holding onto the steering wheel for another few minutes, waiting for the waterworks to abate. They finally did, and I soon piloted my car to the nearby I-75 South ramp, which I imagined as a runway, and "took off" to the south. In my rearview mirror, I consciously watched the distant skyline of downtown Atlanta quickly fade from sight. This chapter in my life was officially closed. I was now on a new journey and had no idea where it would take me—admittedly, I had apprehensions.

As soon as I arrived back home in Jacksonville, I was hit with bad news about a good friend. Leonard Brewer had passed away earlier in the week. He was forty-three years old. I knew Leonard was gravely ill and had visited him a few weeks prior when I was home for a weekend. He was upbeat and didn't seem to be consumed with how seriously ill he was. Ironically, Leonard didn't die from AIDS; he died from an aggressive form of lung cancer. Leonard had long been a nonsmoker. For reasons unknown to any of his friends, he began smoking when he was in his thirties. How tragic: tobacco killed him.

Two Celebrations, and Then a Rough Landing

Thomas and I celebrated my transition back to Jacksonville by taking a Mediterranean cruise, including several days in Mykonos, Greece. It was an incredible trip and the perfect exclamation point to the end of my career at Delta, which was a wonderful, even if at times trying, experience.

On the first Saturday in June, I was astonished when Thomas shocked me with a surprise welcome-home cookout at the house. Nothing had hinted a party was in the works. Rich Krause came down to visit us that weekend, ostensibly for some beach time. I had no idea his actual reason for visiting was to help Thomas orchestrate the party, primarily by getting me out of the house. As planned, Rich and I went to the beach late Saturday morning—without Thomas. He was insistent we go without him because he wanted to peruse the booths at the antique mall. I was a little miffed and interpreted his antique reconnaissance to be impolite. When Rich and I returned from the beach, I noticed Thomas had mowed the yard (it needed the trim), swept the driveway, and cleaned the kitchen. I found this perplexing since Thomas had planned to spend the afternoon looking at antiques. He hadn't. I felt ashamed for being disgruntled with Thomas earlier in the day, and still didn't suspect what he was about to spring on me.

A few minutes after getting back to the house, I heard a knock on the door. Much to my surprise, there stood Beverly Kesterman, a close Delta friend who had worked with me in Jacksonville and Atlanta. She said she was in town, visiting her brother, and dropped by for a minute to see how I was doing. It was evident I desperately needed a shower. After determining Beverly was not in a rush, I excused myself to go upstairs for a shower. I didn't have a clue a "mass of humanity" would be arriving in about five minutes. When I stepped out of the shower and glanced through the bathroom window which overlooked the driveway area, I saw my friend Ilene talking to Beverly.

At last, my radar screen came to life with a series of blips—something was going on! By the time I got dressed and went outside, the driveway was filling up with a throng of folks. Delta colleagues from Jacksonville and Atlanta, as well as my mother, brother, and sister-in-law were in the gathering crowd. Soon, the bar-b-que food truck arrived and we had a fabulous evening. The "Return of the Native" soiree, as it was billed, was the perfect way to be welcomed home. Thomas, with Rich's help, had pulled it off as scripted.

The initial euphoria associated with returning home was quickly tamed by the reality of being without a job and the intimidating task of finding one. It was a struggle. All too soon, it became painfully apparent that finding meaningful employment would be more difficult than I had hoped. Interviews were scarce, and I became increasingly dejected. My emotions assumed control of the driver's seat, and I began to second-guess my decision to leave Delta.

After six fruitless months of seeking "the right job," I decided to take a temporary position as a clerk at a locally-based logistics company. Even though it was a major downshift when compared to my responsibilities and income at Delta, it was easy work and I enjoyed the folks with whom I worked. My spirits were lifted and at least I was a contributing member to society again. In three months, my position was converted to a permanent position, although the lack of a challenge translated into increasing boredom in the months to follow. Opportunities for more suitable positions in the company were limited, so I began to explore other avenues. In the meantime, I continued to lease my house to generate additional income.

Chapter 34

But Dad, I Have No Interest in Insurance

Had my dad been alive today, he no doubt would recall the above declaration. When I was in high school and contemplating various career possibilities, he suggested I consider a career in insurance. Jacksonville was dubbed the insurance capital of the South, which it probably was, and jobs in the industry were plentiful. Even so, nothing about my dad's chosen field of work remotely interested me. Well, things change.

Prior to the time I went to work at the logistics company, one of the companies I had targeted for possible employment was Blue Cross Blue Shield of Florida. This company was headquartered in Jacksonville and had a well-known reputation for being a desirable and inclusive workplace. Accordingly, I submitted my résumé and cover letter in response to a hiring announcement. They were looking to fill a large number of entry-level telephone customer service positions. I was more than qualified, and willing to start at that level to get my foot in the door. To my disappointment, the résumé got lost. Even though a second résumé resulted in an interview, the outcome of the required drug screen, which I passed, was also lost. Accordingly, I missed out on the opportunity.

About a year later, two former Delta colleagues with whom I had closely worked in Jacksonville and who held managerial positions at Blue Cross, came to my rescue. These stalwart friends were able to resurrect my résumé from the death pile, whisk it past the guards, and present it as an offering to the gods residing in human resources. Once the résumé had been appropriately blessed and bathed in incense, another close Delta friend, who lived in Atlanta, contacted a woman she knew who was "further up the ladder" at Blue Cross in Jacksonville. (Gosh, is the world ever connected.) This lady retrieved it, reviewed it, and called me for an "informational" meeting as a courtesy. As it turned out, this delightful and unassuming woman was a vice president at Blue Cross. The meeting was productive. My résumé was soon forwarded to a department head who was actively looking to hire two trainers for entry-level telephone customer service reps. This was the same work area where I had attempted to land a job as a customer service rep a year earlier. Finally, through the assistance of this accommodating lady, my résumé landed on the playing field, and I was soon called for an interview.

The interviewer, Brad Sweeney, was the manager and would guide the ultimate hiring decision. He had a great sense of humor, and we developed an easy rapport. This fascinating gentleman was originally from Gardner, Massachusetts, and formerly served as a representative in the Massachusetts State House. Brad was in his late fifties, a "nuts and bolts" kind of guy, and one of the most articulate and well-informed individuals I had ever met. He was interested in exploring my training philosophies and spent little time asking the usual out-of-the-book interview questions which to me are mostly senseless. He was not concerned that my college degree was unrelated to the job or that I had no insurance background. The interview was one of my best. At its conclusion, I was invited to prepare a fifteen-minute training session on any subject of my choice, to be presented in three days to a panel of four (Brad, plus three trainers).

After much thought, I decided to train the panel on the proper care and nutrition of houseplants. With this objective, I went to the grocery store and bought five small, inexpensive arrowhead plants, one for each panelist and one for me (that I later killed). The short time leading up to my presentation was a flurry of preparation as I designed a brief curriculum and a single-page "Kwik Tips" handout containing helpful hints for proper plant care. Each panelist could take the handout and their plant following the session.

The day came for my training presentation, and although a little nervous, I didn't wilt (nor did my plants). The panelists were intrigued by the subject I chose and even asked general houseplant questions, which I competently answered for fifteen minutes following the presentation.

Yes, forgetting to water is frequently lethal—as is confirmed on my arrowhead plant's death certificate. For this, I humbly apologize to my former professors at UF, who taught me better.

Several days later, I was offered the position. It was ego boosting to hear Brad say I had an innate talent to train, which gave me an edge over the first runner-up. I had never attended as much as a single training and development class, so where did I acquire this ability? Undoubtedly, I was born with it. I didn't choose to have it, yet I did choose to pursue a career, albeit later in life, allowing me to tap into this gift—choices are predicated by what is offered on the menu.

I learned two important lessons from this experience. The first is: We are all born with specific traits, talents, and abilities. It is no accident that certain traits are frequently coupled with certain talents and abilities. Learning to accept, embrace, and capitalize on them is a significant key to success and happiness. The second lesson is: Even the most qualified candidates are usually hired as a result of networking. Chances of being hired "off the street" are difficult without having contacts within an organization. Someone you know will know someone else who can open the door. Once the door is open, the curtain goes up and the stage is yours.

A Tough Start

After beginning my new career, I was made aware that Brad had gone out on a fragile limb when he passed over the second-place candidate and hired me instead. The individual who was not chosen had considerable insurance knowledge, was working toward a degree in training and development, and was an internal candidate. There was some resentment in the area over my hiring, and one coworker curtly told me I would fail. This nearly proved to be the case. I quickly discovered the business was extremely complex—the learning curve loomed like Mount Everest. I worked many nights until 2:00 a.m., trying to avoid drowning in the subject material and convoluted computer programs I was responsible for teaching. This hectic pace went on for several months, as I feverishly hustled to remain a step ahead of my students.

The idea of failure was personally reprehensible, but more so, I didn't want to fail my students or Brad and the panel who hired me. I had a point to prove and never worked so doggedly hard than during those killer months. Much gratitude went to three fellow trainers who provided above-and-beyond assistance while I walked a tightwire.

Finally, I reached the top of "Everest" when my students were consistently outperforming those who were trained solely "out of the book." The "Kwik Tips" handout I designed for my interview was the forerunner of similarly-styled, practically-focused job aids. My students credited much of their success outside the classroom to these "down and dirty" references. One trainer who initially was adversarial to me, became a supporter and even asked me to share the "Kwik Tips" with her—and I gladly did. This was the ultimate vindication.

The Gay Thing Raises Its Ugly Head at Work

In mid-1999, about fifteen months into my budding career at Blue Cross Blue Shield of Florida, I had an opportunity to throw my hat into the ring for an agent training and development position in one of the sales divisions. It offered more personal latitude, was a significantly higher pay grade, and gave me the opportunity to work directly with our sales force. It also included a reasonable amount of travel, which I welcomed. I got an interview, followed by two more. Ultimately, I gave a sales presentation to a panel of ten, composed of sales managers and related staff from throughout the state. The presentation was well received and it was evident I easily connected with the panel. The feedback I received was overwhelmingly positive, and I felt the job was mine.

A week passed, then two, then a month, then two months, and I became as deflated as a blown-out tire. For five seemingly endless months, a hiring decision languished, with no information other than "it has been delayed." Finally, the logjam was cleared and the job was at last offered. I eagerly accepted it.

Several months later, one of the individuals with whom I closely worked, shared a bit of disconcerting information. I was informed that shortly after I gave my presentation, someone from within the company contacted one of the managers in the sales division to alert them I was gay. The implication was clear—being gay should be an exclusion for the position. I never found out who "outed me" or how they knew I was gay. It disturbed and perplexed me since I had been highly circumspect about my personal life at work—I had discussed it with no one. I don't know if the delay in making a hiring decision was related to my being gay. Nonetheless, it didn't keep me from ultimately getting the position and didn't affect my acceptance by work associates.

Incidentally, Blue Cross Blue Shield of Florida was—and is—an active proponent of LGBTQ inclusiveness and nondiscrimination.

Even so, someone didn't agree with official company policy when unsuccessfully trying to thwart my hiring. Based on this experience, I continued to speak little of my personal life at work, yet was honest about it if asked.

I never again experienced any issues at work, based on my sexual identity, and enjoyed other highly rewarding positions at Blue Cross before retiring in 2012. Thankfully, the company remains a vanguard for equality and serves as a positive role model in an area of the country continuing to be resistant to LGBTQ acceptance and equality.

Chapter 35

CHANGES IN LATITUDE

At the height of the Great Recession, Thomas and I began searching for a house to buy in historic St. Augustine, which is about forty miles south of Jacksonville. We were frequent visitors to the area and had toyed with the idea of someday moving there. Even though close in terms of mileage, we knew St. Augustine was a world apart from Jacksonville in attitudes and inclusiveness. This enclave of astounding history, eclecticism, and natural beauty has attracted visitors from all over the world, and we wanted to be a part of it.

By 2009, housing values had plummeted to the point of affordability, which allowed us to pounce on a fairly new, relatively small house in a near-downtown area with jaw-dropping views. It was the first house we jointly owned. We began to spend all weekends in our "slice of heaven," while getting to know our neighbors and making new friends. It was the perfect testing ground to determine if an eventual relocation would be in the offing.

It didn't take us long to determine our "house experiment" overwhelmingly validated our initial expectations, and we fell in love with St. Augustine. The icing on the cake was the genuine acceptance and welcome extended to us by our neighbors. Thomas and I were soon included in neighborhood functions, and we felt valued. Within two years, we made the decision to begin the groundwork toward a permanent relocation to St. Augustine.

A Curve Ball from My Church

What much of corporate America has done to recognize LGBTQ employees' contributions is gratifying. No doubt, the talent and resourcefulness of this minority group has proven to be healthy for business. It also demonstrates that doing the right thing enhances understanding, which in turn boosts employee morale and camaraderie.

Unlike corporate America, most churches continue to grapple with the LGBTQ "conundrum." Some churches recoil at the presence of LGBTQ parishioners within their flock, whereas others give tacit acceptance without offering full fellowship. A few are openly accepting and fully inclusive.

For many years, I had been relatively happy in my Presbyterian church, while mentioning I was never asked to join a Sunday school group, never asked to join a men's group, and never asked to participate in any committees. Fellowship-related activities such as these were something I missed, yet I was able to excuse these "slights" for the most part. My true joy in the church was singing in the choir, which was composed of an accepting group of folks. Importantly, I never heard the LGBTQ community being condemned from the pulpit. Basically, most of my needs were fulfilled by my church. Unfortunately, in 2011, after being a member of this church for over twenty years, reality slapped me in the face.

Due to declining membership and the loss of a number of high-profile members, the pool of individuals who were qualified (and willing) to serve on the church's governing board began to diminish. This board, known as the Session, is responsible for handling church business, among other duties. Undoubtedly, the scarcity of candidates forced the church to begin searching for members who had not previously been asked to serve. During a Session meeting, without my knowledge and without any concurrence from me, my name was submitted for consideration to serve on this board. A member in attendance informed the attendees I was gay. Summarily, my name was excluded from any further consideration. A good friend in the church advised me—in confidence—of what had transpired. I was highly embarrassed and felt stabbed in the back. Being disqualified is not what disturbed me; I could handle that. However, being judged unfit was beyond my scope of acceptability.

I was grateful to be made aware of the truth. Even so, this uncomfortable disclosure placed me in an untenable situation. I didn't wish to betray the confidence of the individual who rightfully apprised me, and therefore I remained silent while considering my options. The first was to remain in the church and forgive what had occurred. I believed in forgiveness, and also recognized that forgetting was a different matter—particularly when reminders would be unavoidable every time I entered the church. The second option was to look for another church where doors were genuinely open to LGBTQ members. The third option was to not attend church anywhere. This third option, which the millennial generation is opting for in increasing numbers, caused the most discomfort.

At least I had gained an enhanced perspective as to why so many folks forego church attendance. Many churches are rightly perceived to be not diverse, not inclusive, frequently exclusive, and selectively judgmental. Sins seem to be conveniently compartmentalized, and ones more or less "acceptable" are glossed over. For example, the "sin of homosexuality" is an easy finger-pointing target since the overwhelming majority of churches are composed of members who are heterosexual. Yet the combination of divorce and remarriage, which usually implies adultery (it gets a lot of billing in the Bible), is seldom the subject of harangues from the pulpit in most evangelical churches. Is this the type of authenticity that would attract millennials or even someone like Jesus?

The first option, of remaining active in a church that "tolerated" my presence (while gladly accepting my financial contributions), would be difficult. Other than in the choir, I had few close friends in the church. My closest friends, Charlie and Brock, were no longer members after their relationship dissolved, and both had left Jacksonville. As much as I hated to leave the church, I felt compelled to do so and carefully considered my exit. Ironically, if I had been asked in advance if it would be permissible for my name to be considered for the Session, the answer would have been no, and I would have been none the wiser. Nevertheless, the church did me a favor because I found out the truth.

Timely Conversation

When I was grappling with exiting my church, two lesbian neighbors in Jacksonville, taking an afternoon stroll, spotted me in the driveway and stopped by to chat. One of the ladies, who was a longtime active member of another Presbyterian church, didn't seem surprised to hear about my recent experience. She recounted that she had recently left her church because it had experienced an attitudinal shift resulting from a pastoral change. The permutation translated into an uncomfortable atmosphere for LGBTQ members, which motivated her to seek out—and find—a more relevant Christian experience. She invited me to go with her and her partner to their new church, which was affiliated with the United Church of Christ (Congregational) denomination. This is not to be confused with the Church of Christ, which is in no way related. The timing for me was uncanny, and I accepted their invitation to attend the following Sunday. However, I had no plans to become involved; I was already scouting churches in St. Augustine in anticipation of our move.

I met my two neighbors at their church and was introduced to a good number of welcoming members. The number of people in the church was relatively small, and the genuine warmth displayed was profound. It was apparent I was among friends—many parishioners were gay—and those who were not gay were equally engaging. I was relaxed and made to feel much at home. The church service was similar to what I was used to, and I liked the pastor. After the service, a fellowship was held, and I met many more parishioners. There was no pretense and no feeling or fear of being judged by anyone. It was unlike any church I had ever visited. In short, I loved it and started to attend regularly. Within a few weeks, I joined this loving, embracing church. Doing so was something I would have never predicted for myself—particularly considering I was looking for a church in St. Augustine.

My pastor and fellow choir members in the Presbyterian church where I had been a member, knew I would eventually be leaving to affiliate with another congregation in St. Augustine. Indeed, this was my stated plan, but plans are like the color of a chameleon—changeable. Without question, I felt the need to give an explanation as to why I had abruptly left the church to join another one—in Jacksonville. Carefully, I composed a letter to the pastor, outlining my reasons for leaving, without going into any specifics that would betray a confidence. In a nutshell, I explained that in a stroke of providence, I started visiting a church fully welcoming to the LGBTQ community and had joined it. I didn't mention anything pertaining to my sexual orientation being discussed in a Session meeting, and instead emphasized I had discovered a more inclusive experience at the United Church of Christ. While direct, the letter was kind and not a condemnation of the Presbyterian church.

My reasons for leaving were also verbally shared with my friends in the choir. I judiciously chose my words, making sure I remained warm and inoffensive—after all, I loved this group of people. I simply stated that through a chance meeting, I had discovered an open and affirming church offering complete acceptance and fellowship to members of the LGBTQ community. My words were few, yet the crux of my message was communicated by my feet when I walked out. I had closure and left the church with no regrets or ill will toward anyone there.

Gladly, I received a graciously written letter from my former pastor. He stated he understood and supported my decision, which he said was a "God thing." Additionally, his letter contained a rather candid and honest admission. In effect, he said he was sorry the climate in the church was such that I felt compelled to leave. It was probable he was unable to change the ingrained attitudes prevailing among some church members. Interestingly, he later moved to another state where he pastored a Presbyterian church that is fully open and accepting of LGBTQ members.

A Great Surprise

Another change in latitude was unexpectedly about to transpire. My good friend Ted Petersen, who lived in Washington, DC, called one evening to tell me his sister and brother-in-law were retiring from their work (also in Washington). They soon would be moving to nearby Ponte Vedra Beach, which was less than an hour from St. Augustine. This was welcome news; I was fond of them and expected Ted would be a frequent visitor, which he was. A couple of years later, Ted made the decision to retire to the same general area, which was an added bonus. He and his partner, Giovanni, now live about forty minutes from Thomas and me. We see them frequently, and they are among our close friends. Ironically, Ted was instrumental (literally) in my search to find a church home in St. Augustine.

Finally!

Our relocation to St. Augustine couldn't occur until several linchpins were in place—the sale of my house in Jacksonville, my retirement from Blue Cross, the sale of Thomas' house in Jacksonville, and the transition of his work to St. Augustine. Lastly, we wanted to do a major renovation to our cozy house. Initially, the pieces started to fall into place fairly quickly: I retired in May 2012 and sold my house in October. Next, we completed the house renovation in December 2012. The two remaining items didn't occur until late 2015, when Thomas' house sold, and he began working full-time from St. Augustine. Up until then, we spent about half our time in St. Augustine, which required a grueling commute two days a week for Thomas to get to work. Even though it was a difficult period, particularly for Thomas, the payoff was worth the wait—the move exceeded our expectations. We loved our surroundings and were among people who embraced us.

Got Church?

There was still one missing piece for me—finding a church home. After much searching, I surprised myself by visiting an Episcopal church, solely because of a circumstance involving Ted Petersen. The curious part of this is I had no intention of ever visiting this particular church. I perceived it to be too far removed from my comfort zone, whatever that was. It is interesting how perceptions can be unmerited, and even so, still remain intractable. Thankfully, I allowed my perceptions to budge and a major growth experience was in the offing.

Misgivings aside, Thomas and I initially visited the church with the sole purpose of hearing Ted play the organ. He had no affiliation with the church, and had been asked to substitute for the organist/choir director, who was on vacation. Ted did his usual magnificent job on the organ, and the church members extended a surprisingly warm welcome to Thomas and me. We were probably assumed to be a gay couple; yet this detail was immaterial. Frankly, it caught me off guard. I had previously—and wrongly—perceived Episcopalians to be rather stiff and with an attitude of "us four and no more."

The positive experience gave me reason to take a second step and visit again, this time without Thomas. The warmth of the congregation was unmistakable and appeared genuine. Accordingly, I felt comfortable in filling out a visitor's card. For the unacquainted, this card, when filled out, acts as a "permission slip" to be contacted by someone from the church. I was not disappointed. The next day, I was called by one of the priests and we soon met to discuss church theology. Additionally, it was of utmost importance to ascertain if the church would welcome me as a gay member, instead of just tolerating my presence. It was the first time I had ever had a conversation with a member of the clergy—in any church—regarding anything so personal. In the United Church of Christ, where I was a member, such a conversation was unnecessary; the church had a stated policy of complete LGBTQ acceptance.

The conversation with the priest was deep and honest on both sides. I was assured I would be welcome to join the church and be encouraged to participate in church activities. It was also confirmed there were other LGBTQ members in the church. I appreciated the pastor's candor in acknowledging the congregation was conservative (at least for Episcopalians) and, accordingly, same-sex marriage ceremonies were not yet sanctioned by the local church. This was no deal breaker, and not surprising, given the diocese was headquartered in Jacksonville. Our theological discussion afforded an extra level of security; I pleasantly discovered my own beliefs were actually closely aligned with Episcopal doctrine. Clearly, my objective to obtain an accurate assessment as to whether or not I wanted to get further involved in the church had been met.

I concluded it would be worth a try and soon attended the three-session "Newcomer's Class." It proved to be time well invested and validated my decision to join the church. Soon, I embraced the traditions and liturgies of my new church, which were refreshingly different from my previous experiences.

I started attending services regularly and within a short time was invited to join a Sunday school class. It was the first time I had become involved in one since I was in my mid-twenties. Ironically, the class facilitators, a dedicated husband and wife team, were former Southern Baptists. Much to my astonishment, there were a good number of us in the church as well as many parishioners who came from other denominations. The church was a denominational melting pot of diversity. This rich "ambrosia" served to make the church unique and appealing; it was a reflection of the city itself.

Before I knew it, I had been asked to participate in a number of church activities. It was great to be included, and I soon joined the choir. It was evident Christ's love, which permeated the congregation, was the guiding force steering the church. This growing, God-loving church became my spiritual lighthouse, and continues to provide illumination to anyone who is seeking a path to Christian relevancy. Of course, many different paths lead to the same address, and this traditional—yet new—path for me was an unexpected discovery.

So why is church so important to me? Good question, given that so many of my LGBTQ brothers and sisters have no interest. And why would they, with the existing incongruities and the rejection being served down from the "high altars" of many churches? My church need, which fueled the pursuit to find the "right" church, is undoubtedly a consequence of being raised in a deeply religious family in the Bible-Belt South. Church attendance was instilled in me and is an undeniable part of my fabric.

Even through all the difficulties I experienced at the hands of the church, I can see beyond the man-made clutter frequently obscuring Christ's true message of love, acceptance, and forgiveness. This includes you and me. It has not been easy for me to forgive the church; yet, in doing so I have found peace, knowing I have followed Christ's directives. Do I think being active in a house of faith makes me any more favored by God than someone who does not attend at all? Surely not. We all pursue different paths, according to our own experiences and individual beliefs

Chapter 36

Leviticus Got Me Thinking

"The heart of the discerning acquires knowledge, for the ears of the wise seek it out" (Proverbs 18:15 NIV). By the time I was in the tenth grade, the seeds of doubt had been planted and I started questioning some of what was being discharged from the pulpit. This was because I had inklings the church's prescribed box of acceptability might not have room for me. My search for discernment had taken flight—although at a low altitude. Even then, it troubled me that the same God who created human nature would condemn anyone for acting upon the nature with which they were born. This deep-in-my-gut thought matured into strong conviction when I became older and was better equipped to confidently process and accept my own God-given gift of reasoning.

According to many "informed" opinions, which to me are subject to debate, gay men are an abomination to God. This is based on a handful of Scriptures, including some from the "far-out" Book of Leviticus that on the surface seems to state God is less than fond of LGBTQ folks. "If a man also lie with mankind, as he lieth with a woman, both of them have committed an abomination: they shall surely be put to death; their blood shall be upon them" (Leviticus 20:13 KJV). (Looks like the lesbians got a "hall pass" on this one.) This same chapter has a lot to say about adultery—with the same death sentence for committing the offense. "If a man commits adultery with another man's wife—with the wife of his neighbor—both the adulterer and the adulteress are to be put to death" (Leviticus 20:10 NIV).

Let's briefly continue our visit with Leviticus for a minute and see some other things that may raise an eyebrow or two. Want to own slaves? Go right ahead and buy some—because Leviticus says it's permissible. "Your male and female slaves are to come from the nations around you; from them you may buy slaves" (Leviticus 25:44 NIV). Of course, owning slaves is unthinkable. And most anyone with a grain of compassion and a jigger of good judgment would agree. Want to eat shrimp or other shellfish? Don't! Eating them is another one of many listed abominations. "Whatsoever hath no fins nor scales in the waters, that shall be an abomination unto you" (Leviticus 11:12 KJV).

It is difficult for me to comprehend that God would find me to be an abomination because of eating lobster and shrimp (and I eat a lot of them)—or to condemn me for my innate sexual orientation. I find it vexing that some people who detest gays the most, and who frequently reference Leviticus to support their views, also consume shrimp while conveniently ignoring the verse condemning them for eating it. Why would God consider something divinely created to be an abomination—whether it be me, or the shrimp (if eaten)? Interestingly, many theologians are now reexamining the original language in Old and New Testament writings referencing same-sex attraction, along with the historical contexts, and are coming to other conclusions.

Didn't Jesus die on the cross to cover our sins? Whether the sin is lying, cheating, stealing, murder, adultery, fornication, lusting, swearing, gluttony, alcoholism, drug abuse, abusing animals, needlessly parking in a handicapped spot, not honoring commitments, or whatever else—we are all guilty. "For whosoever shall keep the whole law, and yet offend in one point, he is guilty of all" (James 2:10 KJV). This is heavy. I was taught, and believe, that Jesus' sacrifice paid for all transgressions. If being gay is a sin (and I don't think it is), then I have to believe it is not an exclusion for forgiveness. This is how I reason being gay and Christian are not mutually exclusive. It is heartening to see some churches are now coming to understand this.

One huge takeaway for me is that being born gay forced me to question much of what I had been taught by the church and society in general. Label me a heretic, but not to question makes me guilty of heresy with myself. Thankfully, an honest self-appraisal allowed me to discover that questions are the seeds of growth. The magnitude of growth I have experienced—spiritually and intellectually—would probably not have occurred had I been born straight.

From a psychological perspective, I am aware that same-sex attraction is manifested in odd ways probably unnoticed by most. For instance, if I am introduced to a woman, chances are I won't easily remember her name. Whereas the opposite is true after being introduced to a man—I will likely remember his name with less effort. Funny thing, I don't remember Charlene Harrelson's birth month; however, I recall Anthony Petrini was born in June. I find this interesting, given my relationship with Charlene was much more serious and longer in term than my brief experience with Anthony. Also, I have no recollection of what perfume Charlene preferred, yet distinctly remember Anthony's choice of Givenchy Gentleman cologne for himself. I have a forty-five-year-old bottle of this cologne, which I recently opened. To my wonder, the fragrance was still recognizable. Amazingly, one whiff evoked reminiscences of Anthony, and I was transported to a time when life's journey was still unfolding with fresh experiences.

My Reality

The percentage of individuals who are gay is frequently explored. No doubt, many of us are included in the LGBTQ community. No matter what the percentage actually is, I am part of the statistic. There are varying degrees of same-sex attraction, and I have friends who are equally attracted to both sexes, which is a curiosity to me. Using myself as an example, on a scale of 1 to 5 (1 being exclusively attracted to the opposite sex, and 5 being exclusively attracted to the same sex), I would say I am a 5. I recognize an attractive woman when I see one and enjoy female company, but never had a genuine interest in touching the female body other than to satisfy a general curiosity (when I was much younger and more inclined to explore the wilderness). The female body is unappealing to me. While straight guys I knew were fascinated with female breasts, my primary interest in them was to gawk at the oversized ones on display at the beach. On the other hand, it was all I could do to keep from staring at any good-looking guy—particularly if well-built and shirtless—there was nothing uninteresting about that! When younger, I could look at a guy of this description and get an uninvited sexual response. My sexual orientation toward men was unsolicited and natural. Not so with girls. There just was no natural sexual attraction and no matter how much I tried, I couldn't create any. Any time I kissed a girl, I envisioned kissing a guy. Initially, it seemed to work. In my heart I knew a long-term relationship could never survive this kind of illegitimacy.

Many years ago, I had a gay acquaintance who yielded to family pressures and married a girl he had known in his hometown. Before he married, I asked him how he expected to maintain a sexual relationship with his wife. He said, "I'll imagine doing it with a man." I wished him well, and reserved any further comment even though I had serious doubts about the ultimate outcome. He moved back to his hometown after getting married, and we lost contact. I suspect his "let's play pretend" approach to marriage yielded a less than blissful, even if socially acceptable, existence.

Something Shakespeare Wrote

"This above all: To thine own self be true, and it must follow, as the night the day, thou canst not then be false to any man" (1.3.78–80). This oft-quoted statement from Polonius, in Shakespeare's *Hamlet*, assumed personal significance when I was wrestling with my truth. This truth eluded me for too many years. Finally, I came to the realization that I had allowed what others *thought* to be true, to supersede what I *knew* to be true. Surely, God didn't create me with the intent that a struggle was necessary in order to develop a sexual interest in women. I don't believe God's will is effectuated through such a contrivance. Unquestionably, many gay men and women find themselves trapped in the middle of the same battlefield.

Admitting to being gay was a soul-ripping process I resisted with every turn. After desperately attempting, for years, to abide by the heterosexual guidelines that had been presented, it became evident they were not written with me and folks like me in mind. It finally smacked me square between the eyes that "all the king's horses and all the king's men, couldn't make 'Humpty' into a straight man." During my struggle, I routinely prayed, asking for God's perfect will to be realized in my life. At last, I removed the veil obscuring my vision and discovered that God's will actually had been realized. My former Presbyterian pastor's wife, who also was an ordained minister, helped me reach this "aha" moment.

Choices?

It baffles me that many people still hold fast to their belief that same-sex attraction is chosen. Of course, to consider anything else challenges "understandings" (usually religious)—hence the stalemate. Unequivocally, I didn't choose to be gay, nor was I "recruited." Who would ever make such a selection in the face of continuous ridicule, damning by the self-proclaimed righteous, and shaming by some parents? A straight friend once told me I had chosen to live a gay life. Well, of course. My internal mechanisms are inherently gay; what else would I do? Does a person born straight choose to live a straight life? Of course. Any other choice would be incomprehensible. Why then would I choose to attempt living in a manner counter to the way God created me? Some churches dispense the instruction that it's okay to be gay as long as you don't live a "gay lifestyle." This makes as much sense as saying it's okay to be straight as long as you don't live a "straight lifestyle." I can't help but wonder how many gays, in an effort to assuage guilt, take the "it's okay" prescription by answering "God's call" to live a monastic life or by attempting to live a life of celibacy. I was not one "so called."

When in college, I took several elective courses in psychology (trying to figure myself out), and have never forgotten the following assessment by one of my professors. He referenced the oft-repeated phrase, "Thou dost protest too much." The professor paraphrased this by saying that in many instances, an individual who continually rants about a much tabooed subject is sometimes guilty of the same offense, or at least has experienced guilt-related insecurities surrounding it. Think about it. How many times have you observed the downfall of well-known or not-so-well-known "religious leaders" whose dirty laundry has been exposed, sometimes on the national stage? Possibly, their protests from the pulpit were rooted in their own insecurities.

Butterflies

My brother Max made an interesting observation not long ago. Regarding this, he sent me the following email:

> *Dear Seth,*
>
> *Yesterday after we left Mother's house, I arrived home and saw two monarch butterflies mating in the front yard. I stopped the truck and watched. The top butterfly had black spots on the veins near the trailing edge of both wings near the center of the butterfly. This identifies the butterfly as a male. As things progressed and the angles changed, I noticed the bottom butterfly also had the two black spots, which identified it also as a male. As you know, we have raised milkweed plants for several years and usually have many monarch butterflies in our yard every year. We know a lot about monarchs, both*

from observation as well as from websites. We have seen a lot with the monarchs and are familiar with their life cycle, and what I saw in the front yard yesterday, I had never seen before. I thought it was interesting that what I observed in our front yard took place just after our conversation. God's creations are interesting.

Incidentally, among the topics Max and I had discussed, prior to his butterfly observation, was my conviction that same-sex attraction is innate. Thus, the timing of Max's butterfly observation was coincidental—or was it? Could it have been an affirmation of God's love for me?

Following the receipt of Max's email, I combed the internet to see if there was any research addressing same-sex behavior among monarch butterflies. I found plenty, which corroborated my brother's observations. This begs the question: Did these butterflies choose to be attracted to the same-sex? I think not. Incidentally, I also stumbled across observational accounts of same-sex behavior among a wide range of animals. Umm … leads me to believe all the debate can be distilled into one statement: It's the way life is engineered.

Reflections

"Happily ever after" is a phrase I frequently heard as a young child, particularly in the context of fantasized storybook endings. In my limited world view I accepted these rosy outcomes and expected real life to mirror them. Of course, the realities with which we are all presented usually paint a different picture. This led me to wonder if "happily ever after," whatever this means, is a realistic outcome for members of the LGBTQ community. My conclusion is absolutely yes; we can and should be as happy as our straight counterparts. However, validation from outside sources and—more important—from one's self are essential components to finding happiness. It would be wonderful if we lived in a world where religious and social hostility toward members of the LGBTQ community didn't exist. Since this is not the case, finding validation can sometimes be challenging.

Now that I am fortified with hindsight, if I could do it over again, would I tell my parents I was gay when I was young? Probably not, assuming the same circumstances. Today, the world is more enlightened than it was back then and many young LGBTQ individuals are finding it comfortable to come out. Still, for some, such "boldness" is extraordinarily difficult and may not be advisable, particularly if families are chasing them with a Bible in one hand and a hatchet in the other. While attitudes pertaining to sexuality have changed for the better, there are still many adversaries who harbor hate-filled viewpoints viciously targeted to members of the LGBTQ community.

I was taught to follow the adage, "Honesty is the best policy." Most of us probably were. Does remaining quiet about one's sexual orientation fall into the realm of dishonesty? I don't think so. Given the possibility that hostility and abuse might occur in some individual circumstances, being smart should override an urge to "confess"—at least until a point is reached where a safe emotional and physical environment can be secured. Individual circumstances vary, and what is appropriate for one person might not be for another. Admittedly, living in the closet is repressive, which greatly diminishes personal freedom and happiness.

There is no doubt my parents would have never disowned me or loved me less had I advised them of my sexual orientation when I was young. However, I expect they would have reacted by seeking some sort of conversion therapy for me, probably from "qualified experts" recognized by the church. For a kid who already had suicidal thoughts, this could have pushed me over the edge. Despite their religious beliefs which rendered attitudes incompatible with my own, I am indeed grateful for being gifted with such wonderful parents.

Did My Parents Know?

Surely, my parents feared and suspected I was gay. I am certain my father and mother discussed my "situation" through the years, but nothing regarding my sexual orientation was ever divulged by me. I knew it was the last thing they ever wanted to hear from my lips. It has been said that a mother is the first to know and the last to say anything about her son's gay orientation. I believe this was true (at least subliminally) with my own mother. However, for my mother to admit something that in her understanding was utterly detestable, would have forced her to question deeply-held religious beliefs—which were unquestionable. Also, guilt may have played a role in her inability to effectively cope. "What did we do wrong?" probably rang in her ears as she sought to find explanations. Of course, my parents did nothing wrong. On the other hand, my deep thinking and quietly questioning father likely acknowledged to himself I was gay. Interestingly, he had several family members who were gay, and I imagine he considered there could be a familial link.

Through the years, my brother Max and his wife Lois have become ardent supporters of Thomas and me as partners. Several years ago, I asked Max if our then ninety-six-year-old mother had ever said anything to him regarding my being gay. He said she hadn't, while at the same time sharing that she had stated on numerous occasions how much she liked Thomas. Several weeks later, Max telephoned me to deliver some surprising news. He stated that during a visit he and Lois had with our mother the night before, she asked them if Thomas and I were a couple. They confirmed to her we were. Max said the revelation rendered her expressionless and speechless. After all those years of silence, for her to ask the question when she did was unexpected. Nothing further regarding the topic has ever been asked, and my mother is now approaching her 100th birthday. It didn't surprise me that in posing her question, Mother chose the word *couple,* instead of *gay* or even *"homosexualist."* Those words would surely have been too direct, too uncomfortable. Nonetheless, she did ask the question. My analysis is she asked the question when she was in a place to handle the answer she already knew.

Interestingly, she recently made the comment to a close friend of mine that she wished I would find a girl and get married. No doubt, she is still holding out hope that my "gay phase" will end.

Personal Catharsis

I can't say I am glad to have been born gay, although I am a happy gay individual. For whatever reason, this more-common-than-you-may-think anomaly was dealt to me in life's deck of cards and I accept this. I am grateful for a life filled with richness and surrounded by abundant love, which comes from friends, family, church, and of course from my life partner, Thomas. My gratitude to him in his role of helping me find my grounding is immeasurable.

Being gay has made me sensitive to the many differences in humankind existing in our world. This in itself is a huge blessing, among others. Having been the subject of scorn, prejudice, rejection, and, in some cases, hate, has rendered me much more accepting and understanding of individuals who also are different. My Christian beliefs make me keenly aware of the need to be compassionate and loving. The Apostle Paul said, "Be kind and compassionate to one another, forgiving each other, just as in Christ, God forgave you" (Ephesians 4:32 NIV). Jesus said, "A new command I give you: Love one another. As I have loved you, so you must love one another" (John 13:34 NIV). My observations make me wonder how many professing Christians really take these verses to heart, based on actions counter to their instruction.

While writing this autobiography, long-dormant emotions and repressed anger associated with coming to terms with my sexuality resurfaced as I reviewed letters, notes, and long-forgotten personal journaling from many years ago. Along the way, I frequently prayed, sometimes cried, and sometimes laughed as I recollected many poignant life-event details. When I later read the completed work, it became apparent a catharsis had taken place within me—the message was as much for me as anyone else.

A Tidbit of Advice

Change is inevitable. I have learned this while negotiating life's twists and turns. Individuals who are the most successful navigators are those who accept change and embrace it. This has never been easy for me; however, I learned to do it—primarily due to many forced changes at my various places of employment.

I look at the quickly changing social landscape in this country with the same set of spectacles. Like it or not, there are two basic choices when dealing with these changes. The first is to remain hostile, trying to force the rest of the world to continue living with antiquated myopic attitudes. Or, accept that change will occur and learn to "love your neighbor as yourself." The first path, in my view, will result in frustration and unhappiness. The second will likely create a richer and more diverse life experience, which leads to inner peace and happiness.

A quote sometimes attributed to George Orwell states: "Happiness can exist only in acceptance." I wish I had written it.

Incidentally, *Big Eden,* a movie released in 2000, explores what life is like in a fictional Montana town where everybody loves their neighbor and gay acceptance is not out of the ordinary. Even though utopian, it is funny, enlightening, safe (PG-13), and illuminating.

My wish is that this narrative will provide understanding and hope to anyone struggling with their own or a loved one's sexual orientation. My suggestion to those of you who are experiencing religious conflict as a result of your sexuality, is to find a family of faith that will support you. While the denominational shingle hanging in front of a particular church is no guarantee of acceptance, some denominations are generally more open. The United Church of Christ (not to be confused with the Church of Christ), the Episcopal Church, the United Church of Canada, the Evangelical Lutheran Church in America (ELCA), and some Presbyterian Church (USA) congregations are becoming more accepting. Also, I have discovered that some individual congregations belonging to denominations that traditionally are not accepting, have opened their doors to the LGBTQ community. It is advisable to check a church's specific website to obtain more information.

Unitarian Universalists are open, accepting, and welcoming to members of the LGBTQ community. Additionally, the Metropolitan Community Church (MCC) has a primary mission of ministering to and serving the LGBTQ community; however, at this time the number of congregations is limited.

As a supplemental word of encouragement, please don't allow anyone or any organization to convince you that you can't be the recipient of God's love because you are gay. Find your truth through unbiased, qualified sources of support and direction. A simple search on the internet will list a number of gay support groups that are able, willing, and eager to lend assistance.

References and Resources

The Internet references and resources listed in this publication are current at the time of printing. They may be helpful but I cannot endorse or guarantee the efficacy of any particular reference or resource.

SCRIPTURAL INTERPRETATIONS

Eastman, Rev. Elder Don. "Homosexuality, Not a Sin, Not a Sickness." Last modified 1990. www.themetchurch.org/#/listen-look-learn/homosexuality-the-bible

Phillips, Adam. "The Bible Does Not Condemn Homosexuality." Last modified July 16, 2016. www.huffingtonpost.com/adam-nicholas-phillips/the-bible-does-not-condemn-homosexuality_b_7807342.html

"Would Jesus Discriminate." Accessed March 1, 2018. www.wouldjesusdiscriminate.org/biblical_evidence/born_gay.html

IS IT A CHOICE?

Ghose, Tia. "Being Gay Not a Choice: Science Contradicts Ben Carson." *Live Science.* Last modified March 5, 2015. www.livescience.com/50058-being-gay-not-a-choice.html

Soh, Debra W. "Cross-Cultural Evidence for the Genetics of Homosexuality." *Scientific American.* Last modified April 25, 2017. www.scientificamerican.com/article/cross-cultural-evidence-for-the-genetics-of-homosexuality/

"The Verdict Is In: Homosexuality Is Not a Choice." *Health 24.* Last modified August 7, 2015. www.health24.com/Sex/Sexual-diversity/The-verdict-is-in-homosexuality-is-not-a-choice-20150807

CONVERSION THERAPY

Drescher, Jack, Alan Schwartz, Flavio Casoy, Cristopher A. McIntosh, Brian Hurley, Kenneth Ashley, Mary Barber, David Goldenberg, Sarah E. Herbert, and Lorraine E. Lothwell. "The Growing Regulation of Conversion Therapy." *HHS Public Access.* 2016. www.ncbi.nlm.nih.gov/pmc/articles/PMC5040471/

Frankel, Joseph. "More and More States Are Outlawing Gay Conversion Therapy." *The Atlantic.* Last modified July 10, 2017. www.theatlantic.com/health/archive/2017/07/states-outlawing-conversion-therapy/533121/

"The Lies and Dangers of Efforts to Change Sexual Orientation or Gender Identity." *Human Rights Campaign.* Accessed March 1, 2018. www.hrc.org/resources/the-lies-and-dangers-of-reparative-therapy

Pappas, Stephanie. "5 Surprising Facts about Gay Conversion Therapy." *Live Science.* Last modified June 4, 2013. www.livescience.com/37139-facts-about-gay-conversion-therapy.html

HOMOSEXUALITY AMONG ANIMALS AND INSECTS

"1,500 Animal Species Practice Homosexuality." *News Medical.* Last modified October 23, 2006. www.news-medical.net/news/2006/10/23/1500-animal-species-practice-homosexuality.aspx

Andrews, Steve. "Gay Monarch Butterflies and Homosexuality in Nature." Last modified February 17, 2017. www.soapboxie.com/social-issues/Gay-Monarch-butterflies-and-the-normality-of-homosexuality-in-nature

Brandlin, Anne-Sophie. "10 Animal Species That Show How Being Gay Is Natural." Last modified February 8, 2017. www.dw.com/en/10-animal-species-that-show-how-being-gay-is-natural/g-39934832

Fereydooni, Arash. "Do Animals Exhibit Homosexuality?" *Yale Scientific.* Last modified March 14, 2012. www.yalescientific.org/2012/03/do-animals-exhibit-homosexuality/

WHERE HETEROSEXUALS ACCOUNT FOR MAJORITY OF HIV INFECTIONS

Kharsany, Ayesha B. M., Quarraisha Karim, "HIV Infection and AIDS in Sub-Saharan Africa: Current Status, Challenges and Opportunities." *PMC US National Library of Medicine National Institutes of Health.* Last modified April 8, 2016. www.ncbi.nlm.nih.gov/pmc/articles/PMC4893541/

Mugurungi, Owen, Simon Gregson, A .D. McNaghten, Sabada Dube, Nicholas C. Grassly. "HIV in Zimbabwe 1985–2003: Measurement, Trends, and Impact." *Springer Link.* Accessed February 4, 2018. https://link.springer.com/chapter/10.1007/978-1-4020-6174-5_10

BOOK REFERENCES

Brownson, James. *Bible, Gender, Sexuality: Reframing the Church's Debate on Same-Sex Relationships.* Grand Rapids, Michigan: Wm. B. Eerdmans Publishing Company, 2013.

Vines, Matthew. *God and the Gay Christian: The Biblical Case in Support of Same-Sex Relationships.* Colorado Springs, Colorado: Convergent Books, 2015.

HELP/RESOURCES

Crisis/Suicide Intervention for Youth
The Trevor Project: https://www.thetrevorproject.org
866-488-7386 (24/7 hotline)

GLAAD (news & support for cultural change leading to LGBTQ acceptance)
www.glaad.org/

GLSEN (champions LGBTQ issues in K–12 education)
www.glsen.org/

Human Rights Campaign (advocating for LGBTQ equality)
www.hrc.org

LGBTQ Civil Rights and Legal Resources by State
www.lambdalegal.org/

LGBTQ Health Resources for Youth
www.cdc.gov/lgbthealth/youth-resources.htm

LGBTQ Religious Support
www.gaychurch.org/
www.reformationproject.org/

PFLAG (the nation's largest LGBTQ family and ally organization)
www.pflag.org/

SAGE (advocacy and services for LGBT elders)
www.sageusa.org/
LGBT Elder Hotline: 888-234-7243

About the Author

Seth Vicarson is a Florida native whose passions led to occupations in agriculture, aviation, and health insurance education. He is an environmentalist and a proponent for protecting the state's agricultural heritage and challenged wetlands.

He has traveled extensively and relishes opportunities to experience cultures and philosophies different from his. He considers diversity a gift to be embraced, and a portal for personal growth and understanding.

Seth and his partner of more than thirty years enjoy living in the historic and enchanting city of St. Augustine, Florida. They savor the area's natural wonders and wildlife, and are the proud parents of their beloved pug, Bella.